# BOTH SIDES
# OF THE LINE

*MY COACH, THE BOSTON MOB ENFORCER*

*MY MENTOR, THE MURDERER*

*THE TRUE STORY OF CLYDE DEMPSEY*

*AND THE 1974 DON BOSCO BEARS*

## KEVIN KELLY

"Mr. Kelly's brand of storytelling is simply elegant. I felt as if I was in the room with him all the while through. At its core, this is a love story, rippling well beyond the realm of sports. Honest and hearty, Mr. Kelly offers the reader a caring lens through which we witness a complex and inspiring coach in Mr. Dempsey, an individual who gave all he had in life—both good and bad. After reading it, I was moved to strive to be a better man."
—Max Williams, Actor and Screenwriter

"A wonderfully engrossing read about the author's journey of discovery investigating the dark side of his high school football coach and mentor—Jack Dempsey, a dynamo who makes an indelible impression on the author (and on us, the readers)."
—Cliff Carlson, Professor Emeritus of English, Springfield College

"A beautiful case study on the positive influence that adult mentors, however imperfect they may be, can unknowingly have on kids over a lifetime."
—Doug Tierney, Principal and Coach (retired), Deerfield, MA

"Delivered from the heart, *Both Sides of the Line* is a riveting account of a devoted disciple's complex relationship with his tormented coach. Kevin Kelly delivers a lesson about how a street-wise, inner-city boy selectively garners moral guidance from a sociopathic mentor. His rendering of the American dream contrasts the glorious emergence of an earnest teenager with the crushing demise of an ethically inconsistent criminal."
— Jim Andreas, Northfield, MA

"Football fans will enjoy this detailed inside story of a high school football player in the Boston of the 1970s. We all idolize most of our coaches, but we really never know what makes them tick. This book vividly demonstrates how one dedicated and devoted Don Bosco senior came to idolize a mentor and coach with a hidden dark side. It really demonstrates that you can't 'judge a coach by his cover!' A must read!"
—Mark Nemes, Fullback, Northeastern University

"Kevin Kelly is a master storyteller who draws the reader deep into the street dynamics of Hyde Park, Don Bosco football, and the aspirations of a young athlete who finds himself in the middle of a dark, crime-ridden enclave of Boston inspired by a larger than life coach and mentor."
—Julie Webster, Educator, Deerfield, MA

"[*Both Sides of the Line*] is an enjoyable and multi-layered memoir that brings the reader through the glory days of school football, Boston city life during the tumultuous 1970's, and the dual personality of a role model coach by day, and volatile criminal by night, who truly played both sides of the line. Even better, this memoir will make a great movie someday. Envision a mix of *Remember the Titans* and *The Departed*!"
—Jack Shea, Sales Executive, Hewlett Packard

"I've known Kevin since he was a little boy. I'm so happy he found some closure with this book. It's a wonderful example of overcoming adversity and the growth that comes with an inspirational figure, clay feet and all."
—Dianne Donnelly, Hingham, MA

Published by Bancroft Press
"Books That Enlighten"
P.O. Box 65360
Baltimore, MD 21209

bancroft
press

410.764.1967 *fax*

*www.bancroftpress.com*

ISBN
978-1-61088-169-2 cloth
978-1-61088-171-5 Kindle
978-1-61088-172-2 eBook
978-1-61088-173-9 Audiobook

Cover and Interior Design: J. L. Herchenroeder
Printed in the United States

*To my wife Xiaofeng and daughters Tianyao and Michelle, thank you for your love and support during this long journey.*

*To my brothers, both Bosco alums, Tommy '71 and John '87.*

*And to the brotherhood, a special group of men, the 1974 Don Bosco Bears.*

# Contents

# Don Bosco Varsity Football
## Catholic Conference Champions
## 1974 Roster

## Offense

### Quarterback

| | |
|---|---|
| Mike Ewanoski | Brookline |

### Fullback

| | |
|---|---|
| Al Libardoni (Capt) | Somerville |
| Stevie Riley | Brookline |

### Tailback

| | |
|---|---|
| Colie MacGillivary | Dorchester |
| Paul Carouso | Somerville |
| Peter Masciola | Roslindale |
| Craig Cemate (Capt) | Brighton |

### Receiver

| | |
|---|---|
| Chester Rodriguez | Dorchester |
| Shawn Murphy | Dorchester |

### Tight End

| | |
|---|---|
| Chris Staub | Revere |

## TACKLE

| | |
|---|---|
| Skip Bandini | Brighton |
| Tommy "Yogi" McGregor | Hyde Park |

## GUARD

| | |
|---|---|
| Derrick Martini | Somerville |
| Abe Benitz | Jamaica Plain |

## CENTER

| | |
|---|---|
| Eddie Dominguez (Capt) | Jamaica Plain |

## DEFENSE

## NOSE GUARD

| | |
|---|---|
| Derrick Martini | Somerville |

## TACKLE

| | |
|---|---|
| Kevin Kelly | Hyde Park |
| Skip Bandini | Brighton |

## DEFENSIVE END

| | |
|---|---|
| Chris Staub | Revere |
| Billy Elwell | Watertown |

## LINEBACKER

| | |
|---|---|
| Al Libardoni | Somerville |
| Eddie Trask | Revere |

## DEFENSIVE BACK

| | |
|---|---|
| Colie McGillivary | Dorchester |
| Paul Carouso | Somerville |
| Craig Cemate | Brighton |
| Chester Rodriguez | Dorchester |
| John Sylva | Quincy |

## LINEMAN

| | |
|---|---|
| Vinny O'Brien | Jamaica Plain |
| Frankie Marchione | East Boston |
| Richie Abner | Dorchester |
| Jerome Frazier | Dorchester |

## RECEIVER

| | |
|---|---|
| Gary Green | Brighton |

# PROLOGUE

In 1998, while placing a call from a phone booth outside the Shady Glen Diner in Turners Falls, Massachusetts, I caught the *Boston Globe*'s front page headline from a nearby newsstand: "Don Bosco Technical High School Shuts Its Doors After 43 Years." I ended my call, bought the paper, found an open table, and tore through the *Globe* trying to understand how a school which, for over four decades, had educated thousands of inner city kids (including all three of us Kelly boys) could be closing its doors.

It turned out that Bosco had tried to change its course and mission, took some financial risks, and ended up bankrupt. Memories of high school—my teachers, my classmates, my coaches, my teams—flooded me. But none were more powerful than those of our 1974 football season. Deep down, I selfishly enjoyed the fact that I was part of the only team in Bosco history to win the Catholic Conference Championship. But with Bosco shutting down, despite its history, despite our stories and triumphs, I realized it was all about to evaporate into obscurity.

Bosco was unique in many ways, not all of them great. Despite having students from every section of Boston, it had a weak alumni association, and so I had seen only two of my former teammates over the previous thirty-seven years. I suppose I could've acquiesced to that reality, put the paper back on the stand, and left things as they were. But that's not how things happened.

I felt a power go through me, a determination I hadn't felt in years: I was going to track down as many players as I could from our '74 season, and together we would keep our memories alive.

That's how it all began, and though it did start out as my story, over time, it became *our* story. And, perhaps most of all, it became our story of Coach Jack Clyde Dempsey, a talented, street-tough football coach who'd shaped up a bunch of undisciplined kids, taken the smallest team in Bosco history, and engineered a miracle season. A coach who'd also had a dark side, a side he did his best to keep hidden. A side that, one fateful night, changed his life forever. And so what seemed like a simple, straightforward football story turned out to be anything but.

Our coaches preached for years that the challenges on the football field would mirror the challenges we would all face throughout our lives. What I discovered was that our team, made up of lower-middle-class city kids from every ethnic background, would do more than simply mirror these challenges.

Over the next fourteen years, I tracked down twenty-four of my teammates and discovered just how extraordinary their life stories are. I discovered that, during our high school years, many of my teammates dealt with things that made the challenge of playing football almost a relief by comparison. We all faced family issues, sure, but for some of us, they stretched beyond the typical and into the almost unimaginable: alcoholism, abandonment, neglect, jail, prejudice, illness, poverty, murder, and suicide.

But with the bad came plenty of good, because these were also all the things that, in one way or another, brought us together as a team. We came from tight-knit neighborhoods and from families that provided discipline (even when those families consisted of neighbors and older siblings who stepped up in place of unavailable parents). We grew up in a time and place where parents knew only tough love and where "survival of the fittest" was all the philosophy we had. I would discover that my teammates took those challenges and disappointments and used them as fuel to become as successful in life as they'd been on the field. They also took with them the undeniable fact that they were *winners*: tough, strong, and driven, with a deep, hard-earned sense of pride.

After forty years, we were finally all back together again, the old team once more.

Players flew in from all over the country. Each man wore his jersey, and each took a turn speaking about his school, coaches, and the '74 season. As I listened in admiration, amazed to be surrounded by them all once again, a swell of pride overtook me. No other team in Bosco history could ever wear the "green and gold" with more pride than the twenty-five of us. Undersized and underestimated, we had accomplished the unthinkable.

In that moment, I knew that the one badge we all still wear—the one that bonds us together for life—is the badge of CHAMPION.

# SUMMER 2010

*"When I came to America, I thought there were three kinds of kids: Catholic school kids, Jewish kids, and public school kids."*
—Frankie Marchione

"Thank God the Boston Police rejected my application," I said, shaking my head. "I'd make lousy detective. After three years, I've only found seven of us."

Max and I had gotten there first, so it fell to us to wait, buzzing with nerves I hadn't felt since my football days. Standing by the Charles River, looking down at our old practice field from atop the Storrow Drive Bridge, I felt my chest tighten with nostalgia.

After four long decades, members from Don Bosco High's 1974 championship team were about to come together once more.

"Don't forget Coach Currier—you found him too, Kev," Max said, smiling. "What made the search so difficult?"

"Well, when Bosco closed its doors in '98, they didn't leave any resources behind for finding alumni. But trust me, I'm not complaining. This is a great beginning."

Max Williams and I met in 2000 at Deerfield Academy, a world-renowned boarding school in western Massachusetts. My wife taught Chinese there. I was an assistant principal at a nearby public elementary school. Max's father, Bob, was Deerfield's athletic trainer who also happened to be our neighbor.

Max, himself a Deerfield alumnus, had been a three-letter man who, after college, went on to play professional hockey until he sustained a career-ending injury. Max is solidly built with long, flowing blond hair more fitting for a man of the '70s. He is polished, well-mannered, and articulate, but with a look that only other athletes can really pick up on. It's that *I'm cool as long as you don't cross the line* look. After hanging up his skates, Max headed out to LA to pursue his lifelong passion to be an actor and writer.

During a Christmas visit, Max's dad looked over at me and said, "Hey, Kev, tell Max about your coach, that Dempsey guy."

"Geez, Bob, it's Christmas, and that's a long story. Maybe some other time? Plus, I'm not sure the Dempsey story is appropriate for Christmas dinner."

"No, no, go ahead," Bob assured me, smiling. "Max'll love it."

Over the next hour and a half, Max hung on my every word. He didn't take his eyes off me for a second. When I finished, Max took a deep breath and exhaled slowly. "I feel like I just sat through a movie. What a story! Kev, you've got to write this down. It would be a bestseller!"

Over the years, off-and-on, I attempted to write what simply became known as *The Dempsey Story*, only to find myself swept back into the real world of Now: working full-time as Assistant Dean of Students at Deerfield Academy while helping to raise my two daughters. But still the story haunted me; I found myself telling and retelling it to anyone who would listen (a bit of the "Irish Curse," I suppose, to know what stories need to be told and then feel compelled to tell them).

Finally, after a full decade had gone by, Max called and said, "Kev, I'm coming out to Boston, and you're either doing this now or you're never going to do it. And guess what? You're doing it. Try to find as many guys as you can, get them together, and let's get started."

He was right. Not only had I always believed in the story, but I knew the collective pieces by heart: Don Bosco High with its Catholic corporal punishment, an entire student body made up of kids who grew up in the roughest parts of Boston, the '74 season, the friends and competitors, and the coach who led the smallest team in Bosco's history to its only championship.

But there was one hidden twist to our journey: discovering Dempsey's dark side—the side that most of us, his players, his would-be sons, refused for years to believe possible. Yet, by the end, we would all come to the stunning realization that the man we'd all idolized and aspired to be had taken his last breath behind bars.

"Truth be told, Max, after Bosco closed its doors, I was afraid that the '74 team would be wiped away. But hold on to your hat, 'cause today is going to stir up some interesting conversations. This is the first time any of us have tried to reconnect in decades. Not sure if we'll ever find all the players, but I'm determined to try. And at least I found Skip Bandini. Skip and I played defensive tackle together. He went on to be an All-American lineman at Massachusetts Maritime Academy, and now he's head football coach at Curry College. I can't wait to see him again after all these years."

"So, this is where you guys practiced?" Max said, looking out over the water. "Hey, this is a beautiful spot. From what you told me, I'd had visions of a sewer pit."

That July morning *was* beautiful; I'll give him that much. Not a cloud in the sky and the air was crisp at 8:00 a.m. A slew of sunfish and sloops sailed lazily west on the Charles River to where the water splits Boston and Cambridge. At our backs, the city streets were quiet, with the Prudential and Hancock buildings looming in the distance (the two largest buildings in Boston, fifty-two and sixty stories tall, respectively).

"Don't be fooled by the scenery," I grinned, pocketing my hands as I breathed it all in. "What you're looking at now wasn't here back then. I mean, during the mid-seventies, Boston was dealing with some major issues. The economy was in shambles and the unemployment and crime rates were high. We were still dealing with the gas crisis, at times waiting in line for up to thirty minutes for gas.

"See that beautiful building there with all the mirrors next to the Prudential? That's the Hancock. During its construction, those fifteen-foot mirrors began popping out of their frames and shattering when they hit the sidewalks. Every window had to be removed and replaced with plywood, and it stayed an eyesore like that for *three years*. The construction ended up costing a hundred *million* dollars!

"But nothing during the '70s—and I mean *nothing*—tore this city apart more than forced school busing. The subway ride you and I took this morning? With every race in the city sitting side by side? That definitely was *not* my or any of the players' experience during high school."

"Why? What made it so bad?"

I shrugged, my eyes stuck on the shining face of the Hancock. "In the fall of '74, a Judge Garrity ordered the introduction of forced busing to address issues of inequality in the Boston public schools. And, well, violence just erupted all over as white and black high school kids were forcibly bused into each other's neighborhoods. Most of us Bosco kids had to take the MBTA subway system to get to and from school, so the busing part of it didn't impact us quite as much, but the atmosphere on the subways was made all the more tense because of it, and often violent.

"Hyde Park High School (not far from where I grew up) was

featured in *Time* magazine for the level of violence in and around the school. State Police with K-9 dogs were assigned to roam the hallways, adult monitors were in every bathroom, and the students were forced to move through the school in single file," I said, shrugging again, shaking my head at the madness of it all.

"For us Bosco kids," I went on, "the forced busing and all it caused was something we had to prepare for every day. I mean we even had to—wait a minute!—Look who's here!" I laughed, greeting Abe Benitez with a hug and healthy slap on the back. "Benitez, Benitez, Benitez—I can't believe it's you! Geez, Abe, you look terrific! Great to see you! Max, Abe was our starting right guard, built like a tree trunk—5'10" and a hundred-ninety pounds," I said, guiding Abe over to exchange handshakes.

Abe was one of those guys who'd always been quiet and shy until you got him on the football field, and then he turned bullet-proof tough. Abe's parents came to America from Cuba, just prior to Castro taking over, and settled in the Jamaica Plain section of Boston.

I remembered a scrappy kid with bruises and grass stains, but that day I was greeted by a neatly dressed, clean-cut businessman decked out in studious-looking glasses, polished shoes, and a noticeably expensive fall parka.

He carried himself with class.

"Hey, Kev, great to see you too," he said, turning to accept Max's extended hand. "Great to meet you, Max—and don't listen to a word Kev says; he's full-blooded Irish, which means he's full of shit more than half the time!"

"It might be forty years later, Abe, but apparently you still know this guy quite well," Max chuckled, happy to throw in a quick jab.

Then a laugh bellowed out from behind us, a laugh that could only belong to one person: Skip Bandini. A tremendous offensive and defensive tackle, Skip grew up in Brighton, the kind of guy who always talked the talk because he knew he could back up every word. He'd played football with a chip on his shoulder. Off the field, he was always extremely intelligent with a surprising capacity for tenderness. Get him talking about his mother or his relationship with Dempsey, and he'll be fighting back tears. Skip's mother raised her children alone, their father only periodically popping in and out of their lives. But Skip never held a grudge against his father, because that's just one of Skip's gifts: his ability to see the world through someone else's eyes.

In terms of size, Skip *exploded* after high school. His bones now carried two-hundred and forty pounds of muscle on a 6'2" frame. In high school, he'd only weighed one hundred ninety-five pounds. A thick-necked, full-blooded Italian with jet black hair and piercing eyes to match, he was intimidating in both looks and person. He wore a Curry College hooded sweatshirt with matching coaching shoes. The only thing missing was a whistle around his neck.

"Well, well, well, Kevin Kelly and Abe Benitez," Skip said, hands on his hips as another great laugh shook through him. "I can't believe I'm starin' at you two again after all these years!"

No handshake from these fellas—the three of us embraced without a moment's hesitation.

"Hey, look who just drove up behind you," Abe grinned. But none of us had to look back to know; Mike "Ski" Ewanoski's voice isn't one a person forgets.

With the horn blowing and the black-tinted window lowered, Mike's big grin hung out in the breeze as he called, "I can't believe I'm spending my Sunday afternoon hangin' out with you knuckleheads."

"Ski," our team's quarterback, had arrived. Sharp and athletically gifted, he'd inherited his father's Polish surname and his mother's Irish good looks. Poised, confident, and cocky, he flashed us a million dollar smile that's impossible not to warm to. Mike grew up in Brookline, a wealthy suburb attached to Boston. To us, he'd been the rich kid, none of us ever realizing that he'd actually grown up in the projects. As it turns out, his father had to work three jobs just to make ends meet, so it'd been left to Mike's mother to keep the family together. Tough, but with an endless well of love, she'd pushed the family forward and nudged Mike (along with all four of his siblings) toward athletic excellence.

Mike entered Bosco during his junior year and, though he'd never played quarterback in his life, he led us to the greatest football run in the school's history, an 18-2 record over two seasons. Mike was always the pretty boy, the one with the John Travolta disco look that got all the girls chasing after him. On the field, though, he was a fierce competitor.

"I see our quarterback is still a cocky shit," Frankie said, stunning us all into another wave of greetings, embraces, and cheers.

Frankie Marchione had been one of many outstanding linemen on our team. He arrived in America from Italy at the age of seven, and settled into East Boston's all-Italian neighborhood. Not speaking a word of English, his father immediately enrolled him in a local Catholic school. You can't help but be drawn to Frank. He can be both sharp and gruff, but if you stop and listen a while, you start to hear a deep thinker with a wide view of life based on experiences that can only be envied.

"When I arrived in America," he once told me, "I thought there were three kinds of kids: Catholic school kids, Jewish kids, and public school kids."

Frank whipped out a couple of white paper bags filled with donuts and other pastries, all from his bakery. "Hey, who brought the fuckin' coffee? I know it wasn't that cheap Irish bastard Kelly!" Frank hooted, throwing me a quick wink. The first words spoken between us in nearly forty years and already he was busting my chops. We both laughed as we hugged.

John Sylva, the only freshman on the '74 team, arrived next. John came from a family of nine who'd lived in Quincy, Massachusetts (one of the few Bosco kids not from Boston proper). Easy to like and easy to talk to, John is quiet, intelligent, and dependable. Starting out as an inside linebacker, he *always* brought his street-toughness to the field.

I think John still views us as the older kids who'd taken him in as one of our own when other upperclassmen would've left him to drift. And I know he's never forgotten his first two years of playing with the '74 and '75 Bosco Bears. "I wasn't sure how a freshman was going to be received by varsity players," he admitted. "I've never forgotten the support and endless encouragement you guys showed me."

Of course, as soft-spoken (and introspective) as John is, it only takes one push before he'll deliver a look rooted in Germantown (then one of the toughest housing projects in the Boston area).

Our old head coach, Bob Currier, was the last to arrive. Now in his late seventies, he grinned when he told us that, even after sixty long years, he was still hard at work in the coaching game. To me, Currier still looked more like a track coach than a football coach: a slender man with glasses and a misleadingly gentle, easygoing smile. Currier grew up in Brighton, and developed a brilliant mind both in the classroom and on the field. He was intense, even brutal at times, in the way he treated his players. Some kids loved him, some hated him, and I, like most, just didn't want to get on his bad side.

By ten o'clock, we were all sitting together drinking coffee and eating Frankie's pastries under the old open-air boat shelter, its platform dotted with picnic tables still wet from the morning dew. The warm breeze coming off the Charles felt inviting, different from my football memories of it as a muggy dust bowl in the summer; comfortable in the fall; and a frozen tundra in the winter.

Nearly half a century had passed since those afternoon practices and games, and yet, here I was, laughing all over again with the guys who'd made it possible: Skip Bandini, Abe Benitez, Frank Marchione, Ski Ewanoski, John Sylva, and Coach Currier—all as if we'd never parted ways in the first place.

"Fellas, it's so great to see you," I said, standing to take the floor. "I know some of us haven't seen each other in a long, long time, but let me just take a minute to introduce Max. He and I met back in 2000 and, after hearing the story of Coach Dempsey and the '74 season, we agreed that Bosco's '74 championship ride shouldn't be allowed to disappear from memory." I paused as a murmuring of agreement drifted through the group. "And though he and I are collaborating on this project, Max is the real force behind why we're meeting here today."

While I could tell that the guys were listening to me, caution remained clearly in their eyes. Max was an outsider. Max hadn't been a part of the team. He hadn't been a part of *us*.

"As you remember," I continued, "we had two miserable seasons at Bosco. Our sophomore year, we had the largest team in the school's history and went 1-8. Our junior year, we were 3-5-1, and lived through a horrible tragedy."

I was forced to pause again as several men shifted uncomfortably, some diverting their gazes, their cheer immediately dampened by the memory.

"So," I continued, sipping coffee, knowing this one area would be especially difficult for us to discuss openly, "it made perfect sense when the *Globe* predicted that Don Bosco would end the season in the Catholic Conference cellar."

"And there wasn't one player who could argue with that prediction," Skip said, shifting the mood back as the guys got to nodding and chuckling once more.

"Yeah, what reason did we have to think otherwise?" Frankie grinned.

"Fellas, would you mind if I ask a question?" Max piped up.

"You're the whole reason we're here today," Mike said. "Jump in any time."

Max nodded his thanks and jumped: "Would you all agree that you wouldn't have won the championship without Dempsey?"

"Absolutely. Without question." It was the unanimous answer as the team traded nods around the table, including Coach Currier.

"So, what was it about him? What did he bring to the table that you hadn't seen before?"

"Max," Skip said, "at 5'7" and two hundred and ten pounds, the man got us to believe that size means *nothing* in the world of football. We were the smallest team in the school's history, but he still led us as champions through a season in one of the toughest leagues in the state."

"It was all about quickness, technique, and desire. That's all he preached. He pounded it into us," Frankie said, his large hands folding together on the tabletop. "We were so small. I think Eddie Dominguez and Yogi were the only solid two hundred pounders we had."

Abe couldn't keep himself from laughing, "Speakin' of Yogi, does anyone remember the time Dempsey went live with him during a pit drill?"

"No. What're you talking about?" Mike asked, confused.

"I sure as hell remember," I said, joining right in with Abe's chuckling. "Dempsey was teaching us line technique and was stressing how important it was to focus on the movement of the offensive lineman's hand."

"I remember, I remember," Skip said, laughing. "Dempsey got pissed with Yogi for not coming off the ball quick enough."

"And of course Dempsey flipped around his baseball cap like he always did when he was pissed," Abe added with a grin.

"Everyone knew shit was going to hit the fan when he flipped his hat around like that," Skip agreed, shaking his head over a nostalgic smile.

"Well," I started up again, "after Dempsey and Yogi went live for a few reps, before speaking to all the rest of us, he yelled: *Hey, Bandini, you gettin' all of this?*, while he's still in his stance, right?"

"Dempsey was a stickler for detail," Currier smirked.

"So then Dempsey looks over his shoulder to say somethin' to one of us and accidentally moves his own hand—"

"Yeah, yeah, that's right. I remember now," Mike said, pointing a bent finger at me. "And so Yogi drills Dempsey right in the forehead with his helmet!"

"All I remember was Dempsey going wild. He grabbed the player closest to him—I think it was Richie Abner—and tore his helmet clear off his head," Abe said.

"Was his head still in it?" Mike asked, grinning.

"Thank God I wasn't a lineman," John muttered, amazed.

"What I remember is Yogi pleading for his life. He threw up his hands, *Sorry, Coach, you moved your hand. I thought you told me to come off the ball when you moved your hand!*" I said, mimicking Yogi backing up, eyes wide.

"I remember all of us taking a giant step backward as we watched Dempsey just dismember the poor kid. I mean, we all loved Yogi, sure, but the hell with him, right? I mean, good luck, pal," Skip said, all of us howling with laughter.

And, just like that, a forty-year gap disappeared.

"Wow," Max said, astonished, clearly not knowing what else to say. "Dismemberment is pretty extreme. So, how big of a role did Dempsey's famous temper really play?"

"It was certainly…part of things," Currier said, all the rest of us nodding along.

"How so?"

"It goes back to the street," Currier said, sobering. "He always had it—everyone always remembers his temper—but you have to understand that the streets ran through him his whole life. The street was what filled him when things got hot."

Silence fell over us once again. Thank God for Skip, always willing to hammer away at our ice.

"Fellas," Skip said, taking the time to weigh his words. "I'm not sure if it's the right time to bring this up, but if we're gonna talk about Dempsey . . . well, what happened to Michael Monahan can't be ignored."

"Michael Monahan?" John said, baffled. "Who's he?"

Looking around, it was obvious how uncomfortable we all felt; everyone was suddenly crossing and uncrossing their arms, clenching their jaws, and avoiding eye contact. All of us—all the vets, the guys pre-John Sylva, anyway—knew the story of Michael Monahan.

After Michael's tragedy, Currier and Dempsey went out on the town to drown their sorrows and ended up driving a Mustang down the wrong side of Storrow Drive, hitting a bus head-on in a Cambridge tunnel.

"Wait a minute, Coach," John began, carefully, unaccusingly, his attention zeroed in on Currier. "Do you mean to tell me that *Bus Left* and *Bus Right* were plays that you and Dempsey created after you *actually* really hit a bus head-on? Shitfaced?"

I can't say which of us was most grateful, but our relief was immediate when a new voice erupted behind us,

"Hey, Bosco's Best!" Chris Staub laughed. "Still sittin' on your asses? Everyone take a lap!"

Chris stepped up to greet us, followed closely by a man I barely recognized. Life, it seemed, had ridden this other man very hard.

"It's great to see that even after all these years, things haven't changed much, you lazy bastards," Chris grinned, exchanging hugs and slaps on the back as we all stood to welcome him.

At a hundred and ninety pounds, Chris had played both tight end and defensive end during high school. Chris came from a family of ten brothers and sisters, all athletes. He was the kind of guy a mother would've called "strapping"; and though skilled in many sports, he'd always had a special love for football.

Chris went on to have a stellar football career at Bosco and in college. His opportunity to even attend and play at college, however, hadn't been his work alone. That opportunity, I later learned, had been due in large part to Dempsey.

"Dear God," Frankie said, jumping to his feet, the first to recognize the man at Chris' side. "Is that Paul Carouso?"

Paul grew up in Somerville, another famously tough section of Boston. Paul had been a gifted running back on offense and a tough-hitting defensive back who weighed in at one hundred and seventy-five pounds. Although we hadn't seen each other in decades, we all had heard of Paul's unimaginable tragedy during the summer of his senior year. We gave a softer greeting to Paul, one that was somehow more respectful than all the others had been up to that point—perhaps it'd even been close to reverent, a shift that I know Max picked up on.

At their arrival, everyone indulged in another soul-healing round of hugs and greetings before settling back into the rhythm of swapping war stories. And, as I introduced Max to Chris and Paul more formally, Paul revealed a magic key to our past: a dazzling memory for details and statistics, many of them stretching all the way back to his freshman year.

"There's no way you could possibly remember all that shit," Frank said, earning another wild laugh from the group.

"Hey, Coach," Chris broke in. "Can I ask you to confirm a Dempsey story for me? I was never actually certain of the truth of this one."

"Shoot," Currier smiled, "though if the story's unbelievable, it's most likely true."

"I'd heard that Dempsey got into a fight in Kenmore Square with four Boston University football players. Dempsey knocked out one of the captains before the rest of the players dove back into their car. Then he pulled a gun, shot open the doors, and beat each player senseless, one-by-one."

Currier sighed but didn't pause a moment to even consider lying. "Yes, it's true. But what you probably don't know is what took place later in the courtroom. Dempsey was brought up on multiple charges, but it took time for a court date to be set. So, by the time they finally got in front of a judge, the players had healed up pretty well. Dempsey went out and bought a polyester suit two sizes too small and walked into the courtroom alone, dressed in that ridiculous get-up and all topped off with his old, oversized Coke-bottle glasses. The judge asked the players' lawyer how they pleaded, and the lawyer stood up and said, *You have it all wrong, Your Honor. We're pressing charges against that man, Jack Dempsey.* The judge leaned forward, looked down at Dempsey, and said, *You mean to tell me this fat, little Jewish guy beat up those four football players? You have to be kidding! Don't waste my time. Case dismissed.* And, just like that, the case was dismissed."

I knew Max was taken aback by our laughter, but there was no way around it. For a bunch of old street kids like us, Dempsey's physical power, ruthlessness, and creativity were still things to be admired.

# HOME FIELD ADVANTAGE

*"At Bosco, we're not ashamed of our dress code; we're proud of it."*
—Dana Barros, Saint John Don Bosco
Technical High School Administrator

It was the fall of 1970, back when Tom, my older brother, was a senior at Don Bosco High. Tom was a varsity football player, and that meant competing in the Catholic Conference, one of the toughest and most talented football divisions in Massachusetts. An offensive tackle, Tom was a quiet, tough kid, lean and quick. I, on the other hand, was an eighth grader, small, athletically uncertain but determined, while anxious to be more like Tom. Our youngest brother, John, was only two at the time, but all three of us Kelly boys, as it turns out, were destined to play for the Bosco Bears.

On a Saturday afternoon, I entered our bedroom to find my brother sitting by himself, his football equipment scattered on the floor. He had this "out to lunch" look on his face, and I knew at once that Bosco must have lost the game. I was kicking myself for not going, as if that would have made a difference. I hardly ever missed a game, but Dad had been asked to cover an additional shift with the Boston Police Department (the BPD), leaving me stranded without a ride.

"Tom," I said. "What happened? How bad was it?"

He smiled, reading my concern, and said, "No, actually, we won. But I've just never played against a tougher group of kids."

The team they'd played that day was St. Columbkille, a small Catholic school in Brighton. Jack Dempsey was their coach. Tom had heard of Dempsey and his coaching talents before, but Dempsey was best known as *street*. Short, and with a deceptively unassuming power, Dempsey was infamous as one of the toughest street fighters in the whole of the Brighton area. St. Columbkille's team was made up of only fourteen players, but they were fourteen who never backed down.

Bosco, with its forty-five to fifty players, won the game only by wearing the Knights down—a fact which didn't go unnoticed by Tom or his fellow players, all of them sharing their astonishment on the bus ride home.

"Boy, could they hit!" Tom said. "They were really something!"

"Those kids are nothing without Dempsey," Bruce McDonald (a lineman) shot back. "Remember them last year? Same kids, different coach, different result."

"Just goes to show ya what a good coach can do for a team," Tom shrugged.

"Dempsey's not just a good coach," Bruce said. "He's one tough son-of-a-bitch. I heard he fought this guy down at The Tap the other night, one of those big muscle-heads—Dempsey was working the door. I think Craig Cemate was actually there—he's the one who told me about it.

"Hey, Cemate, weren't you at the Dempsey fight last week at The Tap?"

With a laugh, Cemate turned from his seat and shouted back,

"Jesus, what a fight! I never saw anything like it in my life. Yeah, I saw the whole thing." Passing around a few excuse me's, Cemate bumpily made his way back to where Tom and Bruce were sitting before continuing: "It was closing time, and Dempsey was trying to clear everyone out. This big dude—he must've been 6'4", two hundred and fifty pounds—was shitfaced, sitting alone at the bar and wouldn't leave. I heard Dempsey say, 'Okay, pal, time to wrap it up.' The big guy takes one look at Dempsey and says, 'Go fuck yourself, you fat little shit.' And then, out of the clear blue, the guy up and smashes a beer bottle right across Dempsey's forehead!"

Tom, mouth agape, pressed Cemate, "So what happened?"

"Dempsey went *wild*," he said, hushed and dramatic. "He lunged at the guy, but before he could get his hands on him, the owner held Dempsey back and told him to settle the matter outside, not wanting to see his place destroyed. He knew there was no stopping Dempsey once he got started. The whole bar emptied out onto the sidewalk to watch the fight. If you were an outsider lookin' in at these two guys squaring off, you'd have felt bad for Dempsey, tellin' yourself that poor little fella doesn't stand a chance."

"Dempsey's what—5'6"? 5'7"?" Bruce asked.

"Yeah, while carryin' two hundred and ten pounds of solid muscle," Cemate said, growing a little impatient, wanting to continue the story. "The moment they stepped outside, the big guy tackled Dempsey, totally engulfing him on the ground. I was like, *Oh shit, Dempsey's gonna get his ass kicked!* But then he just went *berserk* on the guy and—are you ready for this?—Dempsey knocked the guy out while lying on his back! Knocked him out cold! When have you ever heard of anyone knocking someone out while lying on their back?"

"Holy shit!" Bruce chuckled, bright with admiration.

"Then," Cemate said, grinning like a fiend, "just to send an even clearer message to the poor bastard, Dempsey goes and bites the guy's ear clean off, with his *teeth*!"

When Tom first told me this story, I was both horrified and awestruck. How was I to know that one day, this same man who'd removed a guy's ear in a bar brawl would become such a powerful and important influence in my life?

Saint John Don Bosco Technical School was an all-boys Catholic school just outside the infamous Combat Zone, Boston's red light district. Our student body included about a thousand kids from all over the city, most of us taking the subway to school, giving us two educations at once; one that adhered to strict Catholic values, and another that spoke of the world's forgotten: the homeless and the sex workers.

Walking up from the Orange Line, we all got a regular morning dose of porn from the gauntlet of strip clubs located on Washington Street. Every morning, dressed in our school uniforms, our hair neatly trimmed and our shoes tightly laced, we Bosco students walked the last few blocks to school. The hookers loved to taunt us, especially the freshmen, calling out, "Come back when you're all grown up, boys!" Or, "If you really want to be a man, you'll come back and see us soon!"

And though we were city kids coming from some tough neighborhoods, we were all bug-eyed and tongue-tied, not quite knowing what to say to these women (some of them beautiful) when they teased us. Most of us, after all, hadn't even been on a date yet, let alone had sex.

Another Bosco neighbor was the Pine Street Inn, Boston's largest homeless shelter. It was common for students to step over people sleeping in the subway station or in one of the nooks outside the school. But no one except the freshmen were ever shocked by this. These homeless people were part of the fabric of the inner city, a part of us and our days, and eventually becoming our normal.

Located at 300 Tremont Street, the school was originally opened in the 1930s as a trade school known as the Continuation School for Girls. During the late 1940s, Brandeis University purchased the building. After his tour of duty in the Navy, it was here that my father attended night classes and earned his high school diploma. In 1954, the Boston Board of Sales approved a $100,000 purchase offer by the iconic Archbishop of Boston, Cardinal Richard Cushing, who single-handedly ruled Boston from the mid-1940s until his death in 1970. Mayor Hynes of Boston opposed the sale, citing a recent appraisal that valued the building at $308,000, but Cardinal Cushing had done his homework and met with Boston's political powers before Hynes took a look. And just like that, in the fall of 1955, Saint John Don Bosco Technical High School was open for business.

The school was run by priests and brothers of the Salesian Fathers, a Roman Catholic religious order founded in the late nineteenth century by Saint John Bosco. In the early 1970s, the surrounding Catholic schools were releasing their grip on traditionally strict dress codes, but Bosco, taking pride in tradition, maintained the status quo. As we waited for the subway, we were stared at and smirked over. We were the only kids in the city wearing suit coats and ties, our hair cut above our ears, and our shoes polished, but the administration *loved* it. Dana Barros, our dark-skinned, white-haired, slickly dressed administrator, always enjoyed bellowing down the halls, "Boys, at Bosco we're not ashamed of our dress code. We're proud of it!"

The administration didn't draw the "old school" line at uniforms, either. Corporal punishment was also so much a regular part of our school days that not one of us would've ever thought of telling our

23

parents if teachers or administrators hit us. Most parents supported the school's disciplinary code. If I'd gone to my father or mother complaining about getting smacked, they'd have only asked, "So what did you do to upset Brother Julius?"

This conversation would have taken place, of course, while I was getting smacked all over again by one or both of my parents—just to make sure the Brother's message was driven home. Most parents were not only embarrassed if their kid acted out at school, but were afraid it might lead to expulsion. And for the Kelly boys, if you were ever expelled, you might as well just join the Marines, because what was waiting at home for you was much worse than any boot camp. It didn't take long for all of us to learn never to share anything with our parents when we got disciplined at school. The Bosco priests and brothers knew this was part of the student culture, and they took full advantage of it. It was a mainstay of the Catholic school upbringing for students to submit to corporal punishment. Toss some Catholic guilt into the equation, and you've just created the perfect conditions for neatly controlling a population of teenagers.

Bosco was the number one technical school in New England back then. The way it worked, we'd all declare a trade freshman year and continue with that trade for the next three. Each trade comprised theory, mechanical drawing, and a hands-on shop class. Cabinet-making, building technology, drafting, electronics, printing, and electricity were always the most popular trades.

I picked cabinet-making and building technology, and was taught by the most legendary teacher in Bosco history: Brother Julius. He had a glass eye and a thumb the size of a hammer's butt end. He was more than simply "old school." Stories of being poked, slapped, or knocked into the next century by Brother Julius were handed down from class to class for four decades. All three of us Kelly boys ended up on the receiving end of Brother Julius' hand, thumb, and projectile more than once during our time at Bosco.

The most memorable of my Brother Julius experiences, however, wouldn't take place until my senior year.

Shop class with Brother Julius was held on the school's seventh floor, where we had a good view of the nearby streets. So when a homeless man climbed atop a bus stop shelter one afternoon and then fell off, landing on a spiked fence, we had the perfect vantage point. The spike went through the man's kidney, and he bled to death right there on the street as we watched.

Not many of us had seen a dead person before, so we all just stared out the window in horror, watching as the police and firemen pulled the body off the fence. Brother Julius, on the other hand, had absolutely no sympathy for the homeless in general (which I always found unbelievable considering the mission of the Salesian Order). To him, the homeless were nothing but street bums. He felt that God gave everyone the tools to be successful in life, and if you threw away that opportunity, you were committing a mortal sin for which God would punish you.

As I looked out the window that day, gaping at the bleeding, dying man, Brother Julius came up behind me and looked out over my shoulder. Then, in a whisper, his Italian accent thick in my ear, he said, "Dat shoulda bin you, Mr. Kelly."

I turned to him and, without a thought, laughed. He winked at me with his good eye and told everyone to get back to work. Some might struggle to comprehend this interplay between teacher and student but, for me, it was a momentary exchange of affection. It was the moment we both knew we understood each other.

On the last day of my senior year, while we stood together in a line waiting to return our tools, my closest friend, David Killion, was staring out the window, daydreaming and holding up a wooden folding ruler in his hands. Without thinking, David started fanning the back end of the ruler; he spread the ruler as far as he could, then let it snap back into place—something Brother Julius could not only see but hear. He walked over slowly and asked David to stop (Brother Julius always had a calmer demeanor around seniors).

David, realizing what he'd been doing, apologized immediately, dropping his ruler flat onto the desk. Satisfied, Brother Julius went back to collecting our tools. Minutes later, however, David again began daydreaming and staring out the window while fanning and snapping the ruler down. This time, Brother Julius pounced, snatched the ruler out of David's hand, slapped him across the cheek, in line with his jaw-bone, and split his face open. Then Brother Julius calmly handed the ruler back to David and said, "Now you will learn." No one else said a word.

During our high school days, no one would ever think of hitting a priest or brother, but David would certainly have been justified. Kids were surprised and angry, sure, but by our senior year, we were pretty much programmed to keep our heads down and our mouths shut.

After Brother Julius passed away years later, alumni filled the church for his funeral. Over time, we'd begun to realize and strangely appreciate the energy and tremendous attention to detail that Brother Julius had given us. We'd learned to respect and admire his commitment and the unique Julius-brand of caring that he'd always showed us. For many Bosco students (David Killion likely not among them), he became one of the most beloved and memorable of our teachers.

Another colorful icon at Bosco was Father Angelo Bongiorno. Father was unlike any other priest at Bosco. Though he stood but 5'-8", had pure white hair, wore glasses, and came across as a reflective and seemingly mild-mannered intellectual, he boasted a body builder's physique. When my brother Tom had him for math during his freshman year in 1968, he entered class one day with one of those body building spring bars that then were being advertised in the back of every comic book in America. In the ad, a body builder was seen using both hands to bend a thick, metal bar with a heavy-duty spring.

"Anyone who can bend this bar will receive an 'A' in this class for the entire year," he said. Everyone tried but not one kid received a free "A".

Father had an extensive vocabulary and loved to toss out fancy, multi-syllabic words just so he could watch our dumbfounded reaction. "Sullivan, you are phlegmatic and hirsute!" In retrospect, it seems a strange combination of words to describe a kid—"You are calm and hairy." But I guess that wasn't the point.

Father was also in charge of the cheerleaders, who hailed from our sister school from Southie, Cardinal Cushing for Girls. Father often grabbed the pompoms and led the cheers to get the school pumped up at a pep rally. It was hysterically funny to see this muscle-bound priest prancing about with pompoms in the gym of an all-boys school. "Do ya got the spirit? Yay, man! Let the freshmen yell it . . . Go, go . . . go, go, go!" If Father was gay, or if any of the students wondered if he was, there wasn't much conversation about it, because he also had a mean streak, and when he let loose, no one wondered what sexual orientation he favored!

During my senior year, I had Father for Trigonometry, and for some unexplainable reason, Michael May, a classmate, decided to test Father Angelo's patience.

"Okay, boys, please stand for morning prayers," Father said. "In the name of the Father, the Son, and the Holy Spirit, good morning, God!"

Seated in the back of the room, Michael piped up: "Well, good morning, Angelo!"

Everyone froze in disbelief!

Father blew a gasket, "What are we doing here?" he said. "Running a zoo?"

He wasn't too sure who said it, but he didn't care. He suddenly

27

burst forward in Michael's general direction. With an open hand, he whacked every kid he could reach. I wasn't taking any chances, and I certainly wasn't about to announce my innocence, so I went straight into survival mode and dove under my desk!

On the athletic side, Don Bosco was truly unique in that it had no athletic facilities—no gym, no pool, no playing fields, no track, and no weight room. Since Bosco was located downtown, the only way to expand its facilities (short of buying up and demolishing surrounding properties) was to go below ground. In 1957, architectural plans were drawn up for an underground athletic complex, but the project was held up in litigation with The Massachusetts Bay Transit Authority, which was desperate for land with which to build a new tunnel.

Then, in 1973 (my junior year), Bosco finally managed to acquire a new gym, pool, and weight room. Of course, our football team remained without a home field on which to practice, so we had to travel across town to Science Park every day.

Most private school students today are blessed with excellent athletic facilities right on their own campus. Even back then, every other team in the Catholic Conference had a home field at their school. Our pile of weights, on the other hand, was tucked away in the girls' locker room at Science Park's public swimming pool. But though many saw this as a laughable void in our program, we Bosco boys came to regard it with an odd sense of pride and bravado— we were inner city kids at an inner city Catholic school, and if that meant traveling miles across the city to practice on a field where the grass would be destroyed by the second week of September, then so be it.

Science Park was located on the Charles River, in the backyard of Boston's world famous Science Museum. The public swimming pool there served as both our locker room and weight room. During the school year, the pool was closed to the public so, unfortunately, the Bosco kids didn't get the chance to meet any girls at our makeshift locker/weight room. (But then again, I guess God fulfilled our desires by having the strippers and hookers greeting us in the mornings.)

With its riverside walkways; the Esplanade (where the Boston Pops performed every Independence Day); and the world-renowned Massachusetts General Hospital on the opposite side of Storrow Drive, the Science Park area really was quite breathtaking. The Boston Garden, home of the Celtics and Bruins, was located in Boston's renowned Italian North End, and across the river (into Cambridge) were MIT and Harvard. The river itself is where Paul Revere and William Dawes crossed to begin their ride out to Lexington and Concord in 1775. In the 1970s, the Charles River made national news as one of the most polluted in the country. But though swimming in the Charles then would've been hazardous to your health, the river still looked beautiful from a distance.

Practicing out there meant that, each day after school, we hiked thirty minutes with our football bags, shoulder pads, and helmets slung over our shoulders. Everyone knew we were Bosco kids, the only gold-helmeted teenage boys trudging through downtown. And if it wasn't raining, snowing, gusting, or freezing, the walk could be rather pleasant.

The first sights on our daily trek were two scenic landmarks: the Public Gardens, the oldest public garden in America (1837), and the Boston Commons, the oldest public park in America (1634). Thousands of tourists flock to the Public Gardens each year to ride Boston's famous Swan Boats. Being able to close your eyes and smell the endless flowers, or to throw peanuts to the ducks following behind (all while drifting past one of Boston's renowned traffic jams) was a gift.

The Boston Commons has a slightly darker history than the Gardens—it was once not only a public area where farmers grazed their animals, but was also used for the occasional public hanging. Today, it's the front lawn to the gold-domed Massachusetts State House (though even now, if you own livestock and wish to bring in your cattle or sheep to graze on the commons, the laws are still in place for you to do so). For the most part, instead of grazing cattle, the Commons are now filled with students studying, businesspeople walking briskly up from the subway, children playing on the jungle gym, couples strolling, and homeless people gathering.

During the warm autumn months, we all envied the lovers holding hands, lying down on blankets together, and drifting off for nice afternoon naps in the sun. No one would dare say how much we wished we could've traded places with them, but we were all thinking it. To trade our toughness for a nap in the shade with a beautiful girl—that was what toughness was supposed to get you in the first place, right?

On our route to practice were the expensive specialty shops on Charles Street, with sidewalks of red brick dating back to the 1700s. We cut across the street past Buzzy's Roast Beef, Boston's best greasy spoon, and then passed the Charles Street Jail (which dates back to 1851). Hustling across the overpass, across Storrow Drive, we'd arrive (*finally*) at the girls' changing room, and our makeshift locker/weight room.

Each season, it only took about two weeks of practice before all the Science Park grass disappeared. Of course, calling it grass in the first place is being generous. Science Park was nothing but crabgrass and weeds supported by a sandy base. And, after a couple weeks of fifty kids running and tearing up the surface, we were left with what appeared to be competition for the Sahara. During the hot, dry weather, it was a dust bowl. Sweat made the dust stick to every pore on your body. We blew our noses after taking a shower and our towels were covered in black, gooey muck. When it rained, it was a mud bowl. When it froze, it was as hard as playing on a broken, splintered sidewalk.

Snow, of course, was the worst condition to play in. After thirty minutes of practice, the snow turned to slush and, after an hour, we'd lose all feeling in our toes. By that point, we had no feelings in our fingers from either tackling or making catches (gloves weren't permitted then). And if the wind was blowing off the Charles, then our ears (which you couldn't reach to warm while helmeted) felt as if they'd simply fall off during the next hit.

Practice uniforms that had once been fresh and clean were soaked and streaked with mud; the only thing warm in us was the anger and frustration we felt for volunteering for this madness and abuse in the first place.

To the coaches, the field and weather conditions were of little consequence. Somehow, it was all supposed to be character-building for us, and the coaches only seemed to relish in our misery.

It was a well-known (though unspoken) rule to never look at the Lechmere clock during practice. Of course, we all did anyway, and especially during the cold months. It hung across the Charles River, outside the Lechmere building, and it taunted us. Getting caught looking at the clock sent a message to the coaches that we weren't paying attention (or were just thinking of ourselves), and any hint of selfishness on the field was considered the ultimate sin.

"Kelly, I hope I didn't just see you looking at that clock. If I did, you'll being doing laps for the next hour!"

It wouldn't be until my senior year that the city would finally sod Science Park. That our competition had the luxury of athletic facilities (facilities that included actual grass!) right at their school while we only had Science Park seems comical to me now. But during the '72 season, we Bosco boys hiked three miles to practice on a surface that was more conducive for a rock fight than a game of football.

# CURRIER

Our head coach, Bob Currier, was from Brighton (as was assistant coach Dempsey). Bob had attended St. Columbkille's through high school and in 1951, after graduating from college, returned to his high school to begin his coaching career as an assistant football coach. After a few years, he moved up to the Catholic Central league and became an assistant coach at Matignon High School in Cambridge, Massachusetts. While at Matignon, players quickly learned to seek out and listen to Currier rather than their head coach. Currier had a superior understanding of the game and, because he could make adjustments during a game when things weren't working out well, his players trusted him. In 1963, Matignon went on to an undefeated season.

Life was running smoothly for Currier when a friend insisted he apply for the head football coaching job at Don Bosco. Currier had no interest or desire. He felt Bosco's athletic programs were run miserably, he disapproved of its athletic philosophy, and he even disliked the school colors. Sitting reluctantly in front of Athletic Director John Sull, with five candidates waiting in the lobby for their turn to interview, Currier was asked why he wanted the job.

"Truthfully, I don't want the job. My friend Murray said he arranged for the interview, so here I am." A stunned Sull asked what Currier disliked about Bosco's sports programs. "Everything! Your teams are undisciplined, your school colors are embarrassing, and your team records are terrible." Sull was writing it all down frantically.

"The following week," Currier recalls, "I was offered the job, and accepting it was the smartest decision I ever made. Brighton had an excellent Pop Warner program, so I recruited as many of those kids as possible to attend Bosco. I built my nucleus from those kids." In 1969, Bosco would become co-champions of the Central Division. In 1971, Bosco would receive the invitation to the big dance, the Catholic Conference. All of Currier's hard work and dedication had paid off.

He was intense and bright, and he demanded endurance and precision from all his players. He quickly made himself notorious for running a play over and over until it was run to *his* satisfaction, settling only for perfect execution. Nothing frustrated Currier more than mental mistakes—such things as missing an assignment, jumping off sides, running to the wrong hole, fumbling the ball, forgetting a play, or dropping a pass. And want to really get chewed out? Make the same mistake more than once.

"Kelly, how could you possibly block the linebacker on that play? The defensive end is right in front of you! Please explain to me what could possibly be going through your mind!"

Only a handful of players (most often the quarterbacks and running backs) were immune to Currier's wrath. The linemen were the ones most often the objects of his frustration (truth be told, the linemen have the tougher jobs). As linemen, we have to explode into other linemen, and all six linemen at a time have to do their jobs perfectly for a play to be successful. Running backs just need to find an opening, and quarterbacks just have to hand them the ball or toss a pass to a receiver. So, at least during practice, it'd make sense that more mistakes would be made by the line than in the backfield.

As a math teacher at Bosco, Currier ran his classes just like football practice. Every problem had a rule that solved it. If you didn't know the rule, he would get in your face. It was like not knowing your football plays. Some students would lock up in fear as he ranted, grilling us for not knowing one equation or another. I still remember when Jonathan, a small, shy kid in my class, froze up when Currier asked him for the reciprocal of four-fifths.

It wasn't a difficult problem, so Currier asked, "What is the rule?"

But Jonathan became so nervous that, as he started to answer, his words came out in a stutter. So Currier returned to the original question but, again, Jonathan was speechless. At this point, Currier came out from behind his desk, the entire room in an apprehensive silence, all of us just staring at this poor kid.

"Okay, Jonathan, relax. Let's start from the beginning. What's your name?"

"J-J-J-J-Jonathan."

"Great. What day is it?"

"W-W-W-Wednesday."

"Now you're cooking. What's today's date?"

Jonathan paused, looked up at the ceiling, desperately searching for the right answer.

"Within two days!"

We snickered, unable to help ourselves as Currier continued to play with Jonathan.

"The 12th?"

"Beautiful! Now, what is the reciprocal of four-fifths?"

But at Jonathan's continued silence, Currier slowly began to turn red, his demeanor no longer light and easy.

The harder Currier pressed, the more Jonathan stuttered. Currier refused to understand why the kid simply couldn't come up with the right answer. "The rule *never* changes, Jonathan," an exasperated Currier bellowed, "so why can't you give me the rule?"

Why Currier continued to torture the poor kid, I can't imagine. The episode lasted five minutes, but it felt like half a day. And like most Catholic school kids, instead of speaking out, we just put our heads down and thanked God it wasn't us.

While I worried about screwing up on the practice field and hated getting chewed out by Currier, I was never too intimidated by him in the classroom. I just didn't have trouble asking him for help. I can't explain it, but I must've been one of the few who actually enjoyed his classes. He was exceptional in his ability to analyze problems and explain how one might solve them. If he was in a good mood, he'd even inject humor into his teaching. He'd often even drop lessons entirely to switch into a sports scenario or discuss some bizarre football rule that no one had ever heard of. In these times, it was our job—our solemn duty—to ask questions and do anything in our power to keep him going. But whether or not on a digression, when Currier spoke, I never took my eyes off him. He had my complete attention, and he knew it.

Outside of practice, he was a great teacher and storyteller, but he also employed a cutting, sarcastic sense of humor. If you weren't on the receiving end, it was hilarious. But if you *were* on the receiving end . . . Well, just take Johnny Cochran for example.

Cochran was a teacher at Don Bosco. He'd been an All-Scholastic athlete in high school, a big guy, 6'4" and a good two hundred and fifty pounds. But something had happened to him—something *must've* happened to him—because, despite his size and successes, Cochran was often nervous and seemed to lack self-confidence. Because of this, he became an easy target for both coaches and students at Bosco. One day during history class, when Cochran looked particularly uneasy, sweating and shaking, I knew it was only a matter of time before the jokes would start rolling.

Finally, after nearly a half hour of stammering and pacing, he announced to the class that he could not teach. "Boys, something terrible has happened. My mother is in Europe and cannot be found!"

All of us fell silent and for the first time felt genuinely sorry for him. But then, later at lunch, a group of us saw Currier in the cafeteria and heard a very different story:

"Coach, isn't it terrible about Mr. Cochran's mother? The poor guy can barely function."

Currier, rolling his eyes, said, "Johnny Cochran's mother is with forty other people taking a tour of Europe. Cochran just doesn't know where she is *at this moment.* Can't you see Johnny at the airport? *Will the big red-headed kid with the lollipop report to the Lost and Found counter? We just found your momma!*"

Ten of us surrounded Currier as he looked up at us with a deadpan expression; we all walked away howling in laughter.

But while Currier knew how to dish it out with the best of 'em, it was Dempsey's pranks that really hit the mark. One of his most on-point gags took us seven years to learn the truth of.

It all started in the '70s, when Boston was the stolen car capital of the world. Most of us came from neighborhoods where seeing a stolen car was a daily occurrence, and where it was considered fairly normal. In my hometown of Hyde Park, we had our very own neighborhood car thief, a guy named Kenny Whiteman. Kenny was a tiny guy, but he had a giant personality and was a local legend. He'd begun stealing cars in the fourth grade and, during his early days, he'd carry a telephone book along with him to sit on so he'd be tall enough to see out over the windshield.

He also was absolutely fearless. At the age of twelve, Kenny could drive sixty miles per hour down a city street with cars parked on both sides, giving himself just inches to maneuver, and do it all with only one hand on the steering wheel.

Kenny had no problem driving by police sitting in their

cruisers—he'd just beep his horn, "Hey, fellas, think you can catch me while eating all those fuckin' donuts?" and, with a giant laugh, he'd take them on a wild goose chase, never to be caught. Then he'd just show up at school the next day and sit quietly in class as if nothing had happened. Stealing cars was simply a part of who we were and where we lived. Of course, because of kids like Kenny, auto insurance rates went through the roof. So, to beat the system, many Bostonians would register their cars outside city limits under a relative's name.

In the midst of all this, Coach Cochran purchased a beautiful, cream colored, 1974, Ford LTD when, sure enough, he was once again sweating and stuttering his way through class.

"Boys, my new car was stolen last night. I promise, if anyone finds my car, I'll take you to Pier 4 for dinner."

Everyone sat up straight; Cochran had our attention. Pier 4? Only rich people went to Pier 4; my parents maybe went there every five years or so to celebrate something special, but that was *it*. Pier 4? Pier 4 was a beautiful restaurant located on Boston Harbor. Famous visitors to Boston would always head over to Pier 4 for their renowned seafood and giant popovers. The foyer walls were packed with autographed celebrity photos (and always with Anthony, the owner, smiling arm-and-arm).

"Hey, Mr. Cochran, you pulling our legs?"

No, he insisted.

The game was on.

Four days later, a group of us were walking to practice, when suddenly I looked up and saw Cochran's car sitting right across the street from us.

"Hey, that's Johnny's car!" I called out, pointing.

"No shit!" Eddie Dominguez burst out. "Look, the doors are unlocked and everything."

Well, you can imagine how eager Eddie and I were to see

Cochran the next day in class.

"Mr. Cochran, you won't believe this, but I found your car! And it's right near the school—over on Washington Street!"

"Oh, Kevin, that's wonderful!" he gushed. *"Thank you.* I promise when I get the insurance check, we'll go straight to Pier 4."

"Wait a minute," Eddie chimed in, his frown deep and dramatic. *"I'm* the one that locked the car for you, Mr. Cochran. Kelly did nothin'! Why you takin' him?"

"Mr. Cochran," I broke in, "you're not going to listen to Dominguez, are you? He's just lookin' to mooch a free meal!"

"Mr. Cochran, to be honest, I don't even think Kelly *saw* your car," Eddie said, jostling with me to be in front and closest to Cochran.

"Hey, fellas," Eddie added, calling over his shoulder to Skip and Paul. "Did anyone hear Kelly say, 'That's Johnny's car?'"

"Okay, okay, stop," Cochran sighed, massaging the bridge of his nose. "I'll take both of you."

Eddie and I turned and winked at each other and, sure enough, Cochran was true to his word. He took us to Pier 4. Two city kids, living the high-life, eating dinner at Pier 4—what a night!

The story, however, was far from over because the question remained: Who the hell stole Cochran's car, only to return it to the school within a week?

Seven years later, when I was coaching at Bosco (with Currier still serving as head coach), we were both out one night and swapping Bosco war stories when I brought up this little bit of Cochran history and how Eddie and I had put one over on him to get to Pier 4. Currier heard me out but only looked at me in silence a moment before breaking out in laughter—too much laughter. I thought the story was funny, but not *that* funny. Currier could see the confused look on my face so, in between laughing and catching his breath, he informed me that it was actually Dempsey who'd stolen Cochran's car. He'd been driving it to and from Brighton to get to practice on time.

Dempsey, of course, had not been too concerned with how Cochran felt about having his car stolen. "We just needed someone to shit on," he was overheard saying one day at practice.

Dempsey's ability to live on both sides of the line was one we quickly came to both fear and admire.

But it was with Currier that all of us got started in football, and it was Currier who shaped the landscape for Dempsey's eventual arrival and triumph.

Currier had a gift for compartmentalizing his frustrations. He could chew you out unmercifully in practice on Monday and, the next morning in class, act as if nothing had happened. I still remember one particular day back in sophomore year. I'd screwed up in practice pretty badly, dropping a series of passes, and Currier had jumped all over me, making me run laps before replacing me.

So, the next day at school, I was nervous about approaching him for clarification on a math question, though I knew I needed to. Taking a deep breath as he exited his classroom, I straightened my shoulders, called out after him, and asked for his assistance. Not only did he help me with my math problem, but he asked about my brother Tom and discussed the Patriots' recent loss to the Oakland Raiders. I walked away uncertain if he was just a great guy off the field or the most forgetful person I'd ever met.

At Bosco, we all looked forward to our lunch break. We were given thirty-five minutes to eat, socialize, and reboot for our afternoon classes. But, for the football players, one particular lunchtime highlight was listening to the coaches discuss the Patriots,

Boston College football, and the upcoming games on our schedule. The conversations would be light, inviting, and threaded with moments of humor.

But I soon learned that getting chummy with the coaches came at a price. Who we were on the field and who we were in the classroom were two different things. After practice, most everyone showered and got ready to leave. But some began chatting after practice with the coaches and, over time, this group started meeting on a regular basis. They continued to share football stories and lots of laughs, but with losing came special retribution for them.

"Duggan, Finneran," said Currier at practice after our 0-3 start, not to mention our demoralizing 42-9 defeat by Boston College High School the day before. "You have no problem hanging out and laughing with the coaches after practice like we're all buddies, but you can't deliver during the game, can you?"

I made a mental note during my junior year to keep a comfortable distance from the coaches after practices. A quick wave good-bye and I was out of there.

During our two miserable seasons, some of my teammates (including me) wanted to quit at one point or another, but chose not to because of the inevitable social repercussions. To be a quitter at an all-boys' school was to carry a stigma that was awfully tough to overcome. No matter the reason, a quitter was a loser.

There was also the ever-present and simple desire to play football. It was a game we all loved, and it was a big part of our lives. That meant most of us were willing to put up with just about anything to play. We lived and died each week with the Patriots. After school and on the weekends, we played pickup games of both tag and tackle football. Most of us played Pop Warner football. Many of us had older brothers who played high school football. They were regarded as the toughest kids in the neighborhood, and thus kids we all looked up to. We just didn't realize that moving up to the high school level was not only going to be so much more difficult and less fun, but also, for the first time for many of us, carry a tremendous amount of pressure.

Even with all this cultural and social baggage, there were still some very talented athletes at Bosco who refused to even try out for football because of Currier's coaching methods. The word around school was, "It's Bob's way or the highway," and some kids simply never responded well to being yelled at, embarrassed, and publicly humiliated.

From my time as a player at Bosco, there are a few Currier coaching moments in particular that stick out clearest in my mind and that perhaps Currier wishes had never taken place. Once, during my sophomore year, Currier became extremely frustrated. It was a late October practice, and it was cold, cloudy, and windy. The field was muddy from three days of rain and we had just lost our fifth straight game. Morale was low. No one could do anything right, and we simply didn't want to be on the field anymore.

"Run that play again!" Currier shouted, spittle flying and his face red from the cold and aggravation. "How could you possibly miss that tackle, Kelly? If you drop one more pass, I'll have you carrying a football twenty-four hours a day!"

Michael Shea was a good kid and a decent athlete. I can't recall the precise reason why Currier was so upset with him—Michael blew a play or perhaps dropped a pass—but the combination of mediocrity and lack of player enthusiasm caused Currier to come down hard on this poor kid: "Shea! You call yourself a football player? You're a *disgrace*." Then suddenly, the unthinkable— Currier *spit* in Michael's face. A jolt was sent through the entire team; everyone stared in astonishment. It was an unforgivable act by a coach, a uselessly degrading act. How could any athlete benefit from such treatment? Where was the lesson, the mentoring, the inspiration in this? All of us could feel Michael's rage, but he took it and we moved on, none of us ever bold enough to confront Currier about it.

Being yelled at generates different responses from different players. For most, it's a wake-up call to concentrate, to focus, to play for the team. For some, however, it only creates more tension, doubt, and resentment. Being humiliated, though, is another story. Two talented linemen, Billy Dunly and Paul Denny, had simply had enough by the end of their junior year.

Billy, who actually played varsity during the middle of his sophomore year, turned in his equipment with no explanation. To a teammate, none was needed. No one was in Billy's face asking why or what had happened.

I not only got it, I admired the courage it took for Billy to quit.

Paul teetered on the edge of quitting his junior year but ended up coming to camp his senior year. For Paul, the first few days brought a barrage of criticism: "Denny, what's wrong with you? Why are you so out of shape? Jesus, Denny, run the play again!"

After our second day of camp, Paul sat down next to me, head in his hands, and said, "Kev, I'm going to the coaches' cabin, and I'm telling them I'm going home. Hey, maybe they're right. Maybe I don't have what it takes to play football."

"Paul, this is just part of Currier's strategy!" I said, knowing we couldn't lose another star player like Paul without suffering real consequences. "He does this every year. Monday and Tuesday, we can't do anything right, and then tomorrow we'll have pit-drills, and, I promise you, he'll have us all sky-high after practice. Then he'll spend Thursday and Friday building us up for our scrimmage against Watertown—it's all a part of his pattern. Just stay one more day. You're our strongest lineman, Paul—we can't lose you!"

"Nah," he said, though he smiled appreciatively. "I'm done, Kel. But thanks anyway."

For the majority of us, football was the top of the food chain in high school athletics, and we grew to accept gridiron conditions that had been around for decades. Coaches had been pushing players too hard for generations, and it didn't stop at the high school level.

The legendary running back Jim Brown, who played for the Cleveland Browns during the '50s and '60s, once said that he could never have played for Vince Lombardi. "That in-your-face style of coaching would have led to a stand-off between Lombardi and me," said Brown. His coach, the great Paul Brown, was quiet and businesslike on the field and, though intense, known for *not* ridiculing players in front of other teammates.

The great Celtic coach, Red Auerbach, who won eleven world championships in thirteen NBA seasons during the '50s and '60s, employed, in my humble opinion, the best style of coaching. He knew who could take a tongue-lashing and who needed a pat on the back. He knew his players' personalities and how to get the most out of them. Hall of Famer Tommy Heinsohn, who played forward for the Celtics from 1956 to 1965 and helped them win eight world championships in nine years, could take a verbal whipping. But with Bill Russell, voted the greatest defensive basketball center of all time, Auerbach was softer. Heinsohn got inspired when Auerbach was on him, but Russell needed a different kind of motivation and Auerbach knew it.

Much of the time, Currier lacked this flexibility. He had one approach and it didn't matter how a player felt about it. Like many of my teammates, I cringed in fear of getting singled out, knowing all the while that, if he went too far, I'd take it out on the guy in front of me on the field (which, of course, was exactly what Currier was banking on). But, in Currier's defense, his style of coaching never wavered. Year after year, team after team, Currier's method was consistent.

His unknown secret, which he never took any public credit for, was the unending number of kids he recruited to Bosco. Thanks to him, many never had to worry about paying one dime towards tuition. For decades, Currier pulled kids off the streets and gave them the opportunity to receive a top-flight Catholic education along with learning a trade; many went on to college or became independent contractors. Currier was just as committed to his boys as Dempsey, but it came across differently. To this day, there are hundreds of alumni who keep in touch with Coach Currier, who continues to coach football at the age of 80! "Some people my age like to simply retire, travel, relax, or play golf. I like to coach," Currier said.

But during the 1970s and 1980s, all three Kelly boys were targets of his wrath.

Once when my brother Tom was a senior, Currier, thoroughly upset that the team couldn't run a particular play correctly, noticed that Tom had stopped hustling up to the line of scrimmage after the offense broke the huddle. Also, Tom was dragging his feet and keeping his head down as he made his way back to the huddle after the play was completed. He was exhausted and didn't realize that his sluggishness was costing everyone more and more runs of the play. Finally, Currier blew a gasket. He grabbed Tom by the face mask and started beating on it while chewing him out for not hustling.

Playing tight end two years later, I had a similar experience. When the quarterback said "Hit," I was supposed to come out of my stance, move six yards to my right, and stand up like a split end. But I didn't move. I heard the whistle blow and, out of nowhere, Currier kicked me right in the ass, screaming, *"RUN THE PLAY!"* Well, of course, nothing changed on the next play because I still didn't know what the hell I was supposed to be doing. So, he kicked me again.

This lovely pattern continued until, finally, Currier walked up to me and asked, "Kelly, what play are we running?"

"I'm not sure, Coach," I admitted.

"You're not sure? Only a moron wouldn't know his plays by mid-October!"

I didn't dare disagree.

At the end of practice, he had us gather around and take a knee. He explained what we needed to do to get ready for the next day's game, scanning the players and giving instructions when, suddenly, his eyes locked on me.

"Kelly, two years ago, I almost broke my hand on your brother's face mask. This year, I have no desire to break my foot on your ass. Learn your plays!"

Everyone had a good laugh.

For me, it merely took a simple moment of recognition, encouragement, and support from Currier to turn me around.

Currier ignored the fact that some kids were only fifteen years old while others were as old as nineteen. For him, as for many coaches, building toughness, motivation, and consistency isn't always about accommodating personalities and age groups. Most football coaches treat everyone the same in order to weed out the players who are only going to make it so far. Football, like life, is about survival of the fittest. Currier wasn't the only coach in America who coached with that particular philosophy and style in mind. The iron fist approach is still alive and well today in many schools. However, with mandatory coaching courses, the rise in player concussions, and the number of lawsuits now being filed against coaches for negligence and abuse, the pendulum does seem to be swinging in the other direction.

In my sophomore year, Bosco's football team was huge and tough, but we still lost every game but one. We had plenty of talent but no team unity. The players and the coaches turned on one other.

Playing for Bosco became a miserable experience. Every day, practice was nothing but mistakes, followed by ridicule and verbal abuse from Currier and the assistant coaches. It led to a time when I and many of my teammates hated going to practice. During rainy days, we would constantly peek out the windows to check if puddles were being splattered by raindrops, all of us hoping practice would be canceled. It was usually just wishful thinking.

"Hey, Coach, did I hear practice was canceled today?"

"Now Kelly," he'd say, "why would we cancel practice because of rain if we don't cancel *games* because of rain? Don't be late!"

That year, I saw some action during a few varsity games. Often the game was out of reach, and Currier would give some JV players some reps, but it was still a thrill to play at the varsity level, even if we were losing. Although Currier could be tough, I appreciated that he had no problem having fourteen-year-old freshmen and eighteen-year-old seniors play alongside one another. His theory was that performance, ability, and attitude trumped age. As long as a player could contribute, he'd get playing time.

Playing in JV games was great. We had fun, and the JV level gave us a chance to be introduced slowly to high school football with kids generally our age, size, and ability. But each week of the season, JV players also posed as the Varsity's upcoming opponents, both on offense and defense. For the Varsity, such game preparation was great. For JV players preparing to eventually be on the Varsity team, it was good too. Of course, it was still often intimidating to play against the Varsity team. Many of the JV players simply could not compete with the Varsity players, a fact which inevitably made practice a miserable experience (especially if the Varsity team wasn't performing to the coaches' satisfaction).

When Coach became frustrated, he'd shout, "Okay, gentlemen, every play from this point forward is *live!*"

This meant full-contact. As a sophomore, whenever practices

turned live, I used to pray that the guy lined up against me (years older and at least forty pounds heavier) was in a good mood, uninterested in drive-blocking me into the Charles River!

The last game of that year was against New Bedford, a team made up of mostly giant, tough, Portuguese-American kids. Toward the end of the game, things started getting rough. With both teams trash-talking and taunting each other, the refs found themselves breaking up a lot of pushing and shoving.

When the game finally ended (they'd beaten us pretty soundly), a father holding a small child approached our captain, Michael Murphy and, for no apparent reason, shoved him. Michael, weighing in at about two hundred and fifty pounds, spun around and punched the guy right in the face. The father hit the deck as if he'd been blindsided by a linebacker, a move that sent his kid flying out of his arms and onto the field a good ten feet away. I stood fifteen yards behind Michael and watched the whole incident unfold. Within thirty seconds, both teams (fans included!) were brawling. It was a true riot.

Ten-foot high bushes surrounded New Bedford's field. As we made our mad rush for the bus, we could see New Bedford students chasing after us from behind the bushes. We leapt into the bus for a hasty escape but they began pelting the bus with rocks.

"Boys, cover your heads!" yelled Currier, rocks ricocheting off the windows.

We barely got out of town alive. On the way home, the bus was filled with chatter and high energy. For the first time all year, we felt unified. It'd been our fight, and we left feeling as if we'd finally made a statement, the first of the entire season. When we arrived back at Science Park, everyone expected to hear the usual from Currier: "We weren't tough enough, we didn't really want it badly enough, we made mental mistakes, we had no pride," and so on. Not to mention that we deserved a sound verbal-thrashing for engaging in a full-out brawl, with fans and players alike clobbering each other.

But he had something else to say that night: "Boys," he said, "to be honest, I wish this game had taken place six games ago. Even though we lost, you fought together as a team, and team unity is a very special component of football. I haven't seen that level of spirit all year! This season has been difficult for everyone, and I want to thank each and every one of you for being part of it. It's easy to stay with a winning team. When everyone feels good, it seems effortless; it's fun. But it takes a tremendous amount of discipline to come to practice every day when you're losing week in and week out. I especially want to thank the seniors. We all wish your last year at Bosco could have turned out better. For the younger classmen, work hard in the off-season and we'll see you next year!"

Though Currier would never know it, that speech is what made me continue to play football at Bosco. Everything made perfect sense to me then. *Of course* football was going to suck if you lost every week. But we didn't have to lose anymore.

I ended my sophomore season with a new sense of purpose. I knew I was athletic, but I hadn't yet proven to the coaches or to myself that I could be a contributing member of the team. There were still too many demons I needed to overcome, fear being number one: the fear of being hit, the fear of being hurt, the fear of screwing up.

All of us were still in the early stages of discovering ourselves.

But somehow we all knew that things were going to be different junior year. And Currier? He knew he had to try another approach.

In early June 1973, Currier held a mandatory meeting for

all football players at Bosco. Morale was low and no one I knew was looking forward to football camp. School had already let out and it was *hot*. I was sitting in the back of the room half-asleep when Currier walked in and announced that there would be a new face among the coaching staff. "Boys, we have a new line coach, someone I promise you'll all get to know *real well, real soon*. I'd like to introduce Coach Jack Dempsey."

I sat up as if someone had hit me with an electric current, suddenly wide-eyed and wide-awake. Could this be the same Jack Dempsey my brother had described two years earlier? I wasn't sure, but I knew I needed to find out.

What struck me first was how oddly built Dempsey looked. His neck was thick and short, his back was enormously wide, and his chest and shoulders were a single mass of muscle. His legs were so thick he had a sway to his walk, almost an overly exaggerated gait as he moved from left to right and forward all at once. His hands were like Popeye's, small and thick with wide wrists. To the average person, he might've looked dumpy. But to football players, he was a human cinder block with large, square, Coke-bottle glasses. He walked to the podium with an unassuming air, soft-spoken but confident.

He opened with a speech that was short and to the point. He didn't guarantee we'd win every game. Instead, he guaranteed we'd be the best-conditioned football team in the league.

"You boys are going to be a team that earns your opponents' respect because, on the football field, we will never quit no matter what the score. *Never*. Mandatory weight-lifting sessions begin next week at Science Park, and there are no excuses for missed workouts."

Though his speech itself was unexpected in its simplicity, lacking any "we'll-win-'em-all" promises, he had everyone's undivided attention as he spoke. There was something special about him. Immediately drawn to his inner strength, I had a comfortable feeling that he was "in charge" of us all. I could sense that the atmosphere and energy in the room had shifted. Now we players were excited and hopeful for our next season. What we didn't know at the time was that Dempsey wasn't just a mild change in the football weather—Dempsey was a tornado.

Currier knew he needed help with his coaching staff. Although Bosco had six coaches already, none of them could make the commitment or had the ability to forge a team that could truly compete in the Catholic Conference. Dempsey and Currier had known one another for years, both having lived in Brighton. Dempsey had always admired and respected Currier as a coach, and so jumped at the chance to work with him. For the next four years, it would be the ideal coaching combination.

While taking the train home, I felt a rush of excitement, nervousness, and fear, thinking about our new coach. On the one hand, I could tell by Dempsey's confidence that he *knew* football. On the other hand, I liked both of my ears, and wasn't in any hurry to have either of them bitten off.

# NATURE OR NURTURE

*"I love you and I always will."*
—Christine Kelly

Thomas J. Kelly, Sr., poverty-stricken and struggling to survive on his family's two hundred-year-old farm in Athlone, Ireland, arrived in Boston in May 1914. Three years later, he enlisted in the Navy and served on a U.S. submarine during WWI. Upon his return from the war, he purchased a three-decker home in West Roxbury, a heavily populated Irish community on the outskirts of Boston. His was the American dream come true. He'd had his whole life planned out: work hard, raise a family and, upon retirement, collect a pension along with bonus income from renting out the second and third floors of his new home on LaGrange Street.

The dream came to an end, however, when the Great Depression hit in 1929. He lost the house, and was forced to move his wife and five children into the loud, cramped Old Colony housing projects in South Boston. No front yard, no backyard, and no privacy.

My grandfather worked three jobs to provide for his family.

His main source of income came from Wonder Bread, where he worked as lead mechanic and shop steward for more than thirty-five years. My grandfather was a tough, independent, hard-working "Mick" who went far beyond paying his dues. Until he reached his seventies, he never had enough time or financial independence to enjoy his life. The experience made him tough, but that toughness came at a great price, leaving him cold and distant even toward his own family. We convinced him at the age of ninety-two to return to Ireland and reunite with a brother he hadn't seen or spoken to in seventy years.

The visit changed his life. On seeing his mother's grave, he got down on his knees and said, "Often, my mother would take a pound of butter, place it in a bucket of water to keep from melting, and travel twelve miles by donkey to Banlesloe. She'd spend all day trying to sell that butter for fifty cents." With tears running down his face, my grandfather looked over his shoulder: "Many a night my mother came home with that butter."

After returning to America, he opened up even more, sharing memories of his life and beginning to reconnect with his children. I could sense that he knew his time was running out, and he needed someone to confide in. Whatever the reason, he chose me. "I never got over losing the house. It had been my chance—my chance to make it. But we survived. Many rich people jumped to their deaths knowing they'd lost everything, but somehow we managed to pull through." As he turned and looked off in the distance, I noticed his skin as if seeing it for the first time. It was weather-worn but beautiful—the skin of a long life lived hard.

My father, Thomas J. Kelly, Jr., fared much better than his father. In 1953, after following in his father's footsteps with a tour in the Navy, my dad achieved two milestones: He married my mother, Christine Baker, whom he met while working at Boston City Hospital (she was then a nurse and he a lab technician) and he graduated from the Boston Police Academy. That same year, he purchased a two-family home in Hyde Park. We lived on Tyler Street with a mix of Irish and Italian neighbors.

For the most part, my father was an easy-going, good-natured guy. But he also had a cop's black-and-white sense of morality. To him, family image and reputation were all important. "The worst thing that can ever happen to a policeman is to have one of his sons get arrested," he once told Tommy and me (I was only seven at the time, an orange popsicle dripping in my hands). "If you ever get arrested, I'll break every bone in your body. Do you understand me?" I certainly got the message, but Tom must've been distracted by something in our yard's crabapple tree at the time because, over the next few years, he got to know our local police force all too well.

Hyde Park was a middle-to-lower class Irish-Italian neighborhood made up of hard-working, church-going, first-and second-generation Americans. My neighbors took pride in their families and in their properties. As kids, we all played seasonal sports—football in the fall, hockey and basketball in the winter, and baseball in the spring. All of us played together outside after school and on the weekends. Touch football, pick-up basketball, street hockey, street baseball, sledding, skating, hide-and-seek, and bike-riding—it was all part of our kid culture in Hyde Park during the '60s and '70s. To us, it was heaven. My friends were never allowed to mope and sit around the house. "Get outside and get some fresh air or I'll find something for you to do," was often heard from the parents on our street.

Hyde Park was great to grow up in. It was a tough neighborhood, but not a violent one. Sure, there were plenty of fights, drinking, drugs, car thefts, and some minor street crime, but you never had to worry about being murdered or getting jumped for no reason. Most families in my section of Hyde Park never even locked their doors. No one carried guns, and drive-by shootings weren't yet part of our cultural fabric. Neighbors looked out for one another and everyone knew each other's kids. Being disrespectful or foul-mouthed to a neighbor was mostly unheard of, and you paid a heavy price if your parents found out you crossed that line.

Our moral compass was set by the surrounding environment. My group, for instance, wouldn't steal a car or take drugs, but with so many kids in the neighborhood stealing and using drugs, you just came to accept those things as a part of life. We even had a kid in our neighborhood called "Fop"—a great kid, funny, and a constant wheeler dealer. Fop looked like Frankie Valli, short, with a '50s hairdo and a cocky smile, and always well-dressed. If Fop saw you walking down the street, he'd never say hi. He'd just point a finger in your direction and wink at you. Fop actually turned into a hell of a stage performer and sang in many of New England's top clubs.

But as he struggled his way up, he had to make ends meet however he could. So, one night, he and his buddies drove a truck through a store window and stole hundreds of leather jackets. Word got out that Fop was selling the jackets in Curry College's kitchen for forty bucks a pop—and everyone flocked to Curry immediately. How he got away with it is anyone's guess, but a large part of it was no doubt due to the neighborhood's acceptance and tacit endorsement of the crime. After all, who could be that angry at a guy who sold premium leather jackets for only forty bucks apiece?

One day, my father and Fop bumped into each other coming out of our local supermarket, The Stop and Shop. It was a cool, sunny fall day and it just so happened that Fop was wearing one of the stolen leather jackets. At 6'2", my dad towered over Fop, but Fop never showed any signs of being intimidated. My dad always liked Fop; everyone did. He was one of those gifted kids no one could ever get mad at, no matter what he did. But still, my dad was a cop and everyone, *everyone*, knew that Fop was selling stolen leather jackets.

So my dad sidled up to Fop, a full load of groceries in his cart. Fop had his six-pack of beer inside a brown paper bag neatly tucked under his right arm, as if he was protecting a delivery to the Brinks Company.

"Hey, Fop, what's up?" said my father, starting up the conversation.

"Hi, Mr. Kelly. How's it going?"

"How's your mother doing? I saw her but not you in church last Sunday."

"She's doing fine. Thanks for asking. Geez, I think I wasn't feeling very well that day."

"Word down at the precinct is you may know something about the leather coats that got stolen out of Zayres Leather Goods."

"Mr. Kelly, now what makes you think that?"

"I'm also hearing that you're selling the coats for forty dollars a whack out of Curry College's kitchen."

"You don't say."

"Of course, all of this would be speculation if I hadn't seen Kevin wearing a brand new four hundred dollar leather jacket Friday night."

"Hey, Mr. Kelly, what size coat you wear?"

"46-large. Why?"

"I think I have a beautiful green one with your name on it."

"If asked, I'll deny you ever said that, but I do like the color green. Brings out my Irish green eyes, don't you think? Say hello to your mother for me, and don't miss church next Sunday."

"Will do. As always, nice seeing you, Mr. Kelly."

No one ever asked my father how he came to have his own four hundred dollar leather coat; they didn't have to.

But, for Tom and me, Hyde Park would be much more than just our neighborhood. The Hyde Park community would not only rally around us, but save us both.

It was June 29, 1964. I was seven and Tom was ten. Our mother, Christine, was thirty-four, beautiful, and well-respected in the neighborhood. She was also intelligent, reflective, and, it seemed to us, trouble-free. Having graduated second in her nursing class, she worked at the Peter Bent Brigham Hospital in Boston. I knew she loved us, though, curiously, I don't have any memories of feeling all that close to her.

Before dinner that summer evening, she came into Tom's and my shared bedroom and kissed us both on the head, saying, "I love you and always will." I thought it was strange to hear my mother declare those words out of the clear blue. I looked at my brother with an uneasy smile, unsure what was going on. I remember her saying that she was going downstairs to do some laundry, then would pick up my father at the five o'clock train arriving in Cleary Square.

Soon thereafter, Tom and I began fighting. He accused me of stealing his Carl Yastrzemski baseball card, and so I went bounding down the stairs shouting, "Mom, he's lying!" As I turned the corner into the basement, the scene in front of me took away my ability to breathe, and what I saw next has been permanently burned into my memory: the cut rope tossed on the ground, the cutlery knife, the empty chair. If there was a hidden gift to this unimaginable moment, it was not being able to see my mother's face. I had a backside view of her bare feet hovering inches off the ground. At that moment, I knew two things for certain: My mother was dead and she had taken her own life.

Tom, still chasing me, ran around the corner and stumbled into me. Before he said a word, I turned and ran, bursting through the cellar door and sprinting onto the front lawn where, gasping for air, tears filled my eyes and blurred my vision. I felt as if someone had knocked the wind out of me.

Watering his tulips, Joe Hoffman, our neighbor, saw me as I raced, sobbing, across the street.

"Kevin! Are you okay?" he called, dropping the gardening hose as he ran toward me.

"My mother," I said in shock. "She's dead in the basement."

Mr. Hoffman looked at me in disbelief. He grabbed my hand to walk me back home.

"No!" I screamed, fighting like a tiger, trying to release myself from his grip. I couldn't go back to that house. But he picked me up and carried me. We approached the basement door cautiously. He peeked inside, holding me to his chest so I faced the yard. I felt his heart pound and heard him say, "Oh, my dear God!"

I have no memory of what he said to my brother and me as he took us to the Golden family a few houses up the street.

My dad, having waited half an hour at the train station for my mother to pick him up, walked home. He turned the corner onto Tyler Street and discovered policemen, firemen, ambulance drivers, and a street overflowing with neighbors. All of the neighbors kept their distance from our house, standing outside the caution line, but they packed in, getting as close as they could to the drama.

Three of my neighbors—men I admired and would grow to love—were waiting for my father in our living room. My father tried to remain calm, but he was crazed and confused, wondering what disaster had befallen his family that required policemen and ambulances. Was it one of his boys? Had something happened to his wife?

Bob Johnson sat my father down and said, "Tom, before I talk to you, I want you to take off your gun." As my father placed his gun on the fireplace mantle, Bob looked my father straight in the eye. "You're in trouble. Chris is downstairs and . . . Tom, she—she's dead."

My father flew downstairs and cut the rope from which my mother hung. She came down into his arms, and he laid her on the cellar floor and desperately tried to revive her. He held her, begging her to come back, crying into her chest. But she was gone.

My father finally let her go, knowing he had to find his boys. The local priest, Father Johnson, questioned us. I was a wreck; I couldn't stop crying. Tom sat quietly in the living room, stunned, trying to make sense of what had happened. When my father finally came into the Goldens' house, I couldn't stop staring at him—I couldn't believe it; he was wailing uncontrollably. Grief-stricken, he grabbed my brother and me and held us tight.

A few weeks later, my father sat us down and asked us if we should move. Despite our initial shock and fears of the house, we said no—we wanted to stay. Hyde Park was our home and friends and neighbors were part of our lives. I had already lost my mother. I couldn't imagine losing my friends too. For my father's well-being, moving made perfect sense. To come home every day and be reminded of the tragedy that'd taken place must have been hell for him. But he was our rock. He understood what we needed, and stay we did. I attribute my recovery and sense of well-being to my father, my friends, and all our neighbors in Hyde Park. Their generosity and support meant the world to my family.

Tom and I had long ago bonded as brothers but, by experiencing this trauma together, we grew even closer, though we handled it in our own unique way. Tom, as quiet as our mother, refused to talk about her life or death. I, on the other hand, have always been outgoing, and so I never stopped wanting to know *why* she did it. Hungry for an answer, I constantly asked my neighbors for their opinion about what could have caused her to take her own life.

Bob Johnson lived directly across the street from us. A tough WWII veteran (and a Navy guy like my dad), he was short and slim with a no-nonsense directness that demanded respect. I got a kick out of watching him speak without ever removing his unfiltered Camel cigarette from his lips; it was a constant fixture. Bob and my father were close. There was a tremendous level of respect between the two of them. His wife, Kathryn, was also tough, but extremely kind, especially to Tom and me. Whenever I had questions about my mother's death, Bob made himself available to me. But Kathryn would often become overwhelmed and leave us alone with a plate of Oreo cookies and glass of milk, her only contribution to the conversation being, "The whole street was worried about you poor kids. We just didn't know how you would turn out."

Bob told me, "I spoke to your mother that morning and was taken aback by how chatty she was. Your mother was very private—pleasant but private—almost regal. After I said hello to her, she chattered away for the next five minutes like we were old friends. Your mother had lived on Tyler Street for eleven years and never shared anything more than a polite hello or a wave with me. She asked me about my kids and any plans we had for the summer. She laughed, talking about you and Tommy and how you, especially, were a handful. 'Tommy is a Baker, but that Kevin is a *true* Kelly. Uncontrollable,' she said, puffing on a Parliament Menthol. Looking back, I'm convinced your mother had made up her mind that this was the day she was going to end her life and that she was actually at peace with her decision."

It wasn't enough.

I continued to search for answers about my mother. None of my aunts or uncles believed that my mom had indicated anything was amiss in her life. She hadn't spoken with any of them privately about being unhappy with her marriage or anything else. Dad, also, was at a loss as to why. His theory was that she had received some new vaccine months earlier, and perhaps there was a neurological side effect that had caused her to become depressed. I could only conclude that she found herself in impossible pain—a pain she'd hidden well.

Many surviving family members of suicide victims say that they feel anger at the people who take their own lives, that they believe the person who commits suicide is selfish, a coward taking the easy way out. And though my father and brother acknowledged having these feelings toward Mom, I never experienced them myself. I felt it took a lot of courage for her to take her own life. I don't think everyone is capable of such an act. Yet, I remained mystified. Growing up, I missed her dearly, and often wondered what my life would have been had she lived.

The hole inside me from my mother's suicide had a direct effect on my self-confidence. I was always aware that my family wasn't intact anymore. The newest emotion introduced into my life was fear. Before my mother's death, I had never felt any level of fear. I had a nonstop motor, and life amounted to an endless exploration of discoveries: playing, biking, swimming, running, climbing trees, sports. Everything in my life was great.

But the jolt of my mother's death struck me deeply, and fear, doubt, and uncertainty took over much of my life for years to come. I was constantly seeking approval, acceptance, and attention— things healthy parents give their children as building blocks for a successful adulthood. Half of my foundation was gone.

But what my mother's death also gave me was a renewed appreciation for life, a thirst to prove myself, and a new sense of what is right and wrong. For better or worse, I, like my father, began to view the world in absolutes.

Tom, on the other hand, spent his teenage life hanging out at the park, experimenting with drugs, often coming home high or drunk. He even got arrested a few times. That was his way of dealing with our mother's death.

Two years after Mom died, our father remarried. Kathleen Shields became our new mother. She was kind, caring, and emotionally available to us. She and my father would have four children together: Kathy, John, Patricia, and Ann. Tom and I went from an unimaginable tragedy to hitting the family lottery. Katie, as we called her, would become our true mother. We never referred to her or our new brother and sisters as "steps."

We were one family, and she raised and loved us as her own. Eventually, for me, it became natural to call her Mom. She would become my closest and dearest friend. I could go to her with anything. She was always straight and honest with me. When we deserved a tongue-lashing or a whack across the head, we got it, but we knew she was always there for us. She was the perfect mother. Step-parents often have a difficult time winning acceptance in a new household. For us, the adjustment was natural, untainted by resentments, scuffles for control, territory, or love. She was a gift from God, and we all knew it. She saved us.

After the babies were born, Tom and I moved into the basement (that way Kathy and John could be closer to our parents' room). Our new bedroom was eight feet away from where our mother had died. When my parents went out for an evening, I would be the one elected to stay at home to babysit. Tommy was old enough to go out at night and hang out with his friends. My parents would insist, however, that I go to bed at ten.

As Kathy and John fell asleep, the house would settle and I would hear squeaking noises, like footsteps—noises that only grew louder in the silence. As I lay in bed, I felt a terrible sense that someone was in the basement moving about. I have no memory of consciously thinking that it was my mother's spirit. Instead, I remember it more as a fear of a stranger. I would freeze up in bed for hours at a time, lying stiffly awake, waiting for the intruder to leave. When at last I heard my brother stumble in hours later, I raced up the stairs in a panic.

"Tom, I think someone might be in the house! I've been hearing footsteps all night!"

"Okay, calm down," Tom said, gripping my shoulder. "We'll walk through the basement together." He grabbed a flashlight as I followed closely behind.

Not once during these episodes did my brother laugh at me, mock me, or ignore me.

"Alright, no one's in the house. Are you okay now?" I nodded, trying to be brave. "Listen, I'm gonna be here the rest of the night. I'll be in the den watching TV. Go back to bed. I'll be down when Dad and Kate get home." Every time I babysat, I felt a giant burden lift off my shoulders as soon as Tom came home, and only then could I fall asleep.

I've always been grateful to him for that, for tuning into my feelings and worrying about me being alone in the house so soon after our mother's death. I loved Tommy.

And though he may have buried his feelings about our mother's death while I wore mine on my sleeve, I know he found relief in the same place I always have—on the football field. Football was the perfect escape for him. It gave him the opportunity to direct his emotions and release his pain. He was a different kid during football season, calm and at ease. But even with football as his therapy, he struggled because he was easily led astray. When he started coming home drunk, he paid a heavy price with our father, who would not tolerate any of his sons drinking.

"Where the hell were you?" my father demanded one Friday night as Tom staggered drunkenly through the door.

"Dad, I was over at Jackie Gillfoy's house. We were watching the Celtics." My father must have smelled the booze on him—Tom was close enough to his face to kiss him. "Hey, Dad, they're winning by twenty-one points—"

*SMACK!*

I stood in a humming silence until our father managed to aim a hard finger at Tom and say, "Well, let me tell you something, Mister. You're setting a bad example for Kevin!"

I watched and listened. It wasn't as entertaining as I hoped, although it was amusing to see my father try to lay a good smack across his face as Tom reeled around, unable to stand up straight. All I could think was, *Bullshit! Tom's setting a great example!* But I had no desire to be on the receiving end of my father's right hand or to disappoint the man who'd been there for me during those difficult years, so I kept quiet and knew I wouldn't be following Tom's lead. I loved my father, respected my father, and feared my father. For me, challenging him wasn't an option.

Tom eventually came around, turning out just fine, but in those first years after our mother's death, he became the star of some epic family stories to be retold over Thanksgiving dinners for a long time to come.

# DEMPSEY

Clyde John (Jack) Dempsey was born to Francis and Lillian Dempsey on March 29, 1945. His dad was a former football player at Georgia Tech and an amateur boxer. As a young kid, Clyde was often picked on. He later became a ferocious street fighter with an explosive temper and quick hands.

Dempsey also became a two-time All-American lineman at Boston English High School during the mid-'60s. Boston English was so talented at the time, they ranked seventh overall in the nation. Before graduation, Dempsey was told that, if he wanted to play football at the college level, he'd have to complete a post-graduate year to boost his academic profile. Bridgeton Academy had an opening. For years, I attempted to find anyone who played with Dempsey at Bridgeton, but I continued to hit nothing but dead ends. Then, out of nowhere, Wayne Lynch emailed my publisher Bruce Bortz, and within fifteen minutes, Wayne and I were on the phone. "My teammates and I would love to meet with you."

In the fall of 2015, while this book was reaching its final stages, I traveled to Bridgeton, Maine to meet the members of Bridgeton Academy's 1965 football team, gathered to celebrate their 50th reunion. Bridgeton is a unique prep school—a one-year school for high school graduates seeking to better their grades or athletic exposure before entering college. This was where Dempsey had gone after graduating from high school.

Before Bridgeton's game with Navy Prep, eleven men in their late 60s sauntered out to midfield for the coin toss. From the sidelines, it was nothing short of mind boggling to see these highly successful athletic men dwarfed by today's athletes, many of whom weighed close to or more than 300 pounds.

Wayne Lynch, for example, played offensive guard alongside Dempsey, and the two roomed together. Neither broke the 5'-8," 200-pound barrier.

"Dempsey and I were lucky enough to live in a house on campus and to share a room on the second floor. All the other kids had to live in the dorms.

"Hands down, Clyde Jack Dempsey was the toughest person I ever met in my life. Pound for pound, there was nobody tougher, harder working, or more dedicated to his friends, his teammates, and his school than he was!"

After Bridgeton, Wayne would play football and baseball for American International College in Springfield, Ma.

"As far as the rules and restrictions of boarding school, Dempsey complied with nothing! He was impulsive, and he had a very quick temper. Good or bad, right or wrong, he was all in."

"I don't think you understand." chimed in Joe Amico, another offensive lineman and defensive end, who later continued his football career at the University of Massachusetts. "There was no on-off-switch with Jack. If he made up his mind to do something, there was no talking him out of it. He lived in an absolute world."

Dempsey, added Amico, was a natural born leader who had charisma, and everyone wanted to hang out with him. "A lot of people like to focus on Dempsey's negatives, but there were plenty of positives."

"In what way?" I asked.

"Jack had a moral compass, and to his friends, he was ferociously loyal. He was brutally honest, sincere, compassionate, compelling, and enthusiastic. He LIVED! There was something about Jack that the rest of us wished we had!"

"*Ferociously loyal* is a pretty strong term," I said. "Can you recall a moment that captures that quality?"

Duane Johnson jumped in: "Attending the school that year was a kid named Bobby Lynch—no relation to Wayne. He had a minor altercation with a guy who worked in the kitchen. The guy was being a real jerk, so Bobby pushed him. The headmaster dismissed Bobby from Bridgeton. Jack and Bobby were close. The next day at lunch, Jack stood up and said to the entire student body. 'I think what happened to Bobby was unfair. He was my friend!' Jack promptly walked out of the dining hall. One hundred and five students left their lunches and walked out with him. Only three clueless kids stayed behind."

"Was Jack your team captain?" I asked.

"We voted weekly captains," continued Johnson, "but make no mistake: The entire team followed Jack's lead. He never let anyone slack off or get caught up in negative thoughts. On or off the field, he never let us slip. But I have to admit he had a self-destruct button. You could feel it, and when he hit the switch, nobody—and I mean nobody—could talk him down."

"It was quite the thing to see," said Wayne as other players on the team nodded in agreement. "When Jack thought someone was staring him down, or if someone offended a friend, he would work himself up into a frenzy. It could be difficult to go out with Jack socially because you were never sure when or why he would hit the switch."

"I remember sitting with Jack at a restaurant when he turned to me and said, 'I'm going to get that guy,' Alex Moschella, another lineman from the 1965 team, recalled. Moschella attended Villanova after graduating from Bridgeton.

"What guy?" Moschella asked Dempsey.

"That guy right there!" Dempsey said. "He's been staring at me."

"Are you crazy, Jack? What are you talking about? That guy doesn't want any trouble."

"Yeah, well, wait til I get my hands on the prick!"

"Hey, does anyone remember what Jack did to Mr. Tatistcheff's car? Tatistcheff was a math teacher and a real dork. Jack was unhappy with the way he was treating us in class," said Wayne. "That night he said, "Let's go. Get dressed.""

"'Jack, what are you talking about? It's 11 o'clock at night?'"

"'We're going to sneak out and slice Tatistcheff's tires!'

"'Are you nuts? We'll get kicked out if we get caught!'

"'Fuck him!'"

"Just like that, Jack dressed himself in all-black and snuck out the window. Thirty minutes later, he was back in our room."

"'Tell me you didn't do it. You didn't slice one of Tatistcheff's tires, did you?'"

"'One? I sliced all four of 'em!' He was never caught."

"I remember another time in our room when he was really upset with a girl he was dating. Things weren't going well and Jack decided to write her a letter," Wayne remembered.

"'How's this sound for a beginning?'" asked Jack. "'You Greek, diabetic whore!'"

"'Jesus, Jack, you can't say that to a girl!'"

"'Why not? It's true! Okay, I'll take out *diabetic*.'"

"Don't get me wrong," Wayne said. "Jack did plenty of good at Bridgeton. He was responsible for bringing in a weight-lifting program. An all-call went out to parents, and within a few weeks, families were hauling weights in the trunks of their cars to Bridgeton.

After that, Jack and I lifted every day. He was the strongest person on the team. He benched over 400 pounds."

Suddenly, there was a moment of silence in the room and I noticed the players looking at each other and smiling. Wayne finally looked over at me, and with a smile said:

"Take out your pen, Kev, because you're going to want to write this down. The greatest moment in Bridgeton history involves Jack Dempsey.

"Bridgeton is a small town tucked away in rural Maine, and there has always been tension between the local kids and the Academy kids. Truth be told, the local kids always seemed to have the upper hand, and Bridgeton kids for years would come back to campus on the losing end of a street fight. There was this one local kid name Rodney, and everyone feared him. He was known throughout the area as the toughest guy around, and he was brutally strong. Somehow, Rodney heard about Dempsey, and he called him out. The entire school and town turned out for the fight, which took place in front of Gallanari's store on Main St. in downtown Bridgeton.

"Dempsey and Rodney squared off in the middle of the street as everyone else crowded four deep on the sidewalks. Rodney rushed Dempsey and grabbed him in a giant bear hug. Unfortunately for Rodney, this left Jack with both his hands free. Jack took his hands, grabbed two giant handfuls of Rodney's hair, and yanked his head backwards. Jack then bit into Rodney's cheek. Rodney screamed and let go of Jack, who picked up Rodney, slammed him to the ground, and proceeded to pummel him. I honestly thought Jack killed Rodney. It took a team of us to pull Jack off him.

"The whole incident ignited a riot between us and the townies." chimed in Duane. "I was leaning up against a plate-glass window next to a friend, Jim Gamans. Suddenly, a kid walks by, picks Jim up, and throws him through the plate class window. Jim got cut up pretty badly but survived. I thought, 'Holy shit! That easily could have been me!'"

I asked the obvious question: How in the world did Jack not get thrown out of Bridgeton?

"That's the best part of the story," said Duane with a smile on his face. Our headmaster, Richard Goldsmith, presided for thirty-one years, and he ran the school with an iron fist. Given the fact that it was a one-year operation, there was probably no other way to run it. Kids got thrown out for the most minor infractions: missing classes, being late for curfew, or sneaking off-campus. So, the next morning, during our school meeting, most of us were certain Dempsey was going to be immediately expelled.

"Goldsmith began each school meeting in the same way. He stood behind the stage curtain and rang the big school bell. The room became quiet, he stepped from behind the curtain, and went through his agenda. We all held our collective breaths awaiting his pronouncements on the previous day fight. Suddenly, his normally stern look gave way to a broad smile. He raised both his hands above his head and yelled, 'YAY, DEMPSEY!'

"The room exploded! Turns out Goldsmith was sick and tired of the local boys beating on the Bridgeton boys. Jack not only stayed, but he became a legend."

Duane turned to me with a serious look. "You want to know just how much of an impact Jack Dempsey had on this school and this town? I made reservations for us to play golf at the local golf club this homecoming weekend. I went down yesterday and approached the golf shop window.

"'I'm here with the Bridgeton 50-year reunion group.' A pro golfer came out from his office."

"Hey, you didn't go to school with that Dempsey guy, did you?"
"Sure did!"

"Boy, I was at that fight. Never will forget it. I can honestly say that, before or after, there was never an event quite matching that one in this town!"

"Then suddenly, another employee stepped forward from the back room and said to me: "'I was in the eighth grade when that fight took place. I can remember that moment like it was yesterday. What a memory! Kids at my school talked about that fight for years!'"

Wayne looked over, pointed his finger at me, smiled, and said: "'Can you believe all this took place fifty years ago? The legend of Jack Dempsey lives on.'"

Clyde completed a post-graduate year at Bridgeton Academy in Maine, only to have a short-lived, disappointing experience at Xavier College, a Jesuit school in Cincinnati, Ohio. Dempsey went on to play semi-pro football in New England's Continental League during the late '60s; early '70s, Boston Park league; and then end his career as a champion in 1976 playing for the Hyde Park Cowboys in the Eastern Semi-Pro League in Massachusetts.

But no matter where he played or how outstanding his accomplishments, he still had to deal with the stigma of his size and the misconception that short people could not possibly compete against bigger players. Many players would have quit, but not Dempsey; it fed him. He had a relentless drive to prove himself on and off the field. By the time he arrived at Bosco, he was already a legend in Brighton; his street fights were talked about in the projects, at local bars, and on street corners.

All of us encountered tough guys in our neighborhoods who would never back down from a fight, but there was always an elite set of guys no one would ever think of messing with. These guys were different; sure, they were tough, but they had no fear—none. They never quit in a street fight. To end things, you would have to knock them out or kill them, and sometimes not even a knock-out guaranteed an end to the conflict because, chances were, they'd be knocking on your door the next day, ready for more. We all wished we could be that tough, that fearless, but deep down we knew our own limitations. But even some of the elite would think twice before crossing the line with Dempsey—that's how tough he was.

We had plenty of Brighton kids on our team and, by our first workout, the Dempsey stories had circulated throughout the entire team. Before Dempsey had spoken a word, he had our undivided attention, our street admiration. His presence created a mixture of excitement, directness, and nervousness. His words had weight.

"Boys," said Dempsey, "lifting is directly related to football. Football demands that you explode out of your stance to block and tackle. To be the best football player that you can possibly be, you need three ingredients: quickness, technique, and desire. Weightlifting demands the same in order to maximize your strength. They are intermingled and are never to be viewed as separate. We will be focusing on three football lifts: bench press, which strengthens the muscles in the upper body, primarily the chest and arms; squats to strengthen your legs; and, my personal favorite, the football lift, or what are also called power cleans. Almost every muscle in the body benefits from power cleans, and its action mimics the way I want you to hit on the football field. I will teach you the proper technique on how to lift safely and to maximize your strength. No one, let me repeat, no one will deviate from the way I will teach you. This is not a democracy!

"It is imperative that you pay attention to your teammates when they are lifting. If anyone gets hurt because you've decided to be selfish and shoot the shit with your buddy, you will answer to me, and I promise you'll never do it again! Boys, let me be clear: I will never ask you to do anything I haven't done myself, so I expect one hundred percent commitment at all times. Each month we will record your maximum lift in all three areas. Over time, you will see dramatic changes in your size and strength. We'll divide your body weight into the total weight of your three lifts and display the results up on the wall. These results will let us know, pound for pound, who our strongest players are."

Listening to Dempsey, I had a strong feeling my junior year was going to be something entirely new and exciting. I was determined to give him that one hundred percent and make a true contribution to the team. I felt secure and safe around Dempsey, but from a distance. Although he was relaxed and easygoing around us, we had heard enough stories about what he could be on the street to ever get too comfortable with him.

As high school boys, we loved these stories. It put our coach on a pedestal. It was like having a really tough dad. My dad can beat-up your dad type of thing. As football players, we knew Dempsey was the real deal, a truly tough guy—a guy who could walk the walk.

During practice I found myself zeroed in on his every word. His knowledge of the body, and how it would respond to specific exercises and drills, was masterful. He lectured us at the end of every workout, always about what it took to be a football player.

The knowledge and advice seemed endless. What he was giving us as a team, I needed as an individual. I wanted to be a successful football player, but I was hungry for guidance and a roadmap on how to live my life. Dempsey's ability to teach and inspire was unmatched. He convinced us that size meant nothing in the game: quickness, technique, and desire were the holy trinity to being a football player.

"Boys, nature has a funny way of balancing toughness and desire. It's not the size of the tiger in the fight, but the size of the fight in the tiger!" (He stole that line, of course, as he stole many lines from other coaches, but he said it with such conviction that not one of us ever considered suggesting it wasn't his and his alone.)

Dempsey was a player's coach. He would jump right in and go live against his players, with no pads, just to prove a point or to demonstrate a particular technique. When we were on our twentieth wind sprint, he would remind us that he would never ask us to do anything that he hadn't done himself. "Goddamn it, if you can't give one hundred percent of your heart, body, mind, and soul for three-and-a-half seconds, then go play tennis," was often heard during practice. "You will be the best-conditioned linemen in the Catholic Conference!" he would shout as he stood on the back of the two-man-sled that we were driving forty yards down the field. "Fatigue makes cowards out of all of us, boys. Drive those legs, Bandini!"

He wanted us to understand the psychological game that was being played alongside the physical game.

"During my twelve years of playing this game," he said, "I can recall only two players that hit me the entire game. I can't tell you the scores of those games, but I can tell you all about those two players. When the game was over, we had one feeling towards each other, and that was a feeling of mutual respect. There is a great feeling of pride when you walk off the football field knowing you gave it your all.

"Make no mistake: During a game, one of you will dominate the other by the second quarter. But if you plan on playing football for me, you will never allow an opponent to out-hustle, out-think, or out-hit you during a game."

Dempsey was as determined to shape our mental development as he was our physical development. "Players will begin to duck and cut corners when they realize they are being out-hit and out-played. Be ready for it. Anticipate it."

Dempsey often said, "The most dangerous player is the one you knock on his ass and who comes back twice as fast and twice as strong!" He wanted his linemen to out-hit their opponents the entire four quarters, regardless of the score. The tone of the competition, he insisted, was set during the first three plays of a game. We were to dominate our opponent on the line of scrimmage from the start of the game to the finish.

Dempsey also preached God, family, and country, and he

believed that football mirrored life. "You're not always going to win in life, you're not always going to get every girl you ask out, or get every job you interview for. It's not if you win or lose, but how you win or lose. That's the key."

When driving a point home, Dempsey didn't speak with his mouth. He spoke through his eyes, his soul.

"You're going to be asked often if you're any good. If you say yes, you're bragging. If you say no, you're putting yourself down. If anyone asks if you're any good, look them straight in the eye and say, 'I try to be.'"

He preached about living a clean life. Getting caught up with drugs and drinking was a death sentence for us, he said. We always had kids on the team who didn't buy into the coaches' restrictions, who would label it "bullshit," but those kids were the minority. I didn't worry too much about whether or not I'd drink or take drugs; I had watched my brother Tom get his ass whipped pretty good by Dad when he caught him drinking, and that was all the incentive I needed to steer clear of the stuff.

But, more importantly, I didn't want to let my coach down. He was my role model, and I found myself admiring him in the same way I admired my father. I respected and feared Dempsey. I never felt physically afraid of him, of course. It was more like the fear felt when you disappoint someone or embarrass yourself. Great coaches have this gift. They are able to get players to play beyond themselves and to think of the team.

When Dempsey would lift with us, we all got to see just how powerful he really was. Without an ounce of fat on his body, he was as solid as a cannonball. He benched over four hundred pounds, squatted over five hundred pounds, and power cleaned (lifting the weight off the floor to shoulder height) a staggering two hundred eighty-five pounds! Power cleans were his love. He dissected and discussed every movement and would not accept any other interpretations of the lift:

"Bring your ankles to the bar, bend your knees, and grab the bar a little wider than shoulder width. Keep your back flat. Now place your eyes on the ceiling. Your body will always follow your eyes. This will keep you from lifting with your lower back. Lock your elbows. When lifting the weight from the floor, you should never bend your elbows or try to derive momentum from bending your elbows. This will only put pressure on your lower back and expose you to a potential injury. Now, drive the weight off the floor with your legs. Explode your elbows to the height of your ears, and flick your wrists while simultaneously dipping under the bar until it rests under your chin.

"Benitez, come on up and give it a try. Now, say each step aloud so I know you understand what you're doing."

Over and over, Dempsey would repeat the rules of lifting. Benching and squats received plenty of attention, but the power clean was *the* football lift. You had to dip and explode to power clean properly, and that's exactly what he wanted his players to do when they hit opponents on the football field. Dip and explode to block. Dip and explode to tackle. Dip and explode to make a first down.

After workouts, he introduced agility drills. He expected us to be in tip-top shape for camp. Mastering your stance was directly related to how quickly you could come off the ball, he instructed. A poor stance could also give the play away.

"I want quick, light feet—not heavy feet. Jesus, Kelly, pick up your legs crossing over the dummy bags. Eyes up! Look at me! This whole team will be doing sprints if I see one more player looking down at the ground crossing those bags!"

Besides being an outstanding football coach, Dempsey was a master teacher. His attention to detail was unmatched. Everything had to be done perfectly. He didn't care if you were a starter or if you played third string, he wanted his entire team to perfect the techniques of the game.

"Defensive linemen, listen up: You need to study your offensive lineman's body throughout the game. He will begin to give away hints about where the ball is headed, and whether the play will be a run or pass. If it's a running play, he'll want to drive-block you off the line of scrimmage. You'll notice that he's leaning forward and all his weight is on his down hand. If he wants to pull down the line and trap-block, he'll lean into the direction he's heading and put less pressure on his hand. If he's going to pass block, most of the weight will be on his heels, and there will be very little pressure on his hand, because he needs to move backwards quickly to set up his pass block. The offensive lineman knows when the ball is being hiked. You don't. Picking up on these clues helps you to neutralize his advantage. When the quarterback starts his cadence, you are to put one hundred percent of your concentration on the offensive lineman's hand. Why, MacGregor?" Dempsey asked, making sure we were paying attention.

"Because it's the first part of his body that will move on the snap of the ball?"

"Excellent. Did everyone get that?" Collective nods. "Offensive linemen, we will all have the same stance. I will teach you the proper stance, and you will all do it my way. First, we always run up to the line of scrimmage. Place your right toe against your left heel. Slide your right foot out in a straight line, a little wider than shoulder width. Point your toes inward, pigeon-toed, and then sit with your arms resting on your thighs. When you sit, notice that your toes straighten out perfectly. Set your right foot a step back, six to eight inches. Place your hand on the ground with minimum pressure, and always head up. When coming off the line to block, dip, and explode, make sure that your first moment of contact is no higher than your stance. Drive up through your opponent while simultaneously punching your hands through your opponent's midsection.

"I want everyone's undivided attention! Staub, are you listening to me? I hope I didn't just see you glance at the clock across the river."

"No, Coach."

"Good, because anyone looking at that clock will be running laps until sundown. There are three main points on your opponent's body that are critical when blocking a defensive lineman," said Dempsey. "The right hip, left hip, and the center of his chest. If you can come off the ball quickly and dominate one of these three points, you'll be successful. Low man always wins. A quick, little man with the right technique will beat a slow, big man every day.

"Football is a series of angles. If a man weighs two hundred sixty pounds and you weigh two hundred ten, just focus on a third of his body. If your goal is to get your head on the opponent's left hip, then that's the only part of his body you've got to worry about. Your job is to get to that point as fast as possible and, if you're quicker than your opponent, success!"

At the time, Dempsey's instructions about tactics and techniques were all so foreign to us. But, over time and after hours of repetition and practice, everything made sense. He had a way of breaking down every aspect of the game and making it sound simple.

For defensive linemen, Dempsey wanted agile and aggressive players. Defensive ends and tackles were taught to place all their weight down on their hand and come off the ball, as if racing in a sprint.

"Dip and explode while you read your man!"

He wanted his players to be smart. One reason why football is so draining is the mental fatigue of the game. A player's actual playing time during a game is only about six minutes. But the intellectual part of the game—the focus and emotional commitment combined with the physical demands—can feel a little like doing wind sprints while getting beat with a baseball bat *and* taking a math test.

You're coached to not think but to react to what is in front of you. But your reaction is directly related to the time spent in practice and to your own football intelligence. "The most dangerous player you'll ever play against is an intelligent player!" Dempsey said.

Even after years of coaching and playing on high school, college, and semi-pro teams, I have never met another line coach who taught football players to focus on the hand as intensely as Dempsey. Whenever I discuss defensive linemen technique with coaches, reading an offensive lineman's helmet has always been a popular method taught to players.

"The head will take you to the play," is what many coaches teach. Unfortunately, many players, including those on the college level, think that this means for them to wait and read, resulting in hesitation. Many players try to read the helmet and react after the offensive linemen move. Any hesitation on the defensive line gives the offense an advantage. Dempsey believed in focusing on the hand because it is the first part of the body to move. He believed a quick defensive line could wreak havoc by disrupting the timing and responsibility of the offensive linemen.

It is important to read a player while in motion. Hitting a lineman while in mid-stride often disrupts his ability to successfully do his job. Astonishingly, today, many coaches teach defensive players to look out the corner of their eye at the football, and to move at the snap of the ball. Dempsey would have had a field day ripping into that approach. He believed that offensive linemen gave away little hints to what type of play was going to be run. "Reading an offensive lineman's body is crucial. You want to pick up every signal he's giving you. Most linemen will take you to the ball before the ball is in the quarterback's hands."

Dempsey taught, demonstrated, and mentored all of us in

his style of football. When practice went smoothly, he could be relaxed and, at times, jovial. But when there were too many mental mistakes, he became explosive. When he reached his boiling point, he wouldn't hesitate to jump in and "go live" against some poor son of a gun.

On one such occasion, Dempsey grew frustrated that Jimmy Duggan, our captain and one of our most talented linemen, wasn't playing angrily enough. Jimmy was a skilled athlete and a nice kid from Southie. At 6'3" and two hundred forty pounds, Dempsey was expecting Jimmy to tear up the league, play all out, play mean! So one day he kept Jimmy after practice. "Okay, Duggan, I'm going to hike the ball on the second hit, and I want you to come off the ball as quick as you can, okay?"

"Yes, Coach."

Instead of hiking the ball on the second hit, Dempsey hiked the ball on the first hit, catching Jimmy off-guard and knocking him on his ass.

"Oh, Duggan, I'm sorry. Let's try that again. This time it's on the third hit."

"Okay, Coach."

Set hit, hit—bam!

Jimmy was on his ass again, confused and trying to figure what was happening. This went of for ten minutes. Finally, Dempsey exploded at the kid: "Duggan, what's wrong with you? I've been beating the shit out of you and haven't hiked the ball on the proper count once! Aren't you pissed at me?"

"Well, no, Coach. Why would I be mad at you?"

"Duggan, get off the field!"

From a distance, we were watching our captain getting the shit kicked out of him. It quickly sent the message that no one would be spared Dempsey's wrath. We all knew there was only one way to play football for Dempsey and that was his way—the right way!

# CAMP

*"Remember: On the field, there's no such thing as freshmen, and there's no such thing as seniors. You're all equal on the football field."*
—Tom Kelly

By August 1973, just before my junior year started, I figured the team was in good physical and psychological shape. I know I was. During the two months before camp, lifting weights, doing agility drills, and running wind sprints was my daily life. Three weeks before football camp, I left for the Berkshire Mountains in western Massachusetts to work at a summer camp for boys. There were steep hills and trails, and I took full advantage of the opportunity to get into the best shape of my life.

Fear was a strong motivator for me, and I already knew to fear Dempsey for what he was going to put us through. Most of all, though, I knew to fear the bench because the bench, for anyone unprepared for Dempsey's training, was where they'd inevitably end up.

After one workout session in June with Dempsey, he shared with us how he prepared for an upcoming season. "I lifted weights for two and half hours every day, ran three miles every day, put myself through a torturous series of agility drills four days a week, and then ran the Charles River in full pads for nine months."

*That's* commitment, and that's what he expected from all of us. I took Dempsey's words to heart and, though I didn't run any rivers in full pads, I lifted and ran all summer long to ready myself for camp.

Dempsey not only made an impression on the players, but he made sure his presence was felt by the other coaches as well. Coach Smith, for example, a line coach and English teacher for years at Bosco, was one of the first to end up on Dempsey's radar. "Smitty" had a great sense of humor and was extremely popular with the students. Quick-witted and sharp-tongued, Smitty could (playfully) tear you up with sarcasm in the classroom as well as on the field. Truth be told, however, he wasn't the greatest football coach. His knowledge of line technique was minimal, and it never seemed as if he'd played much football himself, even as a kid. Smitty was a good-sized guy, but had a generously-proportioned gut and was out of shape.

Knowing all of this, Dempsey accepted Smitty's invitation to a preseason cookout party at his Cape Cod cottage with the other coaches and friends. It would be Smitty's first time meeting Dempsey and, after hearing endless stories about the man, was looking forward to knowing him.

The weather was beautiful, and everyone was having a nice time, with most of the guests spending their time out on the deck overlooking the ocean, when suddenly there was a large crash inside the cottage, followed by the sound of someone screaming in pain. As the guests rushed in, confused as to what could possibly have happened, they found Smitty pulling himself out of the fireplace.

Apparently, Dempsey had been demonstrating offensive blocking techniques to Smitty, who had expected Dempsey to demonstrate his knowledge *slowly* and cottage-party-appropriately. After all, why would Smitty think otherwise? They were in his living room, not out on the field. Regardless of their setting, however, Dempsey went full speed.

"Currier, get this madman out of my house *right now!*" Smitty yelled, standing, coughing, and covered in soot.

Dempsey's live hit was no accident, of course. He was delivering a message to Smitty and all the other coaches: *Make no mistake, I'm the new line coach here and, while I may be small, I know exactly what I'm doing.*

It was a message that didn't go unnoticed.

For football players at Don Bosco, the first taste of high school football was a two-hour drive away from the city, into the beautiful rolling hills of New Hampshire. Pulling into Camp Don Bosco, we were misled by its beautiful private lake and rustic cabins, which lined the perimeter of a large, open field. The quiet lulled us into believing we were just coming to have a little fun. Well, the next morning, we were all jolted awake by the realities of football.

For first-year players, football camp was a real eye-opener. The only organized pre-high school football programs that most kids played in were for a Pop Warner or a middle school team, where the practices and coaching were less intense. Most athletes couldn't imagine what was in store for them in high school football.

Coaches had a week to get their players into shape and decide where to fit them on the roster. At times, players and their coaches had different opinions on what position they ought to play (though the coaches always won out, of course). For many, it was a new and intimidating experience having a coach scream in their face before having to run laps and additional sprints because someone *else* had screwed up. The day-to-day routine of football camp was not the glorified life one dreamed of while watching Sunday afternoon games from the comfort of a living room recliner, a Coke and a bag of chips in hand. Football camp practice was hard work and little fun. But, for those who survived, it would yield numerous rewards.

At camp, our routine was straightforward and consistent. First, up at six in the morning for a nearly four-mile run. It was always cool in the morning. I hated the feeling of the cold floor greeting my feet while leaving the comfort of my warm sleeping bag. During our early morning run, the smell of wet grass filled the air, the morning dew glistening like diamonds along the blades. The sound of the rooster crowing from the farm next to the camp penetrated my soul. The team ran in thirds. The first third of runners, always a small group, went all out and would disappear from sight after the first hill. The second group ran at a steady pace. This was my group; my goal was to finish the run and conserve my energy. The last third was made up of those who were out of shape. They ran sluggishly, wearing similar looks of dread. Why they didn't prepare for camp was anyone's guess, but one thing was for certain: For those kids, football camp was sheer hell.

"What were you people thinking about over the summer? *Move it!*" Dempsey screamed. Each morning, Peter Masciola and Vinny O'Brien came in first and second respectively in the four-mile run. Both boys were in fantastic shape. Peter was short and stocky, a running back from Roslindale. Vinny, from Jamaica Plain, was a lineman, lean and lightweight. Both were competitive. (Both would become lawyers but, as always, Pete would finish a little ahead of Vinny, eventually becoming a Brigadier General with the Air Force.)

Immediately upon our return, we went to the field for calisthenics, agility drills, and wind sprints. Not many of us knew what it was like to run full speed over and over. My lungs and leg muscles burned while my brain fought to adjust to what was taking place. "There is *no* walking on a football field! *Ever!* Kelly, come back here and do that again!"

After ten minutes, I found myself in the back of the line gasping for air as players moved forward. In a matter of seconds, I was once again in front, lined up for another hundred-yard sprint. The whistles, it seemed, would never stop blowing.

"Okay, boys, bring it in."

*Finally!*

"Some of you boys better wake up and get with the program, or you'll find yourself sitting on the bench the entire season. As a team, you're slow and out of shape. You have fifteen minutes to get ready for breakfast. Be on time."

It wasn't even eight in the morning, yet I was spent. How was I going to survive the remainder of the first day, never mind the entire week?

I was always shocked to see how much food players ate at breakfast. I was so nervous about the morning "full-pad" session that I ate very little. (It was not unusual to see players throwing up at the edge of the field during the morning session.) From nine-thirty to eleven-thirty, everyone was in full pads. Another round of extended agility drills, sled work, and an array of hitting drills would be the norm during the morning session. No football player would willingly give up his warm bottle of salted water during a break at football camp. You could have offered me thousands of dollars for it and I would have laughed in your face. Nothing was more cherished than having that liquid enter your body while the temperature outside was close to a hundred degrees, and the humidity made you feel like you were breathing air from an eighteen wheeler's exhaust pipe.

After the morning session, everyone headed slowly toward the cabins, holding their heavy, hot helmets by the face mask. It was the first time all morning that I'd had my helmet off, and the hot air circling my steaming head felt wonderful. Damp football equipment that hadn't completely dried out from yesterday's sessions stank of sweat, but somehow the rank scent welcomed us into the cabin. The antiseptic smell of Bengay and the vinegary smell of athletic tape provided an odd sense of comfort. For most of us, football camp was a world we didn't want to be in, but something inside us kept us from quitting. Maybe the challenge of pushing ourselves to levels we'd never before experienced was enough to keep us there. The combination of athletic ability, mental toughness, and pride played a role in balancing the apprehension, anxiety, and fear we all had to deal with.

From the moment I woke up, I was dreading the two-hour morning and afternoon sessions. Up in those mountains, it was unbearably hot and humid. Our clothes were soaked with sweat before we even got onto the field. Wearing my uniform felt like wearing a winter North Face ski coat on a midsummer's day in Texas. My head baked in my helmet.

"Martini, who told you that you could take off your helmet? Take a lap!"

The coaches screamed at us for every mental mistake: for jumping off-side, for missing blocks, for missing tackles, for blowing assignments, and for not showing courage.

"What's wrong with you?" yelled Dempsey. "Everyone, take another lap!"

"You have one responsibility this week!" Currier bellowed. *"Learn your plays!"*

"What type of tackle was that?" Dempsey demanded. "Put your helmet between the numbers. Knock someone on their ass! Kelly! Look at you! You had no problem getting a tan at the beach, but you weren't willing to get in shape? Run the play again! What type of stance is that? Get your ass up! Don't put so much weight on your hand! Head up!"

After two days of nonstop badgering, Dempsey had the team gather 'round and take a knee. "OK, guys," he said. "Tomorrow is the big day. Tomorrow we'll separate the men from the boys. We'll find out who really wants to play football and who the dummy heroes are!"

The "dummy heroes" were kids who could play well in practice because they were comfortable playing against kids they knew, but who were afraid to compete against kids they didn't know during a real game. Every team has these kids. I should know. I certainly fit the definition my sophomore year.

"Tomorrow is pit-drill day," Dempsey continued. "For you new kids, a pit-drill is when we lay down two dummy bags parallel to each other and five yards apart. Two linemen will jump in against each other, one defense and one offense. A running back tries to find daylight and attempts to make his way through. Gentlemen, this will be live hitting, full-contact. I expect to see one hundred percent effort out of each and every one of you! So, get a good night's sleep and get ready for tomorrow."

We'd survived Day Two!

After trudging back to my cabin, battered, soaked, and too exhausted to talk, I peeled off my uniform. The air making contact with my wet skin was cool. I could feel my body temperature begin to decrease immediately as the sweat evaporated. My pants and jersey had doubled in weight due to the amount of water they absorbed during the day. I stood under a cold shower for twenty minutes trying to revitalize my body parts. I looked down at my swollen hands, bruised elbows, and cut forearms, wondering, *What have I got myself into? Who would be willing to volunteer for this?*

I was almost too tired to have dinner, but no one had to explain to me how important it was to eat during mealtime. Food was critical if I wanted to survive the next day. We were fed three times a day and that was it. There was no food allowed in the cabins. There was no snack bar, no vending machines, no midnight snacks. So, when it was time to eat, you ate. We were losing five to eight pounds each day in the severe heat, and no one could afford to lose that kind of weight without eating and still expect to be able to perform at the level the coaches demanded.

Not only was the dining hall a place for replenishment of the body, it also provided a psychological boost to all the players. After the morning session, the stress and anxiety felt the night before and during the early morning were lifted. At lunch, the dining hall was loud with storytelling, teasing, and laughter.

The afternoon session was a repeat of the morning session, but with a stronger emphasis on offensive plays and defensive formations. The evenings consisted of the cerebral part of football— team meetings. The football playbook was loaded with football terminology, plays we had to memorize, and strict protocols and routines everyone had to learn. There was an order to the huddle, formations to learn, the team's cadence to rehearse and respond to, blocking schemes to master, and defenses to run. Coaches diagrammed plays on the board, and we were expected to take notes and quickly memorize our responsibilities.

"Now pay attention! Fullback Blast has the fullback hitting the number two hole. If we're running this play against a four-four defense, we have to double-team the tackle! Kelly, are you getting this?" I had no idea what the hell our coach had just said, but I was writing like a banshee. I looked around. Everyone had their heads down and were taking notes, so I assumed everyone else knew what the coach was talking about. By the end of the first day, I had eight pages of notes and couldn't believe that, during my week-long visit to hell, I also had homework!

After team meetings, the day was finally ours; we could relax and hang out before hitting the sack. Our cabins consisted of ten bunk beds and slept twenty. Older players got dibs on who slept on the top or lower bunks. I slept on the top bunk, which worked for me. The air smelled cleaner the higher up you were, or at least I thought so. Each cabin had one bathroom with a single toilet. I have no memory of how the twenty of us managed to share that bathroom, especially before sessions, when nerves were running high and players were eager to relieve themselves.

Then again it wasn't that unfamiliar. Sharing a bathroom at football camp wasn't much different from our home in Hyde Park. We had eight people—four males and four females—sharing one bathroom. How we managed to meet everyone's personal needs and get out the door on time each morning was simply a miracle.

The roofs of the camp cabins were made of tin, and so they would bake during the day, the heat soaking directly in. Each cabin housed a mixture of underclassmen and older kids. The night before pit-drills, most of us had trouble falling asleep. The pit-drill weighed heavily on our minds.

Late into the night, the rain began to fall, drops pelting the metal roof. It was a beautiful sound, almost hypnotic. And, for some reason, it got me thinking of my brother Tom and made me homesick.

Tom had joined the Coast Guard once he graduated from Don Bosco. He wasn't planning on pursuing football in college and felt the military had the most to offer him. We wrote to each other while he was at boot camp, and there was one letter in particular that helped me get through my own first few days of football camp.

Hopping out of bed, I rummaged through my duffel bag and pulled out the letter (rumpled from night after night of rereading):

*August 12, 1973*

*Hi Kev,*

*I just wanted to give a few words of encouragement before you head off to football camp. Try to remember a few important things to becoming a football player:*

*First, always hustle when on the field. Never let the coaches see you walking. Run everywhere they tell you to go! Second, Hit, Hit, Hit! Coaches love a hitter. No matter what size the player is in front of you, hit as hard as you can! Third, remember, on the field there is no such thing as freshmen and there is no such thing as seniors; you're all equal on the football field.*

*Kev, anyone can survive the physical junk they throw at you, but it's the mental stress that wears away at players. Don't take the coaches' comments personally if they chew you out. Two minutes after they're through with you, they'll be chewing someone else out. If you make a mistake, make sure you gave 100%! Coaches are more likely to ease up on you if they see you hustling while screwing up.*

*Boot camp is tough, but all those years of football certainly helped me deal with what they throw at us here every day. Boot camp, like football camp, is 80% mental and 20% physical!*

*Best of luck, (you'll do fine!)*
*Tom*

*P.S. Write me when you get home!*

Tom was absolutely right. Each new year, football camp would get easier to handle mentally, but the first two were hell. I never forgot Tom's advice and it always grounded me whenever I suffered anxiety or exhaustion.

After I put the letter away, I felt better but still tossed and turned, thinking about the next day. As I struggled to fall asleep, I realized someone was talking. What I was hearing didn't make much sense, though. It was a mixture of words and gibberish.

Jerry Cargill, a senior lineman, was sleeping across from me. Jerry was a nice kid, quiet and kind, especially to the younger classmen. As I peered into the darkness, I could make out his silhouette. Jerry was getting out of bed. He grabbed his helmet, secured it to his head backwards, got into a three-point stance, and began reciting plays. When he started speaking directly to the coaches, it became clear that Jerry was not at all awake or aware of what he was saying or doing.

"Triple Right Option! Linemen on or inside. I can do it, Coach! Halfback Counter Left. Pull and trap the tackle!" Some of the players laughed, others just stared in disbelief. After a few minutes, Jerry took off his helmet and laid back down on his bunk, as if the whole episode had never happened. He had no idea what he had done in his sleep until we told him the next morning. Jerry chuckled and asked if he recited the correct blocking assignment for the plays he called out in his sleep. We told him we weren't sure because we were laughing too hard watching him get into his stance with his helmet on backwards.

The pressure we all felt at football camp manifested itself in different ways. Each of us had to learn how to handle the pressure our own way, but no one would dare admit that he was anxious or felt any fear. Football is a warrior's sport that demands courage and fortitude—and, for us kids, that often meant suffering in silence.

As a young teenager, I looked at the older players and thought none of them felt any of the emotion I felt. For *most* of us, though, *Why did I sign up for this madness?* was a common thought. The reality was, we were feeling the same things, and struggling with the same insecurities, but football demands that you either have mental toughness to handle these insecurities or develop it in a hurry. For most, mental toughness is a learned behavior of self-discipline, the ability to make yourself do something instinctively that you wouldn't otherwise do but for pure survival's sake.

Mental discipline is a tapping into that survival adrenaline. Running full speed into someone you don't know and exploding through their chest, head first, is a good example of mental toughness as a learned behavior. It is the relearning of the primal instinct. Most kids initially don't want to hit with reckless abandon but, over time, this mentality develops and becomes more natural and, for some, even enjoyable.

Of course, not everyone plays with true mental toughness. When a game is close and time is running out, players find what they consider to be mental toughness because emotions are riding high and the final whistle is close to blowing. But true mental toughness can be seen in the performance of athletes when the score is 38-0 with seven minutes left on the clock. Players on the losing end will begin to let up physically and emotionally. This happens at every level. Players acquiesce to this and begin to ask themselves, *Why bother? We're going to lose anyway.* They figure they might as well begin to shut it down and preserve their energy to make sure they're not injured during those last seven minutes.

Only the *very* rare athlete will play always with a pure spirit. The Japanese Samurai warriors call this Bushido, which means heart of a warrior. Coaches preach, "Never say die, and play as if the score is 0-0 the entire game. Leave it all on the field. Never quit, no matter what." Players like the Chicago Bears' Dick Butkus, the greatest linebacker who ever played the game; Larry Wilson, defensive back for the St. Louis Cardinals in the late '60s; and the Cleveland Brown's Jim Brown, the greatest running back in the history of football—they all had it.

Jim Brown once talked about being blown away by Larry Wilson. The game was in the bag, Cleveland was up by three touchdowns, and they were just letting the clock run out. Cleveland ran a sweep and handed off the ball to Brown when, out of nowhere, *WHAM!* Brown found himself flat on his ass and a little shaken up. The next play was a screen pass. *WHAM!* Brown got knocked on his ass.

Brown finally looked over at the Cardinals huddle and said, "Who the hell is cleaning my clock?" It was Larry Wilson, weighing in at a mere one hundred and seventy-five pounds and playing with two broken hands! That guy played with *true* mental toughness. Wilson was a purist, and coaches spend their entire careers trying to inspire players to play with that same level of commitment. The Bosco coaches were no exception.

"The rewards of learning this attribute are lifelong, boys," said Dempsey. "The ability to not quit a job, relationships, your family, responsibilities, or uncomfortable or undesirable commitments, will help shape your adult self. Simply never quitting when you've made a commitment is a trait that separates the winners and losers in life."

We all wanted to be winners back then.

Another major attribute that motivates a player's toughness is pride. It cannot be measured by size or age, and it can often trump fear, stress, and anxiety all put together. During a hitting drill, scrimmage, or game, a good player can put aside all of the apprehensions that may be interfering with his play. When the pride button is pushed, *amazing* things can happen. Taking on someone bigger and stronger who, logically, should be able to dominate you suddenly becomes a fair challenge. Dempsey was living proof of this.

His entire football career, Dempsey was told he was too small.

But Dempsey lived what he preached, and he never let taunts and challenges hold him back.

My teammate, Vince O'Brien, at a hundred and fifty pounds, was too light to be a lineman, but he'd come after you play after play, day after day. He had tremendous pride, and his emotional commitment to the game was absolute. I would often joke that if Vince O'Brien weighed one hundred and ninety pounds, I'd never come onto the football field to face him. When Vince went on to college football some years later, I guess his coaches saw this same potential in him, because they started him as an offensive wingback! All I can say is, he must have been miserable to tackle.

In the midst of all the struggle and pressure, we Bosco players always made a few important discoveries during our camp days. For one thing, size has no connection to ability or toughness. Players often got pigeonholed based on their size. It was a sobering sight watching a big, strong kid get knocked down because he lacked the quickness, technique, or desire to excel. For another thing, the kids with the loudest mouths are not necessarily the toughest kids on the team. The kid to watch out for is often the quiet one. He does what he's told, but carries himself with an air of confidence. These kids often turn into hitting machines on the field.

At camp that summer, Wednesday was another scorcher; you could have fried an egg on the sidewalk. By late morning, we were almost looking forward to the pit-drill just so we could get it over with and get off the field. All players respond differently to the anticipation of the pit-drill: with fear, nervousness, and heightened anxiety, or with aggression. Some players will even jump up and down and start jabbering in an attempt to regulate their emotions. Lots of: "This is it, boys!" or "Let's get it on, boys! Yeah!"

Most, however, are quiet. The anticipation of a fistfight is almost always worse than the actual event. Pit-drills are similar. A hidden aspect is ego. No one wants to under-perform or, worse, get their butt kicked in front of their teammates. During other aspects of practice, it's possible to find moments to lighten up and not give one hundred percent, but there's no place to hide during the pit-drill. It's simple—you either win or you lose. Coaches love the pit-drill. Currier would sit back with an intense look on his face, armed with his clipboard, while Dempsey would all but foam at the mouth. With his eyes wide open, he'd bellow at us the entire time. If someone delivered a good hit, he'd leap off his feet, "Great hit, Dominguez! Now *that's* the way to hit!" "Kelly, you keep standing up! Dip and explode—apply the techniques you've been taught!"

While waiting in line for his pit-drill time, every football player checks to see who they'll go up against. On my first trip through the pit-drill that morning, I looked down the line and my heart skipped a beat. Bruce McDonald, two hundred and forty pounds and just over six feet tall, jumped in as the defensive lineman. I was in the backfield running with the ball. Even I knew that the kid blocking for me was going to get killed. I'm sure I looked pretty desperate as I anticipated being face-planted in the turf.

Coach Currier must have noticed, too. He came over to me and whispered in my ear: "Kelly, I want you to imagine that we're on the two-yard line with no time left on the clock and I'm going to give you the ball to win the game for us!" My mind went blank and I blasted through a tiny seam that, by some miracle, opened up for me. To my surprise, I didn't even get bumped, let alone killed. Truth be told, no one knew I ran the drill with my eyes closed!

On defense, it was critical to be quick off the ball, stand the offensive lineman up, shed the block, and make a perfect tackle. Dempsey would lose his mind when a defensive player did well against one lineman, only to then have the running back break a tackle due to another player's poor technique or, worse, lack of courage.

"Kelly, get back in there and do it again!" Dempsey shouted.

"You have to be willing to drive your helmet right through his numbers! Wrap him up with your arms, and then punish him—drive him right into the ground! If you're not tough enough to do that on every single play, then go play a pansy sport like hockey!"

Dempsey had something to say with almost every hit; his intensity was contagious. After the session, when Currier brought us in, we were sky-high.

"Okay, boys," Currier said, "take a knee. Great effort today. This is the type of intensity we need to see on Saturday when we scrimmage Watertown. We have two more days of hard work left. Enjoy your afternoon. Spend some time at the lake. Good work!"

The first two days, I could barely walk off the field I was so exhausted, but that day I was still so pumped up that I ran off the field. I had held my own. I'd had a few successful hits on defense, and believed that this upcoming season was going to be different for me, and for our team.

The next two days were a nonstop blur of hitting, running, and yelling. My body was battered and bruised. Each morning I looked like Frankenstein getting out of bed. My muscles were torn, stiff, and sore. I had bloody blisters on both my heels (the price I paid for not breaking in new cleats before camp). Trying to get dressed was painful. Bending over to slip on my socks and tie my running shoes was difficult. But the moment the coaches told us to line up, the pain simply didn't exist any more and I ran. After ten minutes, my body would loosen up, and I was good for another day. Although football camp was brutal, the routine strangely started to feel normal. I knew what was coming and I learned to adjust.

At the end of the week, we were to scrimmage Watertown, a team with a hundred players (mostly big Italian and Armenian kids). Many of the Watertown kids had mustaches and beards and looked like college players. Every year, it was a tradition to play Watertown at the end of camp. Their football camp was held at a college campus on beautiful Lake Winnipesaukee in New Hampshire. Their players lived in actual dorms, had access to actual locker rooms, and cleaned up in actual shower rooms that could hold forty kids at a time—basically the opposite of our accommodations, where cabins served simultaneously as dorm, shower, and locker room.

When we pulled into Watertown (what we called Watertown's Resort), their players stopped to look us over as they headed back to their dorms. From the bus, we all stared right back, assessing.

Eyes never wavering from out the window, Cemate leaned over and sneered, "Shit, nice to be rich, huh?"

"I wouldn't know," I shot back.

During scrimmages, coaches are allowed in the huddle. In our case at least, that was the last thing our morale needed—Currier and Dempsey were *not* happy. Watertown was teeing off on us pretty good and we just couldn't get it together.

"Kelly, your head's on the wrong side of the linebacker. That's why your man made the tackle!"

"MacGregor, why are you picking a side? You have both gaps when playing a 5-2 defense!"

"Line it up and run it again! I don't care if Watertown can hear me—*RUN THE PLAY!*"

Even during Tom's time there, Watertown seemed to have our number. Bosco never had much success, and losing has an interesting impact on your psyche as an athlete—the more we lost to Watertown, the more it stood to reason that we'd simply keep on losing. When you lose to a team year after year, you just start to believe you *can't* win, even when you know it's a new season with different players.

Of course, winning has the same effect: Keep winning year after year, and you start to believe you can win every game.

"Winning breeds winning, but most importantly, winning breeds *winners*." That was part of Vince Lombardi's opening day speech to the Green Bay Packers in 1957, after he took over the worst team in the NFL as head coach. If you think his message has little meaning, just consider the fact that Green Bay then went on to win five championships and were the victors of the first and second Super Bowls.

But a lot has to come together to obtain a victory, even a small one, and, after one week of brutal football camp, no one was overly concerned about our poor performance against Watertown. We still had three scrimmages and two weeks of practice to go before our opening game. I don't have many clear memories of the Watertown scrimmage, but I know I didn't play well. In fact, I was just thankful to have survived at all, let alone my first football camp with Dempsey.

By the end of it, all I wanted to do was go home, sleep in my own bed, and be held by my mother.

# TRAGEDY

*"Don't ever let me catch you just standing around."*
—Coach Dempsey

Anyone who has ever played football knows that the helmet can be a tremendous weapon—one that can be used to deliver outrageous hits.

Dempsey believed that hitting properly with your head was far safer than trying to hit with your shoulder, which requires you to turn your head slightly to one side, making it all the harder to actually see who you're hitting. Driving your forehead into the opponent while simultaneously dipping and exploding with your legs maximizes the impact of a hit while also protecting your neck. If a player ducks his head, looks down, and makes contact with the crown of the helmet, serious injury can occur.

Keeping your head up and hitting with your forehead is generally a safe way to hit. Hitting with your head, especially if it is a great hit, actually feels good physically. It can give you a rush or a high. Add speed to the equation and hitting can become lethal.

How wide receivers can stand up after some of the hits they receive is amazing. What's even more impressive is their willingness to go back out and do it again, knowing what awaits them.

In my junior year, Bosco would field another football team with a lot of large bodies. We had players who weighed between two hundred and ten pounds and two hundred and forty-five pounds. The team had high hopes for the '73 season. After camp and returning from our traditional scrimmage against Watertown, we had great energy and high spirits. I was playing tight end on offense and linebacker on defense, but I was playing behind two captains, which meant I was on the second team on both squads. Dempsey and Currier seemed pleased after our next two scrimmage performances, and a change seemed to be in the air for the Bosco Bears. Everyone was looking forward to a great year!

However, we came out of the blocks slower than we anticipated. After four weeks, we were 1-3. We would have a great week in practice, only to come up short during the game. Once again, we were struggling as a team. The week leading up to the Xaverian game, Currier brought the team together and informed us that winning was crucial if we wanted to turn the season around. Our practices were intense, with live hitting every day. The coaches felt they had an excellent game plan in place. The mood on the team was one of enthusiasm and optimism.

The first half of game five was a disaster. Our offense, which had looked great during practice all week, couldn't establish a running game, and was just as ineffective throwing the ball. On defense, players were arm tackling, and we seemed sluggish on pass coverage. Currier and Dempsey were so upset with our performance that they refused to join us in the locker room at halftime. As the team sat in silence, a former coach, Bill Campbell, spoke to the team. He looked at Bruce McDonald, my old pit-drill partner, and said, "McDonald, I've coached you since you were a freshman, and all you turned out to be is a two hundred and forty pound pussy!"

With that, Campbell turned and walked out. When the coaches told us to take the field, Chris Staub, a new sophomore who was starting varsity at defensive back, stood up and said, "Hey fellas, I'm ready for the second half. How about you?"

Bruce McDonald stood up, didn't say a word, and smacked Chris on the side of his head. It was a telltale moment for us, showing just how disconnected we were as a team. The majority of us were pissed with Bruce, knowing that taking out his frustration on a teammate for his own poor performance was chickenshit, pure and simple.

Xaverian, which didn't get the chance to hear our halftime pep talk, demolished us in the second half. Dissension grew and, gradually, the coaches displayed their frustration. The key players were simply not delivering during games. Practices began to look and feel like those during my sophomore year. Once again, yelling, running plays over and over, making mistakes, forgetting plays, and losing were part of our weekly routine.

One of Dempsey's rules had been made clear to all linemen at the beginning of the year: "If you're on the field, practice has officially begun, and you need to be working on *something*: stance, blocking, pass rush, coming off the ball, blocking assignments— something that will help you improve as a football player. Don't *ever* let me catch you just standing around."

Well, on one fall day, that is exactly what happened.

A group of us were standing around with our helmets off, shooting the breeze and enjoying the beautiful sights. It was warm and sunny, and a light wind was coming off the Charles. It was mesmerizing—the type of day that begged you to lie down and take a nap under a tree with your best girl by your side. But when Dempsey came onto the field and saw us, he blew a gasket. He was so upset he decided that he wanted to make an example out of his linemen to the rest of the team.

He had the backs and receivers sit on the sidelines while his linemen formed three lines facing each other, fifteen yards apart. When the whistle blew, we were to run full speed, head on, at each other. I was second in my line, and just one thought went through my head: *This drill is* insane.

Running full speed and head on, at that distance, was suicide.

The player in front of me was Michael Monahan. Michael was a big kid for his age but he was still only a sophomore. He ran at three-fourths speed and straight up. Jeff Harris, also a sophomore, ran full speed and delivered a textbook hit. Jeff dipped, exploded, and drove his helmet straight through Michael's face mask. Michael fell to the ground. When Michael didn't get up, the coaches picked him up and tossed him to one side. Currier took a closer look at Michael, and discovered that his helmet had been split wide open, an extremely uncommon event in football. It had been a devastating hit. Even so, we moved the drill over, not thinking too much about the hit. We were all too worried about ourselves.

After about fifteen minutes, though, Michael was still on the ground, and some of us started to wonder about him. A shoulder injury was most likely the worst outcome. After a half hour, an ambulance came onto the field, and Currier went into the ambulance with him. We didn't see Currier again until after practice. Although it's been forty years now, I still vividly remember how pale Currier looked when he returned.

He asked all of us to gather 'round and take a knee.

"Boys, Michael Monahan broke his neck. He is paralyzed from

the neck down. Tonight he is fighting for his life."

The locker room was deadly silent; no one could so much as exchange a glance. That night, I tossed and turned as I replayed the hit over and over in my head. *Why am I playing this game?* I wondered. *Am I playing for acceptance? For status at school?* It certainly wasn't for the love of the game anymore. Practices were relentless and miserable, and yet we *still* weren't winning. The "togetherness" that Dempsey had wanted to establish between us hadn't happened yet, and now, perhaps, he'd made achieving that togetherness next to impossible.

The next day at school, we had a school prayer assembly. Over one thousand boys entered the gym in total silence. The only noise you could hear was the ventilation system blowing cool air— it's the same sound one might hear while sitting on a plane right before takeoff in bad weather. The entire Bosco community was confounded. That afternoon at football practice, no one said much. If there was a speech—and I'm sure there was—I have no memory of it. I was in a fog.

I do remember feeling as if I had no desire to be on the field, and no desire to hit or be hit by anyone. Dempsey could certainly see this taking place among us. No one knew what to say or do. None of us, including the coaches, had ever experienced anything close to this level of injury to a player before. Everyone seemed to be on autopilot. During one play, Dempsey ran up behind me and told me to get my head out of my ass. I knew he was trying to snap me out of my funk, but it didn't work.

Michael pulled through but remained paralyzed from the neck down. All of us players had mixed emotions, but mainly we were angry. Not only did I have serious doubts about continuing to play football but, for the first time, I had serious doubts about my coaches. For the first time, I began to question the purpose of football as a whole. *Why isn't there any joy in the experience? Why do we tolerate being chewed-out and feeling miserable? Why don't we have the courage to quit?*

When we were cleared to visit Michael, he was in good spirits. I was at the end of the bed just staring at his hands and feet, trying to imagine what it must be like to be able to move only my eyes and lips. I kept saying to myself, *If that were me, I'd make my hands move,* but I knew that was the emotional side of me fighting the fear, the reality, that what had happened to him could have happened to me. As I looked at Michael, I kept thinking, *For the rest of his life, he will feel no pleasure, no pain. He'll never experience the joy of going to college, the full experience of dating, of having children. He'll never again feel life!* He'd lost everything in a single instant, and for what? A stupid drill? A drill intended as a punishment! To teach us a lesson! *What lesson did we learn?*

Michael's older sister came into the room and stood beside me. While Michael was speaking with us, she pulled back his bed sheet, and without his knowing, she pinched him, deep into the back of his thigh with her long, red fingernails. If she had done that to me, I would have jumped two feet off the ground. Michael didn't even flinch. A cold chill came over me. I felt lightheaded and stepped into the hallway to catch my breath. She was hoping to get a physical reaction out of Michael. Getting nothing, she was devastated, and couldn't bring herself to believe that he would never feel or move again.

Our coaches were devastated too. They were tough on us, but they cared for their kids. Dempsey had been trying to make a point to his players that, to be the best, you have to make a full commitment to the game. It was a horrendous decision to put his players through such a drill, but we knew he never intended to bring injury to a player. Dempsey never made a public comment about Michael, the drill, or the hit, but everyone could see that all of it tormented him. Dempsey wore his emotions on his sleeves, and he'd always been a ball of energy. But after Michael's hit, you could see the strain in his eyes. He'd lost some piece of himself.

The weekend after Michael's accident, Dempsey and Currier went out, got hammered, and drove home drunk. Dempsey was driving the wrong way through a tunnel in Cambridge and hit a bus head-on. In one week, not only did we have a serious injury to a young player, but two of our coaches ended up in the hospital as well.

The next few weeks, all of us remained in a daze. Who we played, whether we won or lost, or how I performed, I didn't know. I began to believe that football wasn't for me, and I couldn't wait for the season to end.

When the season was finally over, my church held a Mass for Michael. I visited him in the hospital to deliver an advent wreath. His entire family was present. Before I left to go home, his parents asked if I would tell them the truth about Michael's injury. I wasn't sure exactly what they had heard from the coaches or from the school, and I didn't care. I felt strongly that, at the very least, the Monahans deserved to be told the entire story about Michael's devastating hit.

The family entered the waiting room. Sitting with Michael's parents, I explained what made Dempsey put us through the drill in the first place, how we lined up to hit, and what had happened to Michael after he was hit. Listening, the family sat in numbed silence. My heart broke for them as I told them a story they could only regard as a nightmare.

Over the years, I would often think of Michael and wonder how I would have reacted if my son was paralyzed for life because of a punishment drill. Today, any coach would be in front of a judge for jeopardizing the health and well-being of a student athlete, and rightly so.

Jeff, the player whose hit had left Michael paralyzed, reacted to the incident with anger. "When I look back at that moment," Jeff later told me, "what made me so upset is that I wasn't even *with* the linemen when Dempsey flew off the handle! I was with the quarterbacks and receivers." Jeff played center and had been hiking the ball to Jimmy Conrad, our quarterback, as he was throwing passes to the receivers on the other side of the field.

After the Monahan event, there would be no counseling for the team or for Jeff. He never received any reassurances from his coaches, teammates, or even his family. Tragically, he dealt with it totally on his own. He was a sixteen-year-old kid who should never have been put into this situation to begin with. Today, professionals would come out to speak to the team. But no one at Bosco had the tools to address such a tragedy. Not even the priests came to speak to us. It simply wasn't acknowledged. We moved forward as if nothing had happened. It was "buck up and be tough."

Forty years later, though, Jeff was able to admit, "It played with my psyche. I'm sure it impacted my senior year. I didn't have the year I should have. At times, I held back."

The idea that time heals all wounds is a myth, if not a flat-out lie. Trauma is an experience that needs to be dealt with, not hidden away to fester. I have interviewed more than twenty players from the '74 and '75 teams, many of whom I had not seen since that season, and Michael Monahan's hit consistently brought up deep emotions that they'd repressed for years. That dreadful moment stayed with all of us and left a deep scar that never healed completely.

Ultimately, there was a lawsuit against Riddell, the helmet company, and a settlement was paid out to Michael's family.

Michael visited the team once or twice during my two remaining years at Bosco. On one occasion, he was wheeled over to meet the linemen. Everyone stopped to say hello. Coach Dempsey came over and instinctively stuck his hand out to Michael. There was an awkward silence; Dempsey quickly pulled his hand back and patted Michael on the shoulder.

There has always been this weird thing in football, almost an unspoken rule: If a teammate gets injured, you keep your distance, as if the injury is contagious. Perhaps, way back when, coaches kept players away from injured players because they were nervous that being around them too much would take the edge off their aggression—would detract from their willingness to play all out. Whatever the reason, and however silly and unfair it was, we all kept a general distance from Michael, though his accident remained alive within us.

For the longest time, I didn't know where Michael was living or how he was doing, assuming he was still alive. Also, none of us knew how to approach and support Jeff. It only took a few months before all of us lost touch with Michael and ceased speaking of his accident publicly.

After a full forty years had passed, Skip Bandini stood and said to Jeff at our team reunion, "It was unfair that you had to deal with this alone. It wasn't right, and we're all sorry."

At first, the entire room was silent. Skip's words were brief, but he had a look in his eyes that summed up all of our emotions. Skip spoke directly to Jeff with a look of compassion, support, anger, and frustration. It was a profound moment of closure, not only for Jeff, but for all of us.

The room broke into applause.

I know two things: All of us still feel some level of guilt over Michael's accident. And all of us own a little piece of Michael Monahan.

# THE MIRACLE

*"If there is any certainty, Don Bosco is destined for the cellar
in the Catholic Conference."*
—*Boston Globe*, 1974

In May of 1974, I was walking on the historic pathway surrounding Castle Island in Southie with my brother Tom. Castle Island is a Revolutionary War fort located at the mouth of Boston Harbor. It was built after the Boston Tea Party to confront any British ships attempting to enter the harbor. The old cannons can still be seen high on the walls, an intimidating deterrent to unwelcome visitors. The walkway is shaded with beautiful maples and oaks and is cooled by a salty, ceaseless ocean breeze, making it one of the most pleasant and sought-after escapes in the entire city.

"I'm not sure if I want to continue playing ball at Bosco," I told Tom, taking a seat alongside him on a park bench to watch the seagulls fight over a fried clam from Kelly's Clam Shack. "We suck, the experience sucks, and no one is having any fun."

"Kev, I'm not sure how much fun you'll have, but I will tell you this: If you quit, I promise you, you will regret it for the rest of your life. Kellys don't quit. Think it over carefully before you decide."

And that is exactly what I did. During the entire month of June, I weighed the pros and cons of playing football and came to the conclusion that my senior year was too important to walk away from. By July first, I was all in.

I made a renewed commitment to play. I decided I was going to put last year's agonizing season behind me and be a contributing member to the team, regardless of whether we had a winning or losing season. I hit the weights, ran, and pushed myself all summer long like a possessed animal. I wasn't going to try to kiss any coach's ass. For the first time in my three years of Bosco high school football, I actually went to camp with attitude, with confidence. I wasn't playing for Currier or for Dempsey or to assuage the grief I still felt for my mother's early passing. I was playing for myself.

No one—and I mean *no one*—had any inkling that we would amount to anything special in 1974. The *Boston Globe* predicted we would come in last place in the conference: "If there is any certainty, Don Bosco is destined for the cellar in the Catholic Conference." Not only did the *Globe* believe we weren't going to do anything special, none of the players did either.

The Catholic Conference had long been one of the strongest football conferences in the state of Massachusetts, with Xaverian Brothers, Malden Catholic, Boston College High School, Archbishop Williams, and the state's powerhouse, Catholic Memorial (CM). Catholic Memorial had gone undefeated for three and a half years, thirty-three games—a state record. They had played in three straight state Super Bowls. Don Bosco had never beaten CM. My sophomore year, they beat us 54-0. My junior year, they beat us 41-20. They had size, speed, and, most of all, confidence.

Before we left for football camp, CM wasn't on anyone's mind. I was the only person on our team who was reminded of CM every single day. Many kids from Hyde Park attended CM, and they couldn't help but brag about its many athletic accomplishments. They were great in every sport: basketball, hockey, swimming, track, baseball, and especially football. Success in sports is directly related to school pride, and the CM kids were on the brink of an overdose.

I hated CM.

Often I'd have to listen to how great they were with the occasional, "Hey, Kev, you guys going to suck again this year?" I'd burn inside but knew there wasn't much of a defense I could muster.

By August, I was in shape and ready for camp. My mind was focused and my emotions were in check. Before the season, I read two great books that helped shape my attitude: Jerry Kramer's *Instant Replay* and Dave Meggasey's *Out of This League*. Both authors had played pro-ball, in Green Bay and St. Louis respectively, and both had shared the many mixed emotions players experience while playing this crazy game. There is always a mental tug-of-war going on in a player's mind. On one end, there's the love of the game, the desire to compete and do well. On the other end, there's the reluctance to hit, be hit, or work hard enough, consistently enough to win. Maybe it's a natural mental place for most athletes. Like soldiers in war, they don't want to be there, but something deeper drives them to succeed. During battle, they respond to the training and the mission, casting aside normal human instincts to quit and run.

We would often hear from our coaches, especially Dempsey, how football mirrors life, how winners never quit, and that these attributes would benefit us in the future. Many of us weren't sure if this was just a string of baloney thrown out to keep us motivated, or if these words of wisdom were actually wise, perhaps even true. Regardless, it was reassuring to me to learn that from time to time even the pros struggled mentally with all the psychological and physical challenges of playing the game.

By now, I could see a pattern to football camp: Monday and Tuesday would be hell. We would do nothing right. Coaches would chew us out for countless mistakes. The drills would seem endless. We would find ourselves running plays over and over. We would cringe as Currier or Dempsey blew the whistle yet again, stopping practice to highlight mistakes.

Both Courier and Dempsey came straight out of the Lombardi school of coaching. Both regarded Lombardi as the greatest coach who'd ever lived and did their best to copy his coaching style. On one particularly rough Tuesday, during our morning session, Currier became so frustrated with our performance that he stopped practice to yell: "Boys, I'd break both my arms and both my legs to beat CM. The arms would heal, the legs would heal, and we would beat CM, but I'm just not sure if there is anyone here that would be willing to do just that!"

Inspired, Dempsey also chimed in, "You know what the problem is, boys? No one has any of these!" Dempsey made two small circles with his fingers, signifying "balls." They were undoubtedly right. We all wanted to do well and win, but no one was willing to match their fervor.

Wednesday was pit-drill day at camp, and it weighed heavily on all the players' minds. But after the pit-drill sessions were over, everyone's spirits were sky-high. The next two days, the coaches built the team up and we were so filled with confidence for the big scrimmage Saturday, we knew we'd go into the season on a positive note. I was no longer a timid sophomore. I had matured into a ball player, both physically and mentally. I ran angry and hit angry. Dempsey often told us that true football aggression is a learned behavior. I had finally discovered what he was talking about.

Saturday, we once again scrimmaged against Watertown at their beautiful resort for spoiled kids. They were just as big as I remembered them being. They looked plenty tough and had one ingredient all coaches pray for: depth. Yet, surprisingly, we dominated them, perhaps for the first time ever, on both offense and defense. Then, for a change, we were astonished to find that it was the Watertown kids getting screamed at by their coaches for messing up and losing ground—not us. Not any more.

On one play in particular, their head coach blew his whistle and made their offense line up on the line of scrimmage. The coach grabbed the offensive guard I was playing against by the face mask and dragged him toward me, pointing wildly and yelling, "How is it possible that your man could make a tackle on the other side of the football field? Run the God damn play again!"

*Wow*, I thought. That was an exchange usually delivered to one of *us* by *our* coaches, not to a Watertown kid by a Watertown coach.

Dempsey, on the other hand, came over to me in the huddle and patted me on the helmet, "Nice hustle, Kelly."

Coming from Dempsey, that small compliment meant big things, and it gave me the added confidence I needed.

As we departed for Boston, I looked out my bus window, shocked while watching the entire Watertown team running sprints up a monster hill—and immediately after a two-hour scrimmage in the searing heat! Watertown went on to an undefeated season and a win at their first Super Bowl but, on that Saturday afternoon, neither team could have predicted their future. It did, however, allow us to enjoy, just a little bit, the hot air blowing through the open windows of our run-down school bus as we trundled back from Watertown's Resort to our girls' locker room in Bean Town.

Almost every ethnic group from Boston was represented on our '74 team. Our offense was led by our quarterback, Mike "Ski" Ewanoski from Brookline. We would platoon six running backs, two juniors and four seniors: Colie McGillivary from Dorchester and Paul Carouso from Somerville, who were our junior backs; Stevie Riley from Brookline, Peter Marciola from Roslindale, and two of our captains, Craig Cemate from Brighton and Alan Libardoni from Somerville, were our four senior backs (all six of them tough and dependable). Chester Rodriguez from Dorchester, Gary Green from Brighton, and Shawn Murphy from Cambridge were our wide receivers.

Our offensive linemen were all in great shape, quick off the ball, and wielding a true attack mentality. Chris Staub (from Revere) played tight end; Skip Bandini (from Brighton) and Tommy McGregor (from Hyde Park) played tackle; Derrick Martini (from Somerville) and Abe Benitez (from Jamaica Plain) played guard; and Eddie Dominguez (also from Jamaica Plain) served as our third captain and played center.

On defense, Billy Elwell (from Watertown) and Chris Staub started as defensive ends. Skip Bandini and I played tackle, and Derrick Martini rounded out the defensive line as nose guard. Al Libardoni and Eddie Trask (both from Somerville) played inside linebacker. Colie McGillivary, Chester Rodreguiz, Craig Cemate, and our only starting freshman on the team, John Sylva (from Quincy), were our four defensive backs.

We were also fortunate to have a group of back-up players who could fill in on both offense and defense whenever players needed a breather or injuries occurred. Vinny O'Brien from Jamaica Plain, Richie Abner and Jerome Frazier (both from Dorchester), and Frankie Marchione from East Boston played both on the offensive and defensive lines.

Our first game during the '74 season was a non-league contest against North Reading, a suburb just north of Boston. They were an unknown to us, this being our first time playing them. With two losing seasons under our belt, it was nearly impossible to know what to expect. How would we perform? How would we respond if we ended up down by a touchdown or two? And, most importantly, how would we react to each other?

During my three years, Bosco struggled to establish team togetherness—critical for any team sport like football—but this year and this team were different; it only took a short amount of time for us to learn to support each other whenever we made mistakes, whether it was fumbling a ball, dropping a pass, or missing a tackle.

We managed to beat North Reading, but just barely, at 8-0.

Our defense managed to shut out a tough running offense, and it was the first sign that we had players fully willing to hit and gang-tackle the ball carrier.

Staub and Elwell both had outstanding games as defensive ends. They put pressure on the quarterback all day, and North Reading had no success running plays to the outside. McGillivary, Rodriguez, Sylva, Cemate, and Carouso shut down North Reading's attempt to establish its passing game. Our two linebackers, Trask and Libardoni, stuffed Reading's running backs all afternoon. It was a complete and beautiful defensive effort.

Still, Currier and Dempsey were lukewarm in their praise.

"Okay, boys, it is always important to establish a win to open the season—we'll take it. But we still have a lot of work to do on offense. Linemen, you need to stay on your blocks, and we need to sustain offensive drives down the field. Defensively, we played tough; good job, boys. Now it's time to put this game behind us, and start getting ready for BC. They are *big* and loaded with talent. We're going to have to play much better than today if we expect to walk off the field next week with a win."

The *Boston Globe* rated Boston College High School as the

number one high school football team in the state. Their offensive line averaged two hundred and fifty-five pounds. Our linemen averaged, at most, one hundred and ninety pounds. In the '70s, BC's average weight was the size of any Division I college team in the country. Their key running back, Catoria, was just over six feet tall and weighed two hundred and twenty-five pounds. For the '74 season, we were up for a major challenge right out of the gate.

With Dempsey on board, we knew it would not only be a tough week of practice, but that our coaches would have us prepared for BC. So, we settled in for a week of hell. All week long, Dempsey screamed at us that Catoria was going to run over and through us. "If you think we're going to win this game with just one player trying to tackle this kid, you're dreaming!" "Gang-tackle, gang-tackle, gang-tackle" is all we heard that week. "I want to see six Bosco jerseys on this guy every single time he touches the ball!" Dempsey even took the time to remind us that Catoria was being recruited by none other than Notre Dame.

By Thursday, I was convinced that BC had Superman in their backfield.

But then Dempsey kept me after practice the next day, put a hand on my shoulder, and told me a secret: "Listen, in the next game, you're going to play against one of the premier linemen in the state. Gallagher is big, tough, and talented. But you can beat him. I want you to break his body up into thirds. If you're trying to dominate his left side, I want you to explode all your weight and strength into that side. Your quickness needs to negate his strength. You power-cleaned two hundred and twenty pounds and benched close to three hundred—you're plenty strong. I need you to have a great game, Kelly. Don't let me down."

The game was played at East Boston Stadium near Logan Airport. Bosco had no home field, so when we played at East Boston Stadium, we would alternate years as the home team or the visiting team. If we wore white jerseys, we were the visiting team; green jerseys meant we had home field advantage. We wore white jerseys against BC. It was hilarious—only the Catholic Conference could think of something so clever. Regardless of the color of our jerseys, we were still traveling to East Boston.

Tom watched from the stands along with our father. During the pregame warm-ups, Tom turned to him and said, "Looks like a college team playing against a Pop Warner team. We don't stand a chance. I just hope the score isn't too embarrassing, and Kevin doesn't get killed!"

We didn't need to worry about any overconfidence on our side. But our coaches' strategy worked. On defense, we dominated Catoria. We pounded him all day long. Our offense moved the ball up and down the field almost at will. In the middle of the third quarter, Catoria ran the ball up the middle. He got hit by four of us. As he slowly lifted himself off the ground, he turned to his linemen and said, "What the fuck? Why don't you guys block?"

One of the linemen fired back, "Shut the fuck up and just run the fucking ball."

Hearing this, I bounced into our huddle and said, "Listen, they're turning on each other, so let's turn it up a notch! We can win this game! Keep going!"

The BC offensive linemen started to come off the ball slower and with less enthusiasm.

Unfortunately for us, the game ended in a 12-12 tie. It was a disappointment to dominate on both sides of the line of scrimmage and not be able to come away with a victory. BC ran fifty-eight plays on offense for a grand total of fifty-five yards. Bosco racked up two hundred and seventy-eight total yards against a team whose linemen easily outweighed ours by sixty-five pounds. There was no doubt we deserved to win. We all knew it, and we were all still disappointed, certain we were about to get chewed out by Dempsey.

But then, when he finally reached the locker room, Dempsey was beaming. "If they're number one in the state, then where does that put us?" We gave out a giant holler. Even so, I wasn't totally convinced that the BC game predicted anything about our team's future with any kind of certainty. It was too soon.

The game film showed that we had gifted, committed players. We were quick off the ball, we hit with intensity, and we played intelligent football. We also realized that we had no superstars. What we had was a group of players who understood team football. We played for each other, and it was beginning to show. Dempsey's philosophy of getting us to believe that size meant nothing in the game of football as long as we worked together was beginning to take hold.

What we experienced in practice the following week was a rare event. The coaches were actually civil. We worked hard, but the tone was lighter. If there was a mistake, the coaches turned into teachers rather than coaches reaming us out. The only yelling came when it was deserved—someone repeatedly making a mental mistake. Players and coaches alike felt a sense of accomplishment and pride for our efforts against BC. It was a new feeling for most of us. As the week came to an end, there was a cautious sense of confidence.

In coaching philosophy, Currier and Dempsey were similar. Both were demanding, and both believed in the power of endless repetition. But their coaching styles and their ability to connect with players was significantly different—different to the point, in fact, where it's not even fair to compare the two. Currier and Dempsey were a marriage; we needed both of their styles to be successful.

But it was Dempsey who had the unique gift that made us really work. Players felt Dempsey genuinely cared for them, even in the wake of the Michael Monahan accident. Dempsey had a different pull on the players than Currier, whom many kids never warmed up to, never felt any care or fatherly respect from. For me, I respected

Currier as a coach and enjoyed him off the field, but when he got hot, his words could turn belittling *fast*. Dempsey could also display frustration and anger—Lord knows he could do *that*—but when he vented, his words were aimed more toward the team in general and its performance rather than at any one individual.

Dempsey was a player's coach. He was always relating a football experience to a life experience.

"Feeling fear before a game is natural," he told us. "We all feel it. Even the pros feel it. If you didn't feel some fear before a game, then I can promise you you're not gonna play well. The butterflies show you're ready, because it shows you care."

Currier, on the other hand, didn't value these kinds of comments. He wanted tough kids on his team. He wanted results.

But both coaches had the same approach toward injuries. It was nerve-racking and even taboo to approach either coach to say you were hurt. Playing hurt or through an injury was part of the sport. Coaches had a way of making every sign of human imperfection or weakness feel like an act of cowardice.

"Kelly, your elbow is swollen and you want an elbow pad? Hey, Murphy, McDonald, Duggan, raise your arms. Do you see any of these guys wearing any pads on their arms, Kelly? Unless I see a bone comin' through your arm, you don't need any pansy pads on your elbow or anywhere else."

Our next game was against Matignon. Coach Currier had actually coached for Matignon before coming to Bosco. The school was known for its remarkable hockey teams but, in 1974, their football team wasn't as competitive as the other powerhouse teams in the Catholic Conference. Both our offense and defense executed well against them. Bandini, Staub, and Dominguez dominated on the offensive line. Libardoni and Riley had tremendous games running the ball, and Ski threw for three touchdowns. Murphy, our small, quiet wide-out, was turning into a clutch, sure-handed receiver. He ended the game with six receptions, two for touchdowns. We won easily, 33-6.

Yet, once again, the coaches were lukewarm in their post-game remarks. They wanted to make sure we didn't lose our edge.

That game was followed by one against Boston Tech, which was loaded with kids from my own neighborhood. A neighbor of mine, Steven, was the frequent victim of merciless ribbing. I never knew exactly why he was singled out; he'd always been relatively quiet and was a good kid. When Steven turned sixteen, however, and started to hit the weights and put some muscle on his frame, he tried out for quarterback and, when it was our week to play Tech, he got the nod to start at QB. I was happy for him. But his newfound identity had tapped into an arrogance not apparent to me when he was a loner.

"Best of luck next week," I said to Steve on the T.

"Yeah, well, you guys aren't that good," said New Steve. "We watched a game film on you guys. I think you suck. I'm pretty sure we're going to kick your ass."

"Is that right?" I said, taken aback. "Look, I'm all for being confident going into a game, but Steve, it's hard to talk trash when you only have one win under your belt."

I now knew why Steven got shit as a kid: His social skills were more than a little lacking. But even though he was, as I recall thinking, a little prick, I was still pulling for him and for the rest of the Hyde Park kids to have a good game.

On the first play of the game, Steven fumbled the ball on the snap from center, only to have an instant replay moment the very next play. Fumbling two times in a row during your quarterback debut isn't a good sign. He was replaced, never to return to the game.

We whipped Tech pretty good, 28-0. McGillivary had an outstanding game, recording three interceptions and two touchdowns. Our defensive line decimated their offensive running game. Billy Kelly, a tough kid and a good athlete from Hyde Park, was one of Tech's captains and ran in their backfield. Although we'd never hung out, I had known Billy since childhood. On one play, when Billy ran off tackle, I met him at the line of scrimmage. I bent over to help him up when I accidentally stepped on his hand. He let out a yell, jumped up, and got in my face with a, "What the fuck, asshole!" He wasn't aware I'd tackled him.

Looking straight into his face mask, I grinned, patted the top of his helmet, and said, "Hey, Kel, nice run!"

For a brief moment more, he still didn't recognize me. Then, when it hit him, a reluctant smirk came over his face. "Oh shit, I should have known it was you!"

I chuckled, gave him a pat on the ass, and said, "See you again real soon!"

Carouso, Cemate, Libardoni, Marciola, and Riley ran the ball inside and outside almost at will. The defensive line shut down Tech's running game. Staub, Bandini, Elwell, and I put a relentless pass rush on Tech's replacement quarterback. Trask and Libardoni once again dominated the middle of the field with outstanding performances as linebackers. And though this was Ski's first year playing quarterback at the varsity level, his ability to digest the coaches' instructions and, more importantly, quickly implement that knowledge during a game situation was remarkable.

But the game belonged to Colie MacGillivary. He was simply all over the field. "I still think of the Tech game as a highlight moment for me athletically," Colie later told me. "It was just one of those times when everything came together. The game seemed like it was being played in slow motion."

We were beginning to establish ourselves as a team, but it was still too early to believe we were anything special.

As a team, we were humble in our victory over Tech, but Dempsey and Currier weren't about to let their tight rein around our necks loosen anytime soon.

The following week, I saw Steven on the bus. I'd always had a soft spot for him. He wasn't a bad kid, but he seemed to always have a black cloud over his head. So I sat next to him and, without ever looking at me, he muttered, "Don't rub it in."

I didn't say a word.

A few years after high school, Steven and a few other guys tried to rob a jewelry store in downtown Boston. The whole thing unraveled and the police shot and wounded Steven and killed his partner. No one in Hyde Park was terribly surprised.

Despite the beating we'd given Tech, I focused my thoughts on the next game on the schedule. We were heading into the real meat of the season, where our true mettle would be severely tested.

Malden Catholic was known for fielding excellent hockey teams and for always producing tough, competitive football players. Over the last eight seasons, they were consistent contenders for the championship and, during the previous season, they'd gone 7-3. It was a Bosco tradition to play them on a Friday night at their home field—a tradition that would be our first real test since the BC game. We were very much aware that, up till that point, none of our wins had been against teams from the Catholic Conference or against teams with winning records.

The Malden Catholic game was a pivotal moment for the '74 Bosco Bears. We had an excellent week in practice and continued to develop our team personality. We were quiet but confident, small but powerful. During agility and hitting drills, we became almost businesslike. There was little talking or any of that rah-rah nonsense—Dempsey couldn't stand that crap. "Where are all those players during the second quarter?" he'd say. "They're just wasting time and energy. Let your hitting do the talking for you."

Gone were the days of put-downs, sarcastic comments, and insults. We were slowly coming together as a team. Dominguez,

Cemate, and Libardoni were all outstanding captains. Dominguez was easygoing and supportive. Cemate was quiet, and led by example. Intelligent on and off the field, Libardoni was tough as nails, loved to compete, and performed with a college-level intensity. Every football team needs an Al Libardoni; he's the kind of player that defines a team, a player that everyone respects, and a player that can back it up on the field every week. A true leader.

All three of them had played at the varsity level since their sophomore year, and my senior year of that season, we all learned why. Under their leadership, we all started to support one another, both during practices and games, whether there were mistakes or triumphs.

Going out onto Malden's field, we had a level of confidence that we'd never felt before. The first quarter set the tone for the entire game. We scored twice, driving the ball sixty-four yards in thirteen plays and, with eighteen seconds remaining in the quarter, Ski threw a twenty-seven yard bullet to Murphy in the end zone. Once again, our offensive and defensive lines dominated the opposition. We went on to play a near perfect game and beat a very tough Malden Catholic team, 29-8.

Everyone entered the bus elated from the win. All the starters were soaked with sweat, but it was that good-feeling sweat, the kind you don't mind living in for hours. It was sweat from hard work and success.

Losing game after game, year after year, you begin to feel so beaten down—a feeling that only losing teams can relate to. It's like small countries in the Olympics that get the luck of the draw to play a powerhouse country. The Americans in basketball, the Russians in hockey, and the Cubans in boxing—the opponents knew they were beaten before the competition even began.

The Buffalo Bills developed this disease during their four straight Super Bowl losses. You could see it in their eyes during their third and fourth Super Bowls; deep down, they just didn't believe they could win. During their third Super Bowl appearance against the Dallas Cowboys, Dallas scored first. With the score 7-0, the cameras panned the Buffalo sidelines and the looks of despair were everywhere. The Bills were emotionally defeated, and they were experienced *pros!* They played *hoping* to win versus playing expecting to win. That's simply not how champions play. Champions play with a look of defiance that says, *We're going to drive the ball down your throat and, by the way, try to stop us.*

As we basked in our moment of victory, Currier came on the bus and caught us completely off guard. He was steaming hot and told us all to sit down and to keep our mouths shut.

"I don't know what the hell you're so God damn happy about," he yelled from the front of the bus. "You call yourself a football team? The score should have been 29-0! But you decided to give up and let them score with two minutes left in the game. What a disgrace! If you think for one second that you can let up next week against CM, you'll have your asses handed to you. Oh, and by the way, remember how I told you yesterday that you'd have the weekend off? Forget it. Practice is on Sunday morning—eight o'clock sharp."

We all sat in shock, stunned and open-mouthed, trying to comprehend what we'd just heard.

*Really?* I thought. *Can't we have just one moment of joy?*

But this was the type of speech we were all well-acquainted with by then (having heard it many times before). It was bad enough that we were going to have to practice on Sunday, but the subway ran less often on Sundays, which would mean getting up at six in the morning to make it to practice on time.

As we took the long, silent ride back to school, the victory sweat suddenly made me feel cold, and the joy of our triumph vanished. I leaned over from my seat and whispered to Craig, "I may be a little confused, but didn't we just win that fucking game?" We both laughed but kept it low. God forbid the coaches caught us laughing.

Currier's coaching style wasn't for everyone but, as crazy as the moment seemed to us, he knew exactly what he was doing. And it played an important role in helping us zero in on the biggest game in Bosco history.

Catholic Memorial epitomized the term *powerhouse* for Boston high school sports teams during the early 1970s. They were great in every sport and, for athletes, it was one of the most sought after schools in the greater Boston area. CM, BC, and Xaverian Brothers were at the top of the food chain in the Catholic Conference academically, financially, and athletically. There was one entrance exam for all three schools, and they never had any problems meeting their annual enrollment numbers.

Bosco had a different clientele. Not too many suburban kids were trying to get into Bosco. We were viewed as a trade school and therefore were less highly valued than a more liberal arts-oriented school. Many suburban parents assumed that the brightest kids weren't looking to attend Bosco, and that the kids who did attend Bosco were there because they weren't smart enough to get into one of "The Big Three" (CM, BC, and Xaverian).

But what really made Bosco stand out from the rest was its location. The Big Three were all nestled in pleasant settings and boasted outstanding athletic facilities. Bosco, on the other hand, was downtown, with the Combat Zone and the Pine Street Inn as neighbors. Located at the corners of Washington Street and Tremont, there was simply no land at all around the school. There were no trees, no shade, no grass. The school's mass was vertical—seven stories high.

In those days, the CM Knights were always well-coached. With their winning streak of thirty-three games, they had established a football dynasty. They played with a cold, calculated precision that resembled a military drill. Every CM opponent would get sky-high at the idea of being the ones to finally dethrone the mighty Knights, only to collapse the moment CM scored their first touchdown. Against CM, all other teams seemed to simply throw their hands up and say, "Well, here they go again." Smelling the blood of the psychologically defeated, CM became an unstoppable machine and steamrolled their opponent.

The Knights were also explosively fast and possessed depth at every position, especially in the backfield. The flow of their game was seamless, a businesslike, impersonal force, overwhelming opponents with ease and precision. They never antagonized or trash talked. Just stone faces behind face masks.

The '74 Bosco team was going into the CM game undefeated, but before we could take on the Knights, we had Sunday morning practice to deal with.

It was a crisp, bright morning in late October. No one was happy about Sunday's practice, no one was happy about getting chewed out after a great victory, and no one was happy about having to putter around while we waited for the coaches to get on the field. Finally, a player yelled out, "Fuck 'em! Let's start practice without them."

Eddie Trask, our outstanding inside linebacker, proceeded to set up a pit-drill (which usually everyone dreaded). No big speeches. We just started going at each other, *live*! Currier and Dempsey came out of the locker room, two hundred yards away, and stopped, surprised to see what was happening. When they finally did approach us, they had us gather around and take a knee.

"First," Currier began, "I want to acknowledge our victory Friday night. You played well, and Coach Dempsey and I are proud of you. I want us to embrace the win, but I guarantee you that if you mentally let up at any time during next week's game, CM will beat you. It's that simple. A game like next week's comes around maybe once every ten years. You boys have a chance to make Bosco history. You will take this game with you the rest of your lives. Now, let's have a hell of a practice and get ready for CM!"

And, just like that, Currier brought us from anger and mutiny to focusing on one purpose as a team. Our attitudes were in check, and we had one of the best practice sessions I can remember, driving the sled one hundred yards to end the practice. We were in high spirits as we left the field.

The rest of the week went smoothly. The coaches held back, showing no frustration when we screwed up. Instead, they gave us words of encouragement. The players appreciated the tactical switch in their approach.

There was only one thing on my mind the entire week; it didn't matter if I was sitting in class or at home, waking up or falling asleep, the CM game was ever-present. I knew it was the same for my teammates. In the back of our minds, we were haunted by the same thoughts: *How will we perform as a team? How will I perform? Can we beat them? What if we lose?*

"This game isn't about you," Dempsey said, his tone absolute. "It's about *us*, our team. All you need to do is make a commitment to the guy to your left and the guy to your right that you will give one hundred percent for four quarters."

"Boys," Currier snapped, regarding us all with fists on his hips, "I know I don't need to give you a pep talk to get you 'up' for tomorrow's game. If you're not sky-high by tomorrow afternoon, you don't have a pulse."

Without waiting for a response, he turned immediately and walked off the field, leaving us there together for a few moments alone. Not much was said but, as we left the field, we were one.

The night before the game, I lay in my bed and actually prayed to God. I never claimed to be the most devout of Catholics, but I was searching for an intervention from a higher power. More than anything, I feared losing the mental game and suffering a psychological beating by CM. I wanted us, as a team, to believe in ourselves and live up to our potential. Every thought and emotion in my body and soul wanted nothing more than to win this game. I spoke aloud, "God, the game is going to start at one o'clock and end at three, which means that, at three, someone is going to win this game and someone is going to lose this game. All I ask is, please, don't let us quit. Just let us play a full one hundred percent for two hours!"

After my little conversation with God, I was in a state of peace and I soon drifted off to sleep. All night, Dempsey's words played in my head like a broken record: *Quickness, technique, desire. Quickness, technique, desire. Quickness . . .*

The next morning, I woke calm and relaxed. But during the train ride into Bosco, I started to feel those butterflies in my stomach all over again. This was the biggest moment of my life, and the anticipation, excitement, and fear of losing started to overwhelm me. While on the T, I closed my eyes and slowed my breathing down, telling myself to relax.

When I finally arrived at school, I walked into our new gym and noticed that, while all of us were getting our uniforms on, the gym was in total silence. The noise from the ventilation system was the only sound. I walked over to Ski and, when he saw me, said, "Kev, not today!" No cockiness. He said it so matter-of-factly. Ski had this look of confidence that I'll never forget. "Not today." He didn't need to explain what he meant.

There was something tangible in the air. You could feel it, almost taste it. It was unspoken, and all of us were connected to it. Spoken words would have taken away from the atmosphere. We had heard every encouraging athletic phrase ever spoken. But words would have been meaningless. This was truly our game. It was our time, and all of us knew it.

CM was already on the field as we ran out for our pregame

warm-up. Their captains were playing their role, trying to get players fired-up for the game. There was plenty of grunting and hollering and jumping up and down. Their warm-up wasn't anything special. Every team warms up in a similar fashion. Emotion is an important part of the game, and getting up for a game is part of the fabric that makes football so intense.

But something incredible happened to us then. Not one of us, not even the coaches, said a word during pregame. We were so focused and so intense that we hardly noticed how quiet we were. The energy between us was powerful. There was a connection. Every move, every sense, was heightened.

I remember glancing over my shoulder at the CM kids and noticing that many of them were looking over at us, trying to figure out what we were up to. It was as if we were beating them psychologically before the game had even started!

The game was fast and hard-hitting. CM played with exceptional speed, and we had to play at our highest level just to stay competitive with them. One critical play in the first quarter helped to set the tone for the day. On third and four on our forty-six yard line, CM's quarterback pitched the ball to the outside. Sylva, our starting freshman at monster back, made an incredible open-field tackle of the receiver, forcing a CM punt.

We took possession and drove the ball sixty-one yards for a touchdown. It was Bosco's first go-ahead touchdown in the history of all our games against CM.

Our defense played a near perfect first half. Libardoni intercepted a pass on one drive, and Elwell recovered a fumble during another one. Our defensive line gang-tackled on runs and put constant pressure on their quarterback when CM attempted to pass. Shawn Murphy had the game of his life as a wide receiver, with two touchdown receptions in the first half. Ski played flawlessly as quarterback, picking apart CM's defense with crisp, accurate passes.

He also added to CM's frustration with three first half runs for first-downs. Skip Bandini was playing both ways against Smyth, their All-Scholastic tackle, and was doing one hell of a job.

At halftime, we climbed into the bus (our makeshift away-locker room), somehow leading 19-0. We were stunned. Speechless. No other team had put up these type of numbers against CM in a decade.

Yet everyone knew this game was far from over.

"I want you to know," Currier said, standing up at the front of the bus, "that they're going to score on us. It's okay. Listen: Teams collapse when CM scores. I'm telling you that, if they score, it's okay. So when they score, just keep on playing the way you've been playing and we'll be alright." His anxiety was our anxiety. In the back of all of our minds was the fear that CM would punch in one touchdown and, from then on, it'd only be a matter of time before they beat us. These thoughts were perfectly normal, especially since CM had had our number for years.

Well, sure enough, in the beginning of the third quarter, CM marched right down the field. They were looking as unstoppable as the CM of old. The more they moved the ball, the more confident they became and, eventually, our defense was looking at a first and goal on our two-yard line.

CM, the greatest team in Massachusetts state history, had four attempts to move the ball six feet for a touchdown. That's four tries to move the ball seventy-two inches. The first play was stuffed as CM ran the ball straight at me, Elwell, and Libardoni. On second down, Eddie Trask, our inside linebacker, stunted off tackle and made a super hit on their fullback. Eddie's hit breathed life back into our defense.

In the huddle, we held hands in solidarity. On third and one on our own one-yard line, Eddie once again came up with another great hit. Our sidelines and fans in the stands went crazy, and the surge of

BOTH SIDES OF THE LINE

energy jolted through all of us. For the first time in my high school career, I saw doubt on the faces of the CM players.

They had fourth and goal on our one-yard line. I was lined up in the guard/center gap and, though I can't explain why, I somehow knew that no one was going to block me. Bobby Jones, from Hyde Park, was starting in the backfield for CM. Today, Bobby and I are old friends; we even played a bit of semi-pro together for a few years. But during our high school days, he was an arrogant, cocky little shit. Every year on the bus to Forest Hills, I would have to hear how awesome CM was. Wearing his CM jacket, looking down at the big CM letters stitched into its fabric, he'd smirk and say, "Bosco gonna suck again this year?"

I'd have to grin and bear the abuse because there wasn't much of a comeback, except for, of course, "Fuck you, Jones."

The ball was snapped. I blew through the hole. CM ran a sweep left. I dove at the quarterback, reaching out with my right hand. I clutched the right shoulder pad, but as he pulled away from me, I lost my grip and rolled off. However, CM's quarterback lost his balance, and his pass to Jones was too low to catch. It bounced off Jones' feet.

As I ran off the field, I saw Dempsey leaping about wildly, and I remember laughing, watching this human refrigerator awkwardly jumping for joy because his boys had pulled off a "next to impossible" goal line stand. The Bosco fans, the cheerleaders, and the players on the field were exultant. CM's players, on the other hand, jogged off the field, heads down. It was a break in the cycle, a sight never before witnessed. The play sealed the deal. The Bosco Bears not only beat CM. We shut them out 25 to 0.

The bus ride home was insane. But while everyone else was going nuts, I felt a triumphant sense of calm, an ultimate sense of contentment. Everyone cheered as Currier and Dempsey climbed aboard the bus. We hugged and congratulated one another as they told us—*finally*—how proud they were of us.

Currier spoke to the linemen: "I promise never to yell at any of you ever again—well, not until Monday, anyway." We laughed, and a loud cheer came from us all. Dempsey congratulated each player one by one and, when he got to me, we hugged. When I pulled away, I could see he had tears in his eyes. I knew that we never would have been celebrating this moment if Dempsey hadn't joined the coaching staff. I prayed that the joy I felt would never end. I could have stayed on that bus for hours, drinking in every moment. The longest winning streak in Massachusetts' history had come to an end, and we did it on their own home field! Ten weeks after the start of camp, Bosco, unsung and unappreciated, sat in first place in the conference.

You often hear the term "team effort" in sports. Our victory over CM was the perfect team effort. Everyone played an exceptional game; everyone had been poised, efficient, and confident. We dominated every phase of the game: offense, defense, field position, and special teams. We gang-tackled, blocked tenaciously, ran tough, and threw and caught the ball with deadly accuracy. Our coaches called a perfect game. Currier platooned all our running backs, while Dempsey substituted offensive and defensive linemen all day long to keep us fresh. All in all, we had put on a clinic.

That night, I rode up to Reading with my parents. We were late arriving at the annual banquet for Camp Mohawk, a summer camp run by our priest, Father MacAndrews (aka Father Mac). A large contingent of Hyde Park boys helped run his camp, and I was one of them.

The Camp Mohawk banquet was always held on the last Sunday in October, which, that year, happened to coincide with the CM game. Steve Perry, a Hyde Park boy and CM student, was one of Father Mac's favorites. Father Mac had a great sense of humor and, at my expense each year, he'd always make me get up to announce the CM score to the banquet guests. The audience would have a good laugh when the scores were announced while I would receive clichéd words of encouragement from parents, like "Keep your head up, Kev," and "Better luck next year, Kev."

Perry would shoot me a smug grin. Everyone knew CM's football reputation.

So when I walked in that October, they expected the usual.

Steve Perry and Father were at the head table. They looked up at me from their seats as I approached.

"25-nuthen," I said, answering the traditional question.

"25-nothing," said Perry. "Well, that's rather respectable. CM took it easy on you this year."

"Wait," said Father Mac. "25-nothing, who?"

"25-nuthen *us*! Father, we did it!"

No one believed me, especially Perry, who, for three years, had been gloating nonstop about CM's accomplishments, while at the same time laughing at Bosco's failures.

When he was finally faced with proof, his jaw practically dropped to the floor.

Father got up and gave me a hug. He immediately walked me to the front of the room and grabbed the microphone. The room held at least five hundred people, and yet it was completely silent as Father reminded the audience that, for the past several years, he'd made me announce the score of the CM game. He turned to me and asked me to remind everyone of the years' scores.

"54-0, Father."

"And last year, Kelly?"

"41-20, Father."

A light laughter rumbled through the hall.

"And how about this year, Kelly?"

"25-nuthen, Father."

"25-nothing? 25-nothing, *who*?"

"25-nuthen, Bosco!"

And, after a moment of ripe silence, the place erupted into applause!

"Nice job, Kev. Congratulations."

That night, I lay in bed in complete bliss. I knew this moment would stay with us for the rest of our lives, and that my teammates and I would be forever bonded.

Before I fell asleep, Currier's speech from camp floated back through my mind; *I'd break both my arms and both my legs to beat CM. The arms would heal, the legs would heal, and we would beat CM.*

I wondered what Currier and Dempsey were doing at that very moment but, more importantly, I wondered how they were feeling. Before the season, had they believed we had this kind of potential? Regardless, they must have felt proud of each other, having beaten the greatest team in the state with a blowout performance.

The next day, as I waited for the bus, I knew that everyone was fully aware of the CM/Bosco game score. I had three years of frustration to take out on Bobby Jones, and I was justified to unleash a barrage of comments to rub in the victory.

As I walked on the bus, I found Bobby sitting near the back alone. When our eyes met, he looked down at the floor. No, *Good game, Kelly*, or *Hey, you guys deserved the win*. And I didn't say a single word to him either. The fact that all he could do was look down, unable to muster the sportsmanship to congratulate me, was all the justice I needed. The feeling of true victory is intrinsic, and I was overwhelmingly content. To antagonize him with Bosco's dream achievement, with a sarcastic comment or criticism of CM's performance, would've been contrary to how I'd been coached. Dempsey would never have forgiven me if I'd stooped to that level, displaying such a lack of sportsmanship. What's more, it just didn't feel right all of a sudden. It didn't feel necessary to trash talk after such a great win.

Monday's *Boston Globe* published a wonderful article on the game:

*The state's longest winning streak is dead, killed not by trickery, inspiration, or secret strategy. Catholic Memorial's 33-game unbeaten streak died, instead, at the hands of cold precision. It was a matter of execution, pure and simple. "We just did what we've been doing all year," said Bob Currier, head coach of Don Bosco. "Our offensive line gave Ewanoski time to throw with good blocking in the first half."*

*Ewanoski finished with 12 of 14 for 143 yards and three touchdowns. Defensively, the word was also execution. Six times the Bears forced CM to turn over the ball (four interceptions, two by Alan Libardoni). Three of the turnovers led to Bosco touchdowns. There were no alibis or excuses from Jim O'Connor, the CM coach. "Bosco just outplayed us. They forced mistakes with good plays. They just deserved to win."*

Bosco held a victory pep-rally and, to my surprise, the senior class chanted my name, motioning me to come up to the microphone and say a few words. Currier looked back at me and smiled, giving me the nod to go up. I thanked everyone for supporting the team and emphasized that the victory was the greatest achievement in Don Bosco history. I didn't know it at the time, but the 1974 victory over CM would outshine all others in the school's subsequent history.

Next on our schedule was Cambridge Rindge and Latin, which hadn't won a game all year. During practice the following week, the coaches' biggest challenge was trying to bring us back down to Earth and get us back to work. The coaches were nervous that we wouldn't be able to get up for this game in the same way we had for CM. They knew Cambridge would be sky-high to play us, and that it would make their entire season to knock us off our pedestal. And, boy, were they right. We played flat and with zero emotion. At halftime, the score was 12-0, Cambridge in the lead.

All the good feelings from last week, all the pats on the back and the love between the players and coaches, came to a screeching halt. Currier and Dempsey were out of their minds.

"Let me make this perfectly clear to all of you," said Currier. "If we lose this game, the CM victory will mean absolutely nothing. The entire season will be a giant waste of time and a historical disaster for our team and the school."

Somehow, this woke us up for the second half, and we managed to pull off a 20-12 victory. Currier and Dempsey were so relieved that, for the first time in Bosco's history, we didn't look at film the following Monday. Currier said the game was over and he didn't want to spend one more moment thinking about Cambridge Rindge and Latin.

"I'm just so happy we came out of there with a victory. Besides, watching that first half again would only make me sick. Let's move on. We still have three games left, and each one is going to be tough. If we have any thought of becoming the first team in Bosco's history to win the Catholic Conference, we've got to get through Xaverian Brothers and Archbishop Williams, two excellent teams with plenty of talent, size, and incentive."

We were definitely in uncharted territory—opponents now viewed *us* as the team to beat. Teams were saying it would make their season to beat the first place Bosco Bears. It was a strange, wonderful feeling, walking through the neighborhood with friends and neighbors shouting out words of encouragement.

Xaverian Brothers of Westwood, which were our next opponents, had a talented and well-coached football team. Their line had size and plenty of skill. Their running back, Paul Costello, already knew he'd be heading to Princeton, and an All-Scholastic defensive back of theirs was heading to Boston College.

The first half turned out to be a slugfest, with us hanging on to a 12-6 lead. Xaverian was playing all out. I remember looking at the scoreboard, nervous, thinking that Xaverian could really win this game. Because their offensive line was playing tough, they were effectively moving the ball on us. I was playing against a kid named Fitzgerald, and he was a handful. For some reason, my heart just wasn't in the game, and I knew it. I didn't want to be on the field, and I could tell Fitzgerald sensed this as well. All season, I had made it a priority to send a message to the opposing lineman that I was going to be relentless all afternoon.

But I was in a funk, and just going through the motions, hoping for the game to end. On one particular play, Fitzgerald got the better of me and Costello ran through my hole for an eight-yard gain and a first down. As Fitzgerald got off the ground, he looked me in the eye and said, "You're not that fucking tough."

Then I heard Dempsey yell from the sidelines, "Kelly, what the hell are you doing out there? Wake up!"

Well, wake up I did. Fitzgerald's comment was exactly what I needed to get back in the game. I got pissed-off at myself; I'd been playing selfish, letting down my teammates, and I knew it. Refocusing, I played the remainder of the second half angry. I had something to prove to myself but, more importantly, to prove to Fitzgerald. Earning your opponent's respect is a critical component of the game. Costello didn't gain much on our side of the defensive line the rest of the game. During the next two Xaverian possessions, Skip and I each had a quarterback sack, and I was fortunate to block a punt.

But the game was still close throughout the second half until our very own Chester Rodriguez returned a punt for seventy yards late in the third quarter. Chester wove in and out of Xaverian's punting team, and his tremendous effort sealed the deal. We remained undefeated with an 18-6 victory.

After the game, Fitzgerald came over, stuck out his hand, and said, "Nice game, Kelly. Good luck against Archies."

I still wasn't happy with his chickenshit comment from earlier in the game, and I certainly thought about leaving his hand hanging there in midair and just walking away, but I couldn't stoop to that level. Besides, I should have been thanking him for the wake-up call.

As I entered the bus, I paused, watching my teammates celebrate before turning to Peter Masciola. "Next week," I said, "we're playing for the championship. Who knew?"

Masciola, his uniform soaked and dirty, didn't say a word. He just smiled and patted the top of my head.

The following week was special for both the players and coaches as we prepared for our game against Archbishop Williams. Though we all felt the weight of the upcoming game, there were no rah-rah gimmicks. The coaches turned into true teachers. Dempsey brought us back to basics and reminded us that the entire game would be won or lost based on who controlled the line of scrimmage.

"Boys, it's going to come down to who wants it more. Remember, *quickness, technique, and desire*. They're not going to roll over for us. They want this game just as much as you do. The key will be your ability to sustain your emotional commitment, to make the fewest mistakes, and, finally, to convince them through relentless hitting that they can't possibly win."

All week, the defense line worked on technique. We did double-teaming drills, spinning out of blocks, and tackling: "Drive your helmet through his numbers and wrap him up!" Dempsey reminded us. "Anyone who breaks down and tries to arm tackle or, worse, refuses to wrap up after a good hit, may determine who loses this game! That's just selfish, cowardly football."

We reviewed our stunts and ran them to perfection. We watched game films twice that week (a first at Bosco), and what stuck out to us was just how much Archies looked like us. They played good team football and were solid across the board. They could hit, and they made very few mistakes. Emotionally, we were more sober. The year had unfolded as a surprise, but now we knew who we were. We knew we deserved to be here and that we could compete with anyone in the league and, for that matter, anyone in the state.

Our next game was it—the entire season, the championship.

Just one year prior, we'd been playing one another to see who would claim *last* place in the conference. We claimed that title with no problem then, but because of our tie with Boston College High, a loss by us now would allow Archies to be co-champs with Catholic Memorial, and we would end up with absolutely nothing.

Let me put it this way: Championships in Massachusetts were determined by a complicated point system. CM had beat Archie's during the season, and we'd beat CM, but if Archies beat us, then we'd lose the championship because of the tie.

Archies' quarterback, Morrissey, stood just over six feet tall at two hundred and ten pounds, and was the toughest in the league. He had a cannon of an arm, and he not only loved to run with the ball, he could dish it out to any defender trying to tackle him.

Dennis McCarthy, a tough Irish kid from Quincy, was the main running back in Archie's backfield. He was quick with his mouth as well as with his hands and feet.

I played against an offensive tackle named Joe Pellegrini (a tackle I would end up lining up against yet again some years later when I played for Bridgewater State and he for Harvard). He was an excellent lineman who would later start for the New York Jets!

It was imperative that I deliver on my side of the line, that I play the game of my life. All week long, I visualized run plays, trap plays, being double-teamed, rushing the quarterback—I was determined to get into Pellegrini's head. I wanted him going back into the huddle convinced he was in a dogfight—and losing.

Dempsey took extra time to speak to linemen all week after practice. He wanted all of us to be on the same page: We were going to play *relentless* football.

"A key ingredient is getting to Morrissey," he explained. "He's the most talented quarterback we'll see all year. We have the quickest defensive line in the league. If we can put pressure on him and get him to play out of his rhythm, we'll have a chance. Kelly, I'm going to stunt you and Martini often throughout the game, so be ready!"

The game was just what we'd expected. Both teams were playing all out. Currier went back to platooning our running backs, and Ski kept us in the game with key passes.

On defense, our line pursued Morrissey and we gang-tackled their running backs. Our linebackers and defensive backs came up quick to hit, and covered their receivers exceptionally well.

Their defense was also playing a great game. At halftime, Archies held an 8-7 lead. Dempsey was not happy, and he laid into me with particular force.

"Kelly, do you plan on playing anytime today? Get your head out of your ass and hit someone, will ya?"

It didn't matter how I thought I was playing. If Dempsey criticized me, I would get angry and turn it up a notch. Dempsey had a pull on me. He had made me into the player I had become and, more importantly, he *believed* in me. I wasn't about to let him down, especially not during this game. He knew I'd respond. I wasn't in the same frame of mind as in the Xaverain game. I knew what was at stake. We all knew.

The game was a classic, just the type of game a championship should be. Both teams were giving their all on every play and the outcome was going to be determined by the final drive of the game. We took the lead in the fourth quarter. Stevie Riley ran off tackle from the seven-yard line and, with one minute and thirty-seven seconds left in the game, we went ahead 13-8.

Archies didn't flinch. They marched right down the field and had a real chance to win it all in the final seconds. My heart was pounding wildly. I kept looking at the clock thinking, *God, we can't lose the whole season with less than thirty seconds left in the game!*

Archies' players were exuberant. Their fans were on their feet, losing their minds screaming, hoping for a last-second victory. Archies' sense of urgency could be felt as they came up to the line of scrimmage on their own forty-three-yard line.

Wanting to avoid a last, long completion for a touchdown, we shifted into our prevent defense, which called for us to take one defensive lineman out of the game and replace him with an extra defensive back, giving us additional coverage in our defensive backfield. Our defensive backfield played their receivers tight and thus gave us time to put pressure on Morrissey.

With thirty-seven seconds left in the game, Archies had enough time for only two more plays. On a third down, Morrissey scrambled to his right but threw an incomplete pass. The final play of the game, fourth down, would truly be all or nothing.

My career consisted of three years of football, two of which had been miserable. With no time left on the clock, it would end in either complete glory or devastating loss. Our defensive backfield held tight. Bandini, Elwell, and I exploded out of our stances to get to Morrissey as he moved to his left and then to his right before finally setting up for a throw. A receiver broke open just for a second. Morrissey caught his eye and, as he lifted his arm to throw the winning touchdown, all three of us hit Morrissey at once.

The 1974 Bosco Bears were the Catholic Conference Champions!

Archies' fans sat in total silence as Bosco's side of the field went wild. My immediate reaction was one of numbness; I wasn't sure how to feel. After shaking hands with the Archbishop Williams players, Eddie Dominguez and I agreed to go out to the fifty-yard line and absorb the moment. We were the last two players on the bus. Currier and Dempsey waited for us. Shaking Currier's hand in congratulations, I felt so happy for him, and happy that, after all his years of coaching at Bosco, he had finally gotten his big win.

When I turned to Dempsey, he gave me a hug, and I thanked him for what he had given us, and for what he'd given me.

The '74 Bosco Bears, the smallest team in the school's history, sat on top of the Catholic Conference as champions! Every game had been an away game for us; we went into everyone else's backyard and beat every home team. Were the games in the Catholic Conference competitive? Was the caliber of the players tops in the state? Eight players from the conference would end up playing at Division I colleges in 1974, and five would move on to the NFL.

The bus ride home was nothing like the experience of sitting silent and cold after the Malden Catholic game. This was pure joy and, yes, the sweat now felt *great*. No one wanted the feeling or the ride to end. Years of losing, years of coming in last place in the league, years of doubt, of wondering why anyone would want to play this game—all of that was erased. All of the questions were answered with absolute clarity.

Football mirrors life. It teaches that the strong survive and that self-discipline is the key to happiness and success. Learning to never quit, no matter what the odds or how difficult the struggle, produces lifelong benefits. Learning to sacrifice for others, to be a team player at work, in your neighborhood, and in your family is the foundation to a happy life. What the championship gave us was an unalloyed confidence that we could achieve anything we put our minds to—a gift that would be ours for as long as we lived.

I couldn't help hearing my brother's advice echo in the back of my mind, *If you quit, I promise you will regret it for the rest of your life.* The weight of Tommy's words ran a shiver up my spine. I wondered how I would have felt watching this season, and especially this final game, from the sidelines.

The experience of becoming champions would never have taken place without the contributions of our coaches. For the linemen, our success was pinned on one man, Coach Clyde Dempsey. He taught us superior line technique and forced us to play with intelligence. We were all true disciples. And I, in particular, was especially aware that I never would have had the season I'd had if he hadn't believed in me. I had played the season with Dempsey's advice and drive in my head. I had repeated his mantra throughout each game: *quickness, technique, and desire.* During games, I'd imagined Dempsey watching me from the sidelines to determine if I was going all out on every play. I would use any scenario I could think of to give me an edge.

No other coach before or after Dempsey had ever had that level of impact on me as a player.

At the end of each year, Bosco held its Annual Athletic Banquet for all sports. This year it would take place in our new gym. In my freshman year, I'd watched athletes receive the MVP awards. The football players looked like full-grown men, all tall, broad, and tough. The bearded Leo Falter, who'd already become a father, won the MVP lineman my freshman year, and I remember going home and fantasizing about winning the MVP in football my senior year. I remember laughing out loud at the thought.

Our guest speaker at the banquet was Hank Bullock, defensive coordinator for the New England Patriots. He gave a speech about the greatness of sports in our society and how athletes had the amazing gift of being able to dream. If we worked hard, those dreams could come true. But what he said at the end of his speech stayed with me for life: "Some of you will receive trophies this evening for your accomplishments. Congratulations! You should feel proud when you receive these awards. I want you to look at them, and kiss them if you want. Then I want you to go home and stick those trophies in your closet. Because those trophies will mean absolutely nothing next year. If you are lucky enough to play in college, I want you to realize that everyone sitting in that locker room will have won a trophy just like yours. Next year, you will have to prove yourself all over again."

I purposely sat at the last table in the gym. I had not invited my girlfriend to the banquet, as many of the other players had. Instead, I'd invited Tom, who'd said, "No, thanks, but if you come home with a trophy, I'll feel bad for not attending." So there I sat, with my stepmother and father. I just wanted to receive my football letter and head home. I don't remember why I felt this way, but I did. My high school career was over, and I was thinking ahead to college.

The first trophy of the night was for MVP lineman. Coach Dempsey would announce the recipient. I knew that any one of our linemen could easily be awarded this trophy. There was no superstar lineman on our team and, as far as talent was concerned, we were all pretty much equal. I had actually pointed out Derrick Martini to my stepmother during Dempsey's remarks.

"I have always been a man of few words," Dempsey began, standing up at the podium with his thick glasses balanced on his nose. Seeing him there, feeling the anticipation of all that awaited me outside of high school, I felt a sudden rush of memory, of the first time I'd actually seen Coach Dempsey and all the anxiety and excitement that had accompanied the realization that, *This is my coach. This is the guy who's gonna turn it all around for us.* "This player has improved two hundred percent from last year," he went on, smiling, "and if everyone played with his level of commitment, then this gym would be full of banners. I'm proud to present this trophy to Kevin Kelly."

The words took an eternity to reach me. I was stunned. My stepmother, a normally quiet, reserved woman, jumped out of her seat and screamed.

The walk to the stage took forever. When I reached Coach Dempsey, I wasn't sure what to do. What I was supposed to do was stop, shake hands, and look at the photographer. But I was so uncomfortable, having to get up in front of everyone to receive the trophy, that I shook hands with Dempsey as fast as I could, didn't make any eye contact with him, and rushed back to my seat.

In most every other sport, you usually had a good idea of who would be the MVP: the star basketball player, the star hockey player, and so on. But for the '74 Bosco Bears, the MVP lineman just wasn't obvious. Skip Bandini, Billy Elwell, Derrick Martini, and Chris Staub all played both ways on the line. Both Abe Benitez and Tommy McGregor had exceptional years. Eddie Dominguez, our captain, had played both ways since his sophomore year. The trophy could have gone to any of these players. I'd had a solid year, and I'd contributed to my team, but I was not the Most Valuable Lineman. To be honest, I think they should have given the award to the entire line. We were the perfect example of a unit that worked well together. With our lack of size, if we'd had a weak player, it would have been exposed early on and we never would have had a winning season. After the dinner, I received congratulations from teammates, coaches, and even some parents.

All I could do was look for the door.

My father was so proud of me that he took me to the Old Colony Restaurant on Morrissey Boulevard in Dorchester for an after-banquet drink. Smiling proudly, he placed the trophy on the bar for all the patrons to see. The folks in the bar were kind enough to clap and even offer a few thumbs up. I understood that this was a big moment for my dad; it was the first trophy one of his kids had ever won.

When I arrived home, I left the trophy on the kitchen table for Tom to see when he got home from hanging out with his buddies.

When I finally went to bed and was beginning to come down from the rush, Coach Bullock's words about trophies crept back into my head. And so, the next day, I kissed the trophy and put it in my closet.

Before graduation, I would seek out Coach Dempsey to thank him. He greeted me with a warm smile. When we'd first met at the end of my sophomore year, I was still a boy, unsure who I was as a person and an athlete. About to leave Bosco, I had grown to be a young man.

"Coach, I never would have had the year I did if it wasn't for you believing in me, and I just wanted to thank you."

"Kevin, you deserve all the credit. You're the one who worked hard on the field. It's been a pleasure. Best of luck next year in college."

I shook Dempsey's hand, turned, and walked away. It wasn't a movie ending. It wasn't a big emotional moment when we both had tears in our eyes and hugged. It was a natural parting. I wasn't wondering about whether or not I'd see Dempsey again. I was moving on to the next stage in my life. I was ready. Or so I thought.

Little did I know that my relationship with Coach Dempsey was only just beginning.

# FOOTBALL

THE ENGLISH HIGH SCHOOL VARSITY FOOTBALL SQUAD OF 1963

Third Row: Ed Shanley, Bill Janey, Neil McLaughlin (62), Bill Duffy (84), Tom Abrams (51), Jim McCool (50), Gary Krause (73), Ed Powers (65), Mike Ezekiel (31), Bill Petipas (35), Coach John Doherty, Coach Fred Gillis, Jr. Second Row: Sam Penta, Manager; Charles Hamburg, Assistant Manager; Bill Manley (28), Marty Walsh (64), Bob Odoardi (80), Tom Tracey (70), Marty Parlon (61), Vic Pappas (40), Don Hooper (32), Tom Tucker (21), Mario Caporale (30), Coach P. J. King. Head Master Joseph L. Malone, First Row: Head Coach W. J. Stewart, Tim Pukt (27), Henry Stefano (20), Jim Heelen (29), Steven Dixon (60), Henry McQueeney (85) (Co-Captain), Clyde Dempsey (63) (Co-Captain), Leroy Wilson (71), Anthony Bombadieri (72), Larry Ayers (81), Bill Overton (82).

## ENGLISH BEATS GROTON 16 — 6

E. H. S. opened the 63rd season by being outplayed in the first half, but winning its 15th consecutive game in a 2nd and a 3rd year span. Q.B. Tom Tucker opened the scoring for English with a quarterback sneak from the two yard line and then Q.B. Hank Stefano came in to give to Jim Heelen for the 10 yard conversion. On the kickoff by English, the smart Groton man, who let the ball roll to the four yard line, and didn't touch it. But one of our tacklers who knows his football jumps on it and recovered it for English. Q.B. Hank Stefano then handed off again to Jim Heelen for another tally. Q.B. Tucker came in, and threw a pass to co-captain Butch McQueeney for a two point conversion, giving E. H. S. the final score of 16-6.

| Won | | Lost | |
|---|---|---|---|
| E.H.S. | 16 | Groton | 6 |
| E.H.S. | 26 | B. C. High | 6 |
| E.H.S. | 30 | Dorcester | 12 |
| E.H.S. | 34 | B. Trade | 6 |
| E.H.S. | 28 | South Boston | 0 |
| Rindge Tech | 8 | E.H.S. | 0 |
| B. Tech | 20 | E.H.S. | 16 |
| E.H.S. | 18 | B. L. S. | 12 |

Above: Boston English team photo: Jack "Clyde" Dempsey, co-captain (63). The smallest starter and also the only two-time All-American.

Co-Captain
Clyde Dempsey

Co-Captain
John McQueeney

## DOUBLE BLUE THUMPS B.C. HIGH 26 — 6

Bill Manley scored the first of his two touchdowns at the one minute mark of the first quarter to pace English on to victory. After co-captain Clyde Dempsey recovered an eaglet fumble, scampered 15 yards for a touchdown. B.C. High scored following an interception at E. H. S.'s 33 yard line, but this didn't stop English or Bill Manley. On the kickoff Manley received, and raced 81 yards to put English out in front 12-6. English's defense forced an eaglet punt, but Bill Overton recovered a bad snap from center putting E. H. S. on the two yard line. The next play Tim Pukt bulled over, giving English a lead of 18-6 after the first period. The Blue and Blue scored their final points when Jim Heelen went over the goal line and Overton received a pass from O.B. Tom Tucker adding the final two points.

### E.H.S. PASSES BY DOT. 30–12

In the first period a stunned English High scored their first touchdown when Bill Manley went around the left end. The Blue and Blue was held to 6 points, and a tie for the first half of the game. The first half was a surprise to everyone, but English caught hold of itself during the third period. With E.H.S. near the goal post, on a Q.B. sneak, Hank Stefano scored to give English the lead and their confidence. Later Mike Ezekiel intercepted a Dot pass and ran it to the four yard line before being hauled down. Then two downs later Jim Heelen drove over for another tally. English's defense forced Dot to punt, and English recovered. Two downs later Q.B. Tom Tucker threw a T.D. pass to Larry Ayers to end the scoring in the third period. In the fourth period Dot scored but Bill Murphy retaliated with the final T.D. of the game. Another win for Coach Stewart but not a happy one.

### LETTERMEN

Thomas Abrams
Lawrence Ayers
Anthony Bombadieri
Mario Caporale
Clyde Dempsey
Steve Dixon
William Duffy
Michael Ezekiel
Charles Hamburg
   Manager
James Heelen
Donald Hooper
John Kohler
Gary Krause
James McCool
Neil McLaughlin

John McQueeney
William Manley
William Overton
Victor Pappas
Martin Parlon
Samuel Pento—Manager
William Petipas
Edward Powers
Timothy Pukt
Edward Shanley
   Manager
Henry Stefano
Thomas Tucker
Martin Walsh
Leroy Wilson

Upper right hand corner: Dempsey talking with his coach during a time-out;
he had the look of a warrior.

CLYDE F. DEMPSEY
85 Turner St., Brighton
*School:* Thomas
*Ambition:* Coach
*College:* Syracuse University
*Hobbies:* Sports
*Honors:* Football 2, 3, 4
Co-capt.; Patrol 2, 3

LETTERMEN

J. Brack
C. Dempsey
G. Desimone
E. Doherty
J. Donato (Mgr.)
R. Donovan
W. Ferreira
C. Hamburg (Mgr.)
J. Heelen
J. Hughes
R. Joyce
J. Kelly
T. Legge
F. Loud
B. Tarpey
W. Wadman

Above: Senior High School Picture – Ambition – coach
Below: Dempsey as a member of the swim team

# Class Prophecy

Lenny Burman graduates from Mass. College of Pharmacy and becomes a carbonic engineer for Sparr's.

Mark Davis becomes editor for Jack and Jill Magazine.

Gerry DeSimone and Johnny Gilmore open a Bunny Club.

Otto Kehrmeyer writes the musical score for James Dubro's new hit play.

After collection of Class Dues Bob Jarvis spends a weekend in Las Vegas.

Joe Cohane leads a Buddist revolt in India.

Gartz Gets.

Freeman is imprisoned.

Louis Lopardi becomes the fifth Beatle.

Borr becomes interesting.

Al Bovarnick buys a new sweater . . . at last.

Diamond gets cut.

Bird goes Surfin'.

Arthur Crosby bings.

Barry Applebaum replaces Jack LaLanne.

Fredberg becomes an engineer . . . for the Pennsylvania Railroad.

Steve Dixon and Larry Ayers play football for Peru U.

Goldman tarnishes.

We see the Jones boys as Co-Presidents of the class of 1968 at the U. of Miss.

Al Marston gets a "B" from Mr. Russell.

Clyde Dempsey goes to class.

The Ezekiel brothers finally discover which one has the Toni.

Ricky Rubin come to school . . . tucked and tied.

Jimmy Heelon passes . . . for a touchdown.

Dickie Diaz becomes a full-fledged M.O.T.

Jimmy Ryan performs bird calls daily at the Museum of Science . . . don't miss him.

Al Pepsi Cola drinks DiNicola.

Stan Drobnis finds his place.

Steve Drooker signs with the New York Mets . . . as a bat boy.

"Moose" Goldstein goes on record as saying "_____."

Flip Flops.

Harry Sandler becomes very Tillie — I mean silly.

Leroy Wilson SHRINKs.

Steve Klein buys a outfit valued at more than one of BZ's Ties.

Butch McQueeney replaces Debbie Drake . . . but not completely.

From the pages of the 1965 Bridgton Academy Yearbook, "Stranger"
Above: Headmaster Richard Goldsmith and teacher Michael Tatistcheff
Below: Wayne Lynch, Dempsey's rommate and Clyde "Jack" Dempsey

Richard L. Goldsmith

A.B., Bowdoin College; M.Ed., Bates
College; Graduate work, New York
University

Michael A  Tatistcheff
B S., Boston University; Graduate Work,
Boston University; Mathematics, Stranger
Advisor, Photography Club Sponsor

Wayne C. Lynch
"Wayne"
81 Old Essex Rd.
Manchester, Mass.
"The whole driveway Mrs. Parker?"
    "It's Jack's turn isn't it"

Clyde Dempsey
"Jack"
369 Lexington St.
Auburndale, Mass
"Wayne's buddy"          "Wipe out
at Gallanari's"

FIRST ROW: Mgr. Simpson, Gammons, Young, Desilets, Stagg, Rodes, Chinappi, Furbush, Graham, D<
Lynch, Merullo, Ramia, Lynch, Patten, Saporito. SECOND ROW: Bioty, Damlin, Tuminski, Taylor, K<
Socha, Turati, Doran, Loranger, White, Craw, Amico, Hanlon, Freeman, Kaloust, Mgr Morrill THIF
ROW: Mgr Thurber, Mgr. Clark, Williams, Quigley, Collinson, Tiedt, Gingrande, Stankus, Schlosberg
Wingate, Murphy, Ketchum, Gagne, DeSantos, Moschella, Wilcox, Mgr Robinson

# Football

Coach Robert Walker, in his final season at Bridgton Academy put the team throug
rough preseason workout beginning on September 9th  The season started with a t
ing last minute victory over Worchester Academy  On October 2nd Bridgton came
behind to outscore the Colby Freshmen 33-6  In their third game of the season B
surpassed their opponents by a score of 7-6 in a hard fought game at the Universi
of Maine  Traveling to Vermont they brought home their fourth victory. At this ti
the Bridgton Academy football team  was rated the number one prep team in New E
land. B A. suffered their first defeat in a hard fought battle at Tufts University  >
their last two efforts the B A. eleven were outscored, at Bowdoin and B U. Both R
Walker and his team should be congratulated on a fine season

Bridgeton Academy Team (1965): Dempsey (66) (first row),

Dempsey and a group of players shaved their heads to boost team morale.

## The Season's Record

| | | | |
|---|---|---|---|
| B.A. | -- 12 | Worchester Academy | -- 8 |
| B A. | -- 33 | Colby Frosh | -- 6 |
| B A. | -- 7 | Maine Frosh | -- 6 |
| B A | -- 15 | Vermont Frosh | -- 0 |
| B.A. | -- 6 | Tufts Frosh | -- 14 |
| B.A. | -- 0 | Bowdoin Frosh | -- 13 |
| B A. | -- 12 | Boston Univ Frosh | -- 34 |

Stagg strikes back

Follow me

Leggo, ya slob

63

set of photos from our '74 season. I'm
umber 70. Al Libardoni 20, Chris Staub 84,
illy Elwell 77, Derrick Martini 63, Stevie
iely 46, Shawn Murphy 81, Paul Carouso 32,
olie MacGillvaray (running with ball 33).

Our starting offense: kneeling, (L to R): Chris Staub, Skip Bandini, Derrick Martini, Billy Elwell, Abe Benitez, Tommy "Yogi" McGregor, and Shawn Murphy.
Back Row: Craig Cemate, Stevie Riely, Mike Ewonoski, and Paul Carouso.

Our defense, kneeling (L to R): Billy Elwell, me, Derrick, Jerome Frazier, Chris, Craig, Chester Rodriguez, Al, Eddie Trask, Colie McGillivary, and freshman John Silva.

Our seniors, kneeling (L to R): Bobby Clark, Vinny O'Brien, Mark Beale, Eddie Dominguez, Abe Banitez, Tommy McGregor, and me. Back Row: Peter Masciola, Craig Cemate, Al Libardoni, Gary Green, and Stevie Riley.

Our three captains and coaches, L to R: Al Libardoni, Eddie Dominguez, and Craig Cemate, Head Coach Bob Currier, Assistant Coach Jim Smith, and Defense and Line Coach Jack Dempsey.

The Team

# Forty Years Later:
## Reunion

Vinny and Abe put together a Bosco tribute that was a big hit among the players.

Between Abe and Skip is Peter Masciola, ¿ Air Force one star general. At 54, he was t oldest serving officer in Afghanistan. A tr hero and one tough Bosco brother.

A rough attempt at a team photo: Coach Currier on the left. Holding the football is Captair Al Libardoni. With the black scally cap: Captain Craig Cemate. Smiling in the back is Mik Ewanoski, our quarterback. Number 63 is folded over a chair in memory of Derrick Martini who died too young.

Top Row: Chris Staub, Stevie Riley, Frankie Marchione, Gary Green, and Paul Carouso.
2nd Row: Colie McGillivary, Vinny O'Brien, Rich Abner, Abe Benetez, and me.

Abe, Skip, and me. Skip is head coach of Curry College and exemplifies the very best of
Dempsey. Abe's dad sacrificed everything to get his family to America from Cuba.

Above: The banner celebrating the victorious 1974 season
MVP Lineman—Kevin Kelly. I was an average, dependable player, but not the MVP of ou
team. This trophy belonged to all our linemen.

Hank Bulloch from the Patriots was our keynote speaker during our sports banquet. "Som
of you will receive trophies this evening for your athletic achievement. Congratulations
Take your trophy home, hold it, kiss it, and then throw it in your closet, because next yea
that trophy will mean absolutely nothing." That is exactly what I did. Even my kids hav
never seen this trophy on a shelf or a mantel piece. I always kept it in a box.

These photos were taken in December 2014 as I retraced memories with my daughter Michelle.

on Bosco Technical High School, whose ors closed in 1998. Today, sadly for all Bosco umni, it is a Double Tree Hotel.

Laughing at the thought that Science Park was completely fenced in, and unsure exactly who the city was trying to keep out.

low: Standing outside the old sex Street subway station. The mbat Zone and all the strip bs and hookers are long gone.

Science Park with grass? Wow! The Hancock Building that lost all its mirrors during its early construction is a stunning building today. The Prudential Building is to the far right.

The Charles River. The Lechmere Clock that was taboo to look at during practice is no more. It once hung from a building across the river in Cambridge.

Our locker room and weight room were located in the girls' side of a changing room for a city outdoor public pool. The weather-beaten pool is now closed, a sad and unexpected sight.

Here I walked with my daughter along the perimeter of Don Bosco. It was a bitterly cold day, but I barely felt it; I was flooded with memories from four decades ago. It started out my story, but it rightfully turned into *our* story.

# 1975

*"When I look out at this team, I don't see white football players on this team, and I don't see black football players on this team, I don't see Irish or Italian football players on this team.*
*I only see football players on this team."*
—Coach Dempsey

The timing was perfect. We'd been at Bosco for four years and all of us were ready and even excited to move on with our lives. The strict Catholic philosophy, the coat and tie attire, and the all-boys environment, were now joyfully behind us. Some goodbyes with certain faculty and dear friends pulled emotional strings, but they quickly faded by the time I pulled into Forest Hills.

But as we seniors looked forward to the next chapter in our lives, our city was still being torn apart by forced busing. Boston was gearing up for its second year of the program and the emotional and financial cost to all was crippling.

A strange twist to the busing issue for me, however, was the awareness that my father, for the first time in his career, was actually making some money. The city simply didn't have enough police to handle the issues created by forced busing. Schools needed police in the morning during the arrival of students, and again at the end of the day when students were being bused home. Demonstrations and mini-riots were popping up all over the city.

Boston cops were given the green light to work as much overtime as they could handle. My father, who'd struggled financially for years, was simply never home during this time. He worked double shifts three to four times a week and never once complained about being tired.

"Dad, take it easy," Tom said once. "You're not that young anymore. Try to pace yourself."

"I'm okay. Just make sure you're helping your mother with your brothers and sisters."

"How bad is it out there?" I asked, craning my neck from the car's front passenger seat to look at my father's riot gear in the back.

"Southie, Charlestown, Hyde Park, and Dorchester are the most troubled areas; the residents in those sections will not consider the slightest compromise. A lot of people are getting hurt on the subways too."

My dad was fully aware of the rampant trouble between blacks and whites on the T.

Interestingly enough, as many cities around the country struggled with forced busing laws in the mid '70s, racial tension and prejudice in sports was actually making some positive headway. In the '50s and '60s, many college and professional football teams struggled to find racial harmony. Black and white players never roomed together. Many teams with black players traveling throughout the country, especially in the South, weren't welcome in restaurants or hotels there. Vince Lombardi of the Green Bay Packers and George Halas of the Chicago Bears were exceptions to the rule. They were the first pro coaches in the '60s to room black and white players together in the NFL. Lombardi was once told during an away game that his black players couldn't enter through the front door of a restaurant and had to enter through the kitchen, so Lombardi said, "If one of my players has to enter through the kitchen, we all will."

At Bosco, Dempsey had addressed the forced busing issue before we ever even left for camp in the fall of '74. Dempsey, knowing that forced busing was having an impact on all of us, wanted to address it up-front and make his opinions on the matter known. His speech was straightforward, pinning our attentions down with a *this-is-non-negotiable* look:

"Everyone gather around and take a knee. I want to be clear with everyone: When I look out at this team, I don't see white football players on this team, and I don't see black football players on this team, I don't see Irish or Italian football players on this team. I only see *football* players on this team. Regardless of what is taking place in your neighborhoods or throughout the city, we are a *team* first, and we can win only if we play as a *team*. Let me also make this clear to everyone: Beating on someone because of the color of their skin is pure chickenshit.

"All over the news you're hearing about black and white kids getting jumped, sometimes being outnumbered by four or five to one, sometimes more. That's not anyone's definition of being tough. You'll find out what you're made of when you're put into a position to stick up for someone, and then don't. Tough to look yourself in the mirror the next day knowing you're a coward." Dempsey paused, his lips tight, his eyes glaring at the faces in front of him. "Any questions?" he barked. At our silence, he nodded, pleased. "Good. See you tomorrow."

It was short and sweet, but it put us in the right frame of mind. I knew Dempsey was right, though I had no idea that later that same year, I would have my moment—the moment to prove what I was made of, to prove whether I was willing to stand up for what was right or confront the reality that I was a coward.

Although forced busing was daily news, seniors from the '74 team, for the most part, tuned out the city's problems as their minds drifted off to upcoming college days. Before school ended, the seniors met one final time to discuss our futures and reminisce about the last four years, knowing full well that it might be years before we saw each other again, if ever. Sitting on the bleachers, after school, in our beautiful new gym, looking out over our stunning, first-of-its-kind, green and gold, rubber-floored basketball court, we were silent, just taking in the moment.

Suddenly, our captain, Al Libardoni, broke the ice: "I'm heading off to Springfield College in western Massachusetts to play baseball."

"Baseball?" we all said in unison.

"What about football? You were MVP of the Catholic Conference for Christ's sake," Vinny said, gesturing to the rest of us to show our support.

"I met with the head coach, Ted Dunn," Al shrugged. "He's an old-timer who has a few years left but seems to be out of his mind."

"Why?" asked Pete.

"Here's what he told me: 'Al, I don't think you can play at the college level. Your arms are too short and you won't be able to tackle anyone.'"

We were all dumbfounded, trying to digest what we'd just heard.

Our leader and one of the most talented players to ever come out of the Catholic Conference had seemingly played his last football game—in high school. If any of us could have walked onto a college football field and had an immediate impact, it was Al Libardoni.

"What about you, Pete?" I asked.

Peter Masciola, a halfback and defensive back, was strong, durable, and bright, and had ended his high school career as an all-around athlete.

"I'm going to attend Stonehill College in Easton, Mass," he said. "They don't have a football program, but I plan on playing hockey."

"Me too," said Craig. "I'm off to American International in Springfield to play hockey as well."

Craig Cemate, another talented halfback and defensive back, was also one of our captains. Hailing from Dempsey's hometown of Brighton, he was a quiet and multi-talented runner who liked to hit. He was also one hell of a hockey player.

But it was Vinny O'Brien who truly surprised us. "I'm off to Fairfield in Connecticut. I'm too light to play on the line, so I'm going to give running back a shot." Vinny gave one hundred and fifty percent on every play in high school and was what Dempsey would've called an "all in" athlete. Although we were surprised by the news, none of us doubted his ability.

"What are your plans, Eddie?" asked Pete.

Eddie Dominguez, our third captain, was one of our best liked and most admired players. Eddie wore a smile every day at school, and made you feel good whenever he was around. Eddie had been a two-way starter for three years, tough and smart, with a caring heart, but he had a falling out with Currier that cost him his starting position mid-way through our senior year.

It stemmed from the Boston Tech game. We'd defeated Tech pretty easily, but the offensive line hadn't performed very well. Although our performance was, admittedly, sub-par as a whole, Currier used Eddie as the scapegoat and demoted him from the starting line-up. What was really troubling, though, was that Currier ignored Eddie for the remainder of the season. It was a baffling decision that made no sense to any of us. Calling that coaching decision unfair and undeserved is an understatement.

"I'm off to the Police Academy for the city of Boston."

Next up was Abe: "I've been sitting on the fence trying to make up my mind, but I'm heading to the Berkley School of Music in Boston," he said. Abe Benitez, our starting guard and a baseball standout, had a passion for music and wasn't sure if he should attend college to follow his passion or be more practical and pursue a business degree. Ultimately, he sought out Dempsey for advice.

"Abe, let me tell you something. When I was a kid, everyone made fun of me because my mother made me play the violin. But I actually enjoyed playing. Listen to your heart and follow your passion," advised Dempsey.

We got a kick out of hearing our line coach, legendary for his street fights, giving advice on the study of classical music, but none of us would've ever dared tease him about it. We all smiled in wonderment, proud of Abe's decision.

"I'm not attending college," Stevie said. "It's not for me." Stevie Reily, our tough-as-nails fullback, grinned at our astonishment. "I'm going to work with my dad in roofing."

Stevie had played both football and hockey during high school. I liked Stevie; he was blunt and direct when others weren't brave enough to be. On the team, though, he kept his distance and didn't have much fondness for Currier. "A couple times, after I was out of high school," Stevie later told me, "I approached Currier and extended my hand, but both times he walked away from me. To this day, I still don't know why. I heard he didn't like hockey players."

"Yogi, you're awful quiet over there," Al said. "What're your plans?"

"I'm staying in Hyde Park," Yogi replied. "I'm hoping to settle down and start a family. I'll be living close to home for a while." There was a long silence as everyone drank in the moment. *This was it*, I realized. For the '74 champions, high school was over. As I looked around at my teammates, I couldn't help wondering what was in store for us at college and beyond.

For Dempsey and Currier, the new football season in 1975 would be a dream year. For once, they were predicted to be at the top of the Catholic Conference, with Bosco widely considered the powerhouse to beat. The many juniors who started varsity in '74 had returned as seniors. Everything went their way. They were bigger and stronger, and loaded with confidence. With them, there would be no doubting or hoping for victory. They carried experience into every game and were champions from the start.

What a difference a year makes. In '74, we had no idea what was about to unfold. We'd had two consecutive losing seasons, and there was no indication that anything would change. But for members of the '75 team, an emotional mindset was locked in. They knew exactly what they had as a team, they knew how they were going to perform, and they came into the year with a strong indication of where they were headed.

They would tear through the Catholic Conference.

"Practices were joyful, and the coaches were much more relaxed," Carouso said, reflecting back on those days with a smile. "Sure, we worked hard, and both Currier and Dempsey kept us from becoming complacent, but they knew what they had. We kicked ass throughout the conference, and all of us, coaches included, rode the wave."

Bosco went 9 and 0, with one game left on the schedule. St. John's Prep from Danvers, Massachusetts had joined the Catholic Conference that year. They were a solid football team with an experienced, seasoned coaching staff. Bosco needed one regular season victory to clinch the conference and qualify for its first Super Bowl appearance. But Bosco lost in a heart-breaker, 17-7.

That meant sharing the championship with another school in the Catholic Conference. That meant no invitation to the State's Super Bowl championship game.

Ski, our quarterback my senior year, would receive a hockey scholarship to Boston College, and later be drafted by the Philadelphia Flyers. Billy Elwell would play football at Northeastern. Colie MacGillivary played baseball for Bay State. Chris Staub went on to play football at the University of Rhode Island. Chester Rodriguez played football and basketball at Boston College. Skip Bandini would become an All-American lineman for the Massachusetts Maritime Academy. And John Sylva would play for U-Penn, our only teammate to go Ivy League.

Dempsey's bond with his players started to grow even stronger. He prized loyalty, and his boys paid him back by performing flawlessly on the football field. The 1975 season brought him his second championship in three years, and he knew this group was special. He also had a keen sense that many of his players didn't have a clue about what they wanted out of life. Dempsey was determined that his players were going to have two major opportunities that he hadn't had: playing college football and receiving a college degree.

Dempsey touched so many lives with his unorthodox methods and remarkable coaching but, back in '75, this wasn't something we took the time to appreciate. The culture was at a violent peak and we had a tendency to keep our minds in the moment rather than in the future.

# TAKING DEMPSEY TO COLLEGE

As Boston was coming apart at the seams, I had one thing on my mind, and that was finding the opportunity to play football in college. Bosco had a terrible college counseling office (if we even had one). We didn't know the meaning of an elective or the term "drop-add"; neither had existed at Bosco. Our courses had been laid out for us year after year, no negotiation, no choice.

I was off to Northeastern University to play football in the Yankee Conference. Jack Freeman, Assistant Coach at Northeastern, had previously coached at Don Bosco, and the connection gave me a strong foot in the door. We spoke briefly on the phone and, within two weeks, I had my acceptance letter.

Mark Nemes, one of my hometown's most gifted athletes, was a star running back at Northeastern. We were both excited about playing together in the fall.

"It's going to be great having two Hyde Park boys playing for the Huskies next year! Kev, we'll work out all summer and be in great shape for football camp."

Pound for pound, Mark was one of the strongest athletes I had ever met. With bullet speed—running a 4.5 in the forty-yard dash—

Mark finished his freshman year as the Huskies' starting halfback. The campus had been all abuzz about this new exciting kid from Hyde Park.

But, as excited as I was about playing for Northeastern, I was concerned about money: I hadn't been offered a scholarship. I was, however, offered the opportunity to *earn* a scholarship. I had no problem with proving myself, but I simply couldn't ask my father to pay my way up front and hope that financial help would somehow arrive the following year. But still, I was hopeful. Camp was going to begin on August 17th. On August 3rd, I called the coaches' office to set up a time to swing by and pick up my equipment, only to be informed that, as a freshman, I didn't need to report to the team until September 28th—the first day of classes. I was stunned. The season ended November 2nd. If I didn't report until late September, there'd be no way to earn a scholarship. This suddenly put Northeastern out of the question.

Rich Moran, another football icon from Hyde Park, had had a similar experience. Rich, like Mark, was a huge athletic talent and had set his sights on attending Brown University, but it all fell through at the last moment. Instead, Rich ended up at Curry College in Milton, Massachusetts. Rich was entering his junior year at Curry as captain, All League, and All New England in football, as captain of the baseball team, and as a forward for the hockey team. He was a legend at Curry. To this day, he's the only three-sport college player I have ever met. Rich was one of those players who I'd always idolized as a kid growing up in Hyde Park. He was a tremendous athlete who had a strong street ethic that was admired by all.

After getting in touch with Rich, he brought me to Curry to meet the coaches. They were wonderful and seemed excited to have me join the team, especially after being endorsed by Richie.

"Nice to meet you, Kevin," Coach Champa said. "I understand you played for Dempsey at Don Bosco. Clyde is a good friend of mine. You boys had a hell of a year this year. Sure, we'll help you get into Curry, but we don't have any more financial aid to give out—not till next year." Once again, I was stuck. Tuition at Curry was a staggering $2,800 a year and, seeing as my father's base pay was $13,500 before taxes, paying tuition out of pocket just wasn't possible.

To play with Mark would have been a dream come true, and the same was true with Rich, as we'd have both played defense together. Curry really made me feel welcomed and I left the campus feeling great, but enrolling just wasn't in the cards. The toughest phone call I ever made was to tell Rich that I simply couldn't afford to attend Curry. Rich's true friendship was solidified with the following statement: "As a football player, I'm telling you to come to Curry but, as a friend, you have to play at Bridgewater."

Nothing more needed to be said; Rich fully understood.

Bridgewater State College had shown some interest in me in the spring of my senior year, which I knew about only because of a brief conversation I had with Coach Currier. Bridgewater never spoke directly to me nor I to them, but their tuition, at $600 a semester, was much more affordable.

I called their head coach, Coach Mazafarro, and not only did he remember me, but he said he'd be excited to have me try out for the team. I knew no one at Bridgewater and was clueless as to whether or not I'd actually be admitted into the school, but I was ready to play football. I had been preparing myself all summer and, for some strange reason, knew in my bones that I was going to play *somewhere*. So, two days before camp, I found myself sitting across from the school's Dean of Admissions.

"What's your name again?"

"Kevin Kelly, sir."

"What can I do for you, Mr. Kelly?"

"Well," I began nervously, fidgeting in my seat across from

him, "I was recruited to play football here, and I was hoping I could attend camp next Monday."

"Did you apply here, Mr. Kelly? We can't seem to find any paperwork from you."

"Well, actually, I haven't filled out any paperwork yet, sir."

"So, let me get this straight," the Dean said, taking off his glasses and folding his hands up under his chin, as if he was getting ready to scold a four-year-old. "You're sitting in my office on a Friday afternoon, while my staff is ready to head home, and you're asking me to admit you *today* so you can attend camp on Monday?"

"Yes, sir," I said sheepishly, realizing that I must be coming across like a complete moron. Thoughts of Brother Julius immediately flashed through my mind, and I found myself simply grateful that this guy didn't have a ruler of his own to smack me with. I started to realize that playing college football this year might not happen after all.

I was alone and on my own.

"What high school did you attend?"

"Don Bosco, sir."

"And what was your team's record?"

"We were undefeated in the Catholic Conference, sir."

"Don Bosco? Was that the team that beat Catholic Memorial?"

"Yes, sir!" I said, sitting up taller, surprised that he knew about the CM game. Perhaps there was a glimmer of hope.

"You any good?"

Dempsey's warning flashed into my head: *If anyone asks if you're any good, look them straight in the eye and tell them—I try to be.*

"I try to be, sir," I said, nodding, looking him straight in the eye.

I could tell he was taken aback by my comment—and that he liked what he'd heard. To this day, I'm convinced that it was that single comment that enabled me to attend Bridgewater.

Monday morning, my father dropped me off at football camp, beaming with pride. As I waved goodbye and watched him drive out of the parking lot, I realized that, as a freshman, I knew no one on the team, that I had never met any of the coaches, and that I had no idea where I was supposed to sign in.

Not the best way to begin my college career, but I was ready for whatever they were going to throw at me.

In the summer months leading up to that day, I'd put myself into overdrive. I lifted, ran, swam, biked, and put myself through a brutal routine. Everything Coach Dempsey had taught me about preparation, technique, and attitude would now be tested at Bridgewater.

"Welcome to Bridgewater, Kelly. I'm Coach Mazafarro and this is our defensive coach, Coach Braun. What position did you play at Bosco?"

"Defensive tackle, Coach."

"Really? How much do you weigh?"

"About a hundred and ninety-five, sir."

Dempsey had always told us that, in football, size really meant close to nothing. It hadn't occurred to me that I was actually extremely light for a defensive lineman. I'd been brainwashed into believing that quickness, technique, and desire were the only ingredients necessary to play good ball.

But all I got from the coaches at Bridgewater was a flat, "Well, we'll have to wait and see."

It was also then that I met my new roommate, John Censulu from Stoneham, Massachusetts. John was an All-Star Scholastic quarterback with a rocket for an arm. As we entered our first team meeting, I was stunned by the size of the players. Bridgewater was Division III and, though I'm not sure exactly what I was expecting, it certainly wasn't players as big as these guys.

"Jesus, John! Look at the size of these guys. I hope I can at least make the kick-off team!"

I would later discover that many of the players had had offers to play at Division I or II schools but, due to their grades, lack of money, or minimal exposure to big school scouts, had been overlooked. What's most obvious at the college level is that everyone can play football and play it well—a stark difference indeed from high school ball. College players are self-motivated, and your amount of playing time is determined by you and you alone. No one cares if you're a freshman, if you're homesick, or if you're hurt. It's a fast-moving machine that won't wait for anybody.

I was not only physically prepared for camp; I was prepared mentally as well, determined to hustle everywhere I was told to go. During agility drills, I was always in the top five. And when it came to long-distance running, I was in the top three of the linemen. Where players get the most attention, however, is during the hitting drills. This is what counts most. Over and over, I chanted in my head: *Quickness, technique, desire. Quickness, technique, desire . . .*

During our first day of hitting, the coaches called for a drill that was simply impossible to do without getting your head handed to you.

The coaches had a player lie on his back and then, when the whistle blew, he'd roll over, get up on his feet as quickly as possible, and run head-long into three huge linemen who had a running start. The drill was designed to prepare us for busting the wedge during a kick-off return. During a kick-off, the return team usually has four of its biggest linemen join together in the center of the field (called the wedge) and form a wall as they run down the field. Their job is simply to destroy anyone willing to get in their way while the return man follows them up the middle of the field with the ball.

Most players feared having the responsibility of breaking the wedge due to the high risk of injury (along with the insane task of sticking your head into the middle of a gigantic, moving mass of muscle). Of course, there are always three to four players on every team with a few screws loose who *love* this part of the game. I, however, was most definitely not one of them.

During this particular drill, I studied the guys who performed first, and came away with sheer terror. The first seven guys got pancaked, and not a person on the field was laughing because we all knew we'd be next.

Dempsey had taught us back at Bosco how to break a wedge. He'd said that no player ever wants to receive a knee injury, so when you're going in to dismember a wedge, go for the knees. Many times, Dempsey preached to us about the importance of protecting our knees, saying, "Boys, remember our knees are like our mothers, so protect them. If anyone ever plays dirty and tries to take out your knees, punish them! Just place your hand on the back of his helmet and face-plant him into the ground."

Naturally, he also recommended that, when you run down the field during a kick-off, sprint as fast as you can and then aim your helmet knee-high, because your opponents will always lift up their legs to avoid being hurt. While Dempsey's advice on becoming a gridiron kamikaze might sound easy, trust me when I say it took a lot of courage (and no small amount of stupid recklessness) to carry out his theory.

So here I was, a freshman, eighth guy on the ground, coaches curious to see how the new kid would do and the upperclassmen watching to see some fresh meat get initiated to the team. But when the coach blew the whistle, all distractions melted away and I spun out as fast as I could, sprinting at full speed into the wedge and, at the last moment, barreling my helmet directly into the two middle linemen, knee-high. Both players jerked their knees up, and I blew through the wedge unscathed. Coach Braun went wild, ran over, and grabbed my face mask to read my name from the white athletic tape stretched across my helmet.

"Where'd you play ball, Kelly?"

"Don Bosco, Coach," I said.

"Well, looks like I just found my wedge breaker. Nice hustle!"

My heart skipped a beat. I feared the wedge. I wanted to explain what I'd done and the rationale behind it (as well as the rationale behind why I definitely *shouldn't* be a wedge breaker), but I knew that would've been athletic suicide. Either way, I was screwed. If I told my coach I was scared to death of breaking the wedge, I'd have been sentenced to the bench and viewed as a coward. And if I said nothing, I'd be placed next to the kicker on every kick-off with the sole responsibility of sprinting forty yards down the field to break the wedge, and possibly my neck. It was like being in the front lines of a battle while crossing the field to face the enemy—the odds were high that you wouldn't last long.

During a subsequent moment in camp, I was put in a category that had me hated by the upperclassmen, but one that also gave me some level of status and respect on the team.

Rich had given me some sound advice before I went off to camp.

"Remember," he said, "if they ask you to take out the bags or sing a song in the dining hall, do it. But when you're on the field, there is no such thing as a freshman and there is no such thing as a senior. If anyone takes advantage of you or tries to take a cheap shot, fight like a tiger. You may not gain any friends, but everyone will respect you."

I kept this information always in the back of my mind. When I was at camp, I was friendly and outgoing. I would be the first person to say hi in the halls; in the locker room, I spoke to the players near me regardless of their class; and during hitting drills, I'd pat guys on the back after each good hit.

But on day four, all that team camaraderie came to a screeching halt. We were performing another new hitting drill where I, again, was eighth in line for the chopping block. The drill was simple enough on the face of things: a mock fumble designed to train players to react quickly to a loose ball.

Here's how it happened. First, the coach tossed the ball ten to twelve yards, had two players sprint after it, and one player returned the ball to the coach. It's a high-spirited drill, and the players need to be very aggressive to be successful. Again, I watched the first several players and thought, *This drill is nuts*.

Once again, Dempsey entered my mind: *The most dangerous athlete on the field is an intelligent athlete.*

When I counted down the line, I noticed I was going up against our defensive captain, Benji—the kind of guy whose presence and performance demanded respect. I could feel the butterflies in my stomach. When it was our turn and Coach threw the ball, I saw Benji turn, look in the direction of the ball, and run towards it. So instead of running at the ball, I ran at Benji, exploding right into his chest and knocking him on his ass. What made matters worse is that I then casually walked over, picked up the ball, and tossed it back to the coach. Laughing, Coach Braun went over to Benji and announced, "I want to let you know that a freshman just knocked you on your ass!"

While there were a few laughs from the upperclassmen and a little ribbing coming Benji's way, what I *didn't* know is that I had unintentionally embarrassed our captain, and now he was out of his mind upset—at *me!* As he paced in the back of the line, it was clear to everyone that he couldn't wait to get his hands on me.

Benji, as it turns out, would eventually have his revenge, and it would affect my relationship with players and coaches alike.

Coach Braun blew the whistle and moved the defense to the pit-drill. We had so many players that each one of us would rotate in and out to play defense and then offense. Coach Braun ran the drill by simply saying "Set-Hit." When he said *hit*, he would toss the ball to the running back, and two linemen would go at it. The ball would then be returned, and the next pair would step up to make their play. But when it was my turn to block as an offensive lineman, Benji cut in line and shouted, "Get out of my way! He's mine!"

And Coach let it happen. I was to block Benji for the running back five to seven yards behind me. Coach Braun held the ball, and the entire team stopped to see what might take place between us, the team Captain and the Crazy Freshman. Coach lifted the ball to heft it, calling, "Set—"

Except Benji didn't wait for "hit." He came off the ball fast and drove a shivering forearm straight into my face mask. He didn't care about the running back; he just wanted to take my head off. As he kept on clubbing me with his forearms, I did my best to ward him off to one side. We pushed and shoved each other some, but the coaches broke us up quickly enough. By the time I went to the end of the line, I was smoking hot! My previous hit on Benji was clean; I'd simply outsmarted him in the drill. But I wasn't going to let him get away with a cheap shot that could've easily injured me. I hadn't been prepared for him to cheat in the drill, and after he'd jumped the gun, I'd felt a burning pain down the back of my neck.

And I knew that the one shot wouldn't be enough to satisfy Benji.

So when our turn came up again, everyone was fired up and the upperclassmen really wanted Benji to kick my ass, to make an example out of me. I could hear them snickering, *Kick his ass, Benji!* and *Yeah, he's only a little pussy freshman!*

I can remember Dempsey sitting us down and speaking to us about toughness. "Boys, toughness exists in everyone; it simply depends on the situation. Take a bully in your neighborhood that everyone's afraid of. On Monday, he beats you up, and you do nothing, but on Tuesday, the same kid says, *Fuck you,* to your mother. Then you'll be the one sending *him* crawling home with a black eye."

Dempsey's words raced through my mind, and this time, when Coach Braun called "set," I was the one exploding early out of my stance and tearing into Benji, my helmet striking right under his chin. I then took my right hand and made a fist and slammed the left side of his helmet right into his ear hole. The hit stood him up and he paused for a second. That pause gave me enough time to grab his face mask and pull him to the ground. By the time I got on top of him and started throwing punches, the players and coaches had jumped in. Everyone was yelling, coaches and players alike.

Benji went *wild!* We were both yelling at each other and the coaches were really pissed with me. After they chewed me out, we ended the drill and joined the offense. The upperclassmen were glaring at me and the freshmen all wore looks of *Wow! Who the fuck is this kid?*

As I was jogging over to join the team, I found myself running behind Coach Braun, just close enough to hear him mutter to one of the other defensive coaches, "Did you see that? When's the last time you ever saw a freshman go after a team captain? I like this kid!"

What was becoming obvious to me was the extent to which I had taken Dempsey with me to college. Every thought, every hitting drill, and every experience on the field had me reflecting on a shared moment or lesson taught by Dempsey. It was like watching the pieces of a puzzle coming together to create the hidden picture you couldn't see earlier. Everything was starting to make sense to me.

But, during my first week of college football, I was creating an impression I'd hoped not to make. On the one hand, the fight was important and gave me some much-needed street cred. On the other hand, deep inside, it bothered me. It had emotionally and socially cut me off from the upperclassmen. What made matters worse is that Benji and I had lockers right next to each other. I was and wanted to be a team player. I wanted to like Benji as a friend and a captain.

But, for the time being, I was an outsider.

Benji and I would spend the next few weeks dressing beside each other in awkward silence. But after a week, I could tell that both of us wanted some way to reconnect; we just didn't know exactly how to do it.

The first game of the season was coming up—an away game. I would receive devastating news that Thursday during practice. For away games, we could only dress forty-two players, and I hadn't made the cut. Although it was common for freshmen not to make the away games, I could not remember ever feeling so low—three weeks of sacrifice and hard work with nothing to show for it. I was ignored by the upperclassmen, and now I couldn't travel with the team. I couldn't even play on the kick-off team to break the wedge.

The night before the game, we had a team meal together. Before everyone left, I went over to the varsity players and wished them luck. I could tell that they too felt enough time had passed, and responded with sincere thanks. Making my way over to Benji, I stuck my hand out and said, "Best of luck tomorrow, Captain."

He looked me straight in the eye. "Thanks, Kelly. Thanks."

That would be the last time I would miss suiting up for a game. After that, I buckled down, determined to make my mark on the team. As a second-string defensive tackle, I got playing time during every game, and was, at last, a true member of the team. Of course, I was also the wedge breaker on the kick-off team, but I didn't mind one bit compared to the alternative. Breaking the wedge or sitting on the bench? That choice was a no-brainer.

To dress for a game after busting your ass all week, only to sit on the bench and watch the game be played, was painful. Whether the team wins or loses, you never really feel part of it. And besides, being a wedge breaker is a position of real status on the team. No one really wants the job, so there's mutual respect given to anyone willing and able to do it, willing to sacrifice life and limb diving head first into a sea of oncoming jerseys.

Benji and I grew to be good friends. We played on the same side—defense—and, for the upcoming away game against Plattsburg, he actually agreed to room with me. I was on cloud nine! Life couldn't have been better for a freshman playing college football. I was going to start my first varsity game, was on the travel squad, and was now rooming with the defensive captain.

After a nine-hour ride, we found the Plattsburg campus in full Halloween swing. I was surprised with how much freedom we had to roam the campus. With an eleven o'clock curfew, we hit a few parties, walking into a few mixers and a frat keg party. I was surprised at how comfortable Plattsburg students made us feel on their campus, especially after it was discovered that we were football players from Bridgewater State—their school's arch rival.

"Hey, come on in and have a drink!" they'd cheer.

"Should be a great game tomorrow—we heard you guys are undefeated. Here, have two drinks then!" called some smart-ass with a smile.

And, as much as we were tempted to party with these (admittedly pretty cool) kids, I knew there was no way I was going to risk being benched for drinking or missing curfew. It was painful, but both Benji and I returned to the hotel early. When I went to sleep that night, I was very much aware of how calm I was. I'd imagined myself being much more nervous the night before the Plattsburg game, or at least that I'd have difficulty falling asleep. Instead, I just thought back to Coach Dempsey and what he would've said to me if he'd known I was starting varsity as a freshman: *Don't let me down, Kelly! You better play well!*

I was calm during the team breakfast, but once I started getting dressed for the game, the butterflies came creeping in. Ask any athlete about pregame nerves and they'll tell you that it's when you *don't* get the butterflies that you should really start to worry. Again, I thought of Dempsey and his advice to meditate on your responsibilities and conserve your energy. Moving to a corner, I laid down and closed my eyes, visualizing every offensive play and all of my corresponding responsibilities on defense.

While in the corner, Benji came over to me, slapped me on the back, and said, "You're going to do just fine, Kelly! Any questions, don't hesitate to ask me!"

I nodded without saying a word. Looking Benji in the eye, we shared a small *ready* grin, and ran out onto the field together.

We came out of the gates quickly and scored two touchdowns in the first quarter. On defense, we were shutting them down. Both of our starting defensive tackles were down with injuries, so it was up to Danny McSweeney and I to come through and not be a burden to the defense. I was *not* going to let that happen on my end.

But on one play, Benji screamed, "Kel! Quick! Eagle down!"

I knew exactly what Benji wanted me to do. He wanted me to move down one position and line up against the guard. And I knew exactly why. Benji had read the play and knew the fullback was going to try running between the guard and tackle.

I froze.

The ball was snapped, and the fullback ran up the middle of the field for a twenty-five yard gain. And I had let it happen.

Needless to say, Benji was hot in the huddle. "What the hell are you thinking about, Kel? Wake up!"

"Sorry," I squeaked, my voice coming out as high and pathetic as a guilty little kid's.

Everyone in the huddle burst out laughing. And I guess Benji couldn't help himself because he smiled too, shaking his head at me.

I should have felt good from all the support my teammates were giving me, but instead I only felt embarrassed. I'd let them all down.

But then the old CM game came clanging to mind, and for once it wasn't Dempsey but Currier's voice that echoed back to me: *I'm telling you that, if they score, it's okay. So when they score, just keep on playing the way you've been playing and we'll be alright.*

My mistake hadn't enabled Plattsburg to score on us yet, but I knew it would if I let myself get rattled by it. *Just keep on playing*, I thought. *Just keep on playing.*

We beat Plattsburg 44-0.

The following Monday, the school played the film of the game throughout the day in the new Student Union Building, so Danny McSweeney and I got the chance to watch ourselves perform. We also listened to the announcer talk about the two freshmen starting for Bridgewater's defense and who, as he put it, "did one hell of a job."

After that comment, the two of us thought we were something special. Danny would lean over, grinning, and yell out, "Hey, Kel, who the hell is that number seventy-two on defense? Did you see that tackle?"

"Geez, I think that's Danny McSweeney, that outstanding freshman defensive tackle!" Of course—and you know what's coming—I'd then hit Dan with, "Hey, Dan, who the hell's that number seventy-eight? Did you see him make that quarterback sack?"

"Geez, I think that's Kevin Kelly, the other outstanding freshman defensive tackle!"

This adolescent dialogue went on for the entire showing of the game. We thought we were funny, showing off for the freshmen co-eds, but we were sadly disappointed. Eventually, it was just Danny and I sitting alone watching the game. But we didn't care. We basked in our own glory before ending up at the campus pub to toast our victory properly.

Bridgewater wasn't Notre Dame but, for us, it surely felt like it.

Freshman year was when all of the work ethic, drills, lessons, knowledge, and ability inspired by Dempsey came together for me. Dempsey was constantly on my mind in practice and during games. On game day, as a defensive lineman, you have to transform yourself into an intense, calm, aggressive, intelligent, and unselfish player. There's no room for being reflective, for being concerned about your opponent. It's really just a street fight, and there's only one way to play: all out, hard, and tough. None of this could have happened without my years of growth at Don Bosco.

Dempsey taught us that, on the line, there's always someone who will emotionally quit—you just want to make sure it's never you. Before each game, I made an emotional commitment to give my all on every play. And I would discover that Dempsey's words rang true: Players did eventually start to duck and cut corners rather than hit "head on" every time. I, on the other hand, continued to evolve as a player and learned to relish any opportunity to dominate those who wouldn't dedicate themselves likewise.

It's difficult to put into words, but there's a real high that comes with the realization that your opponent has begun to quit and ceded you total control of the line of scrimmage. It's always unspoken, but all players know exactly what's going on when this kind of concession occurs. During a game, there's always a breaking point when one player begins to quit, either because he believes he's already given his best to no avail or because he's checked the clock and decided his team can't possibly win. With all of these factors, a player can pretty easily sense the level of intensity changing during a game. If you were outhitting and outplaying your opponent, and sensed he was quitting, *that's* when you'd turn it up a notch.

But, to be able to perform at that level, a player needs to start by focusing on the upcoming game way in advance. During the week, we'd have only one day to study films of the upcoming team. Coaches would try to pinpoint tendencies in the offense but, as a lineman, I also had to see if I could pick up any clues about the specific guy I was most likely going to be pitted against. Each night, I'd review my responsibilities and work to visualize my opponent, imagining how I would play each run, pass, trap block, and so forth.

A perfect example of my being mentally prepared for a game was our performance against Tufts University. The offensive lineman I played against must've stood around 6'4" and weighed close to two hundred and forty pounds. His nose was smashed wide like a boxer's and, when he got into his stance, his wrists and forearms bulged to an awe-inspiring size. A jolt of fear ran through me as I realized, *Shit. This guy looks like he snacks on nails!* But I swallowed, settled my nerves, and switched into Dempsey-mode: *quickness, technique, and desire.* Calmed, I studied the player's body and split him into thirds, asking myself: *How would I play against this guy if Coach Dempsey was on the sidelines watching me?*

For the first series of the Tufts game, I paid no attention to where the ball went. But when I finally did come off the ball, I came off it like someone shot me from a cannon, reminding myself that because size doesn't have to mean anything, I could plow through any player on the field. And, sure enough, by the beginning of the third quarter, I owned my opponent. I wasn't tougher or stronger than he was— not by a long shot! He just simply began to submit. He was coming off the ball slower; he was conceding control to me. But his coach or his buddies must've given him shit on the sidelines because, in a moment of frustration during the fourth quarter, the guy punched me square in my stomach while I was fully extended. The wind knocked out of me, I was forced to the bench for a few plays.

Of course, all that time spent sitting out only made me hungrier for another play—hungrier to get back in and punish this kid.

Back on the field, my eyes never left him, and I saw right away how his stance gave away the play, telling me that a pass was coming. When he moved his hand, I exploded off the ball and my helmet smashed into his face mask, my hands grabbing the inside of his shoulder pads. I jammed his pads high into his neck, standing him up and throwing him off balance. Then, with one last hit of my helmet to his face, he landed on his ass. That was it. For the rest of the game, he played passively.

And, just like that, we had beaten a very good Tufts team, 23-21.

After the game, outside the showers, I found him, walked over to him, and shook his hand.

"Hey, sixty-three—nice game."

"Thanks," he said, surprised. "You too. What position did you play?"

"What do you mean?" I said, confused. "I played against you today. I'm number seventy-eight."

His mouth dropped wide open as he took in my height and weight for the first time. "There's no way I played against you today—the guy I played weighed *at least* two hundred and thirty pounds."

"Well," I grinned, pleased, "I guess I just have a big pair of shoulder pads."

Our biggest game of my freshman year was against Harvard. Harvard came out with what appeared to be a hundred kids, all of them poised and sharp. By comparison, we looked and felt like a group of misfits. All the same, we went on to shut them out, winning 21-0. I had two quarterback sacks and one interception. The ball got deflected and ended up in my hands, so I ran sideways with it for forty yards, desperately trying to turn the corner. Everyone on the sidelines was laughing as I ran the entire width of the field. After I finally managed to turn the corner, I gained a truly unimpressive two yards.

Coach Braun laughed as I jogged over to the sidelines, gasping for air, "That's why you're a lineman, Kelly!" he hooted.

After the game, I shook hands with Harvard players Joe Pellegrini and Dave Singleton (both outstanding players from the Catholic Conference). But the real highlight of the day came because Harvard agreed to feed us. Their dining hall was *beautiful*: rich wood paneling, high ceilings, and lighting reminiscent of a cozy, early-1900s dining room. They served us prime rib, and we all had to laugh, comparing Harvard's dinner to our own state-run café back at Bridgewater.

It was easy to laugh at the Harvard kids. We might've been in college, but we were still immature enough to look down on them for having what we didn't have. We looked down on them—the rich, snobbish brats we'd all grown up envying and hating. They were kids who we were all certain didn't really appreciate where they were going to school, kids that wouldn't survive two minutes in our old neighborhoods. But, in all honesty, mocking them was just our way of hiding and deflecting the truth: Most of us would have loved to have attended Harvard and played for a school with such a rich history and tradition—and for a school that served such decadent prime rib!

After the Harvard game, I went home for the weekend. Although the city was still at a boiling point over forced busing, my section of Hyde Park was comparatively calm except for two areas: the high school and my own backyard. A black family (I'll call them the Jones family) had purchased a house across the street from Moynihan Park. They were a family of six, and couldn't have picked a tougher spot to move into.

Located across the street from Moynihan Park and the Roosevelt School, their house was at the epicenter of where forty or so white kids from the neighborhood tended to hang out most days. As a result, they were the victims of nonstop harassment, vandalism, and threats. It was so bad that the city of Boston actually paid to have a police cruiser park in front of their home every day and night for the next six years.

Of course, there were neighbors who didn't like the way the Joneses were treated, but they were a small minority. Only pride and fortitude could make a family stay in that prison of a home for as long as they did—either that or they had no other housing options. Every time they left the house, fear, anxiety, and anger had to have registered high on their emotional meter. When I look back at the whole experience, it amazes me how we can turn on each other solely because we look different, because of such uncontrollable components of our lives as skin color.

Come to think of it, no one who had ever lived in that house had had it easy. There was never any privacy or peace. It was always too noisy and disruptive for folks, and so no one ever stayed long at that corner—no one except this family.

The Moynihan Park is fairly large—roughly one square mile—and it's completely enclosed by an eight-foot high fence. There's a baseball field, two basketball courts, a tennis court, a shallow pool, and swings and slides for the younger kids. Asphalt paths weave throughout, and wooded and grass areas for benches and picnic tables are scattered everywhere. It's a well-conceived park for city people looking to get away from their urban environment for a while. There are four entrances, one of which sits directly across the street from the Jones' home.

So when I came home for the weekend on a beautiful, cool fall day, I decided to stroll through the park, feeling perfectly safe and comfortable. And why wouldn't I? This was my hometown. I leaned against a pole, one foot in the park and one foot out of the park, on the sidewalk. A group of kids were gathered at the entrance near me, but I kept to myself.

The MBTA ran its city buses through Hyde Park, and two stops were at Moynihan Field. A bus pulled up, and Mr. Jones got off. He wore a yellow turtleneck and a brown leather jacket. He stood about six-foot-three, looked to be made of solid muscle, and was probably twenty pounds heavier than me.

As he walked toward his house, about fifteen teenagers started yelling and cursing at him from behind the park fence.

"You fucking nigger!" they yelled. "Get the fuck out of Hyde Park! We're gonna kill you and your family! Come on, you pussy! Come over here and fight us!"

Mr. Jones didn't say a word, but he didn't give an inch either. He gave a quick glance over at me, unsure as to how I fit into the mess. If it wasn't so tragic, it would have been comical. I knew every one of the kids making such a sick spectacle of themselves, and not a single one of them could have fought this man without ending up in the ER.

I now think back on Dempsey's wisdom with pride and appreciation: *You'll find out what you're made of when you're put into a position to stick-up for someone and then don't. Tough to look yourself in the mirror the next day knowing you're a coward.* But in that moment, I didn't need his words to know the right thing to do. Watching those kids humiliate that guy was more than enough to make my blood boil.

"Chucky," I called over to the hooting crowd, recognizing a kid named Charles as one of the loudest voices in the group. Everyone paused at my shout, waiting for me to join in. "You want to fight this guy?"

Chucky looked to me, sizing me up just as Mr. Jones had. "Yeah," he bragged, kicking the fence. "I wanna kill him."

"Fine. Then get your ass over here and fight him one-on-one. Fair fight. But if anyone jumps in, I'm fighting with him," I said, pointing to Mr. Jones.

Everyone was stunned, but I was too angry to let it go.

"Come on, tough guy," I said. "Come out and fight him. Don't talk about it. Do it."

No one moved.

"Yeah," I said, disgusted. "Just what I figured. Just another loud-mouth pussy."

Mr. Jones had a stern look on his face, and I knew he'd heard and seen enough.

Two cars pulled up and a kid who lived near Farmount Hill jumped out, shouting about how he wanted "a piece of the nigger." From a distance, it must've looked to that kid as if all of us were surrounding Mr. Jones. He was just another punk who couldn't fight one-on-one. At this point, I was not only ready to tear someone's head off, I *wanted* to. So I walked toward the kid's car, jabbed a finger in his chest, and told him just what I'd told the rest.

He jumped right back in his car and sped off, another loud-mouth pussy.

But still, I felt compelled to do more. So as Mr. Jones turned toward his house, I approached him. "I know this sounds crazy," I said, "but the people who live in this area are good people. I wish I knew what to say to you that would help. I'm sorry."

And though he looked forlorn, he shook my hand and thanked me.

Walking home, I couldn't stop imagining what it must have

been like for him to live that way, to worry about the emotional and physical safety of his wife and children every single day. I often think about what happens to kids who grow up influenced by racial hate. What happens to them when they become parents themselves and have to face so many of the same problems and dilemmas that their parents faced? And what happens to kids who perpetuate racial hate and later become parents? Years later, when they look into the eyes of their own children, do guilt and regret ever enter their minds?

The following Monday, I was back in college to complete the rest of our season. As I sat in class daydreaming, pretending to pay attention, my mind drifted back to the episode with Mr. Jones in Hyde Park. I thought of the many speeches from Coach Dempsey and realized that he too must've seen the world in a linear, absolutist form, much as my father had: black and white, right from wrong, fair and unfair. And, what's more, I realized that I, in turn, comfortably held the same view. Though I'd long ago begun to adopt my father's more absolutist approach to the world, there was something about Dempsey's perspective that finally made me feel at peace with the idea. There was something about Dempsey that made me finally understand his belief that the challenges on the football field often mirror those in life.

The Bridgewater State Bears ended the '75 season 7-2. We came in second place in the conference. We had a great team and our freshman class was loaded with talent. Still, nine of us would not return for our sophomore year. We were good kids on campus, but we were immature academically, and so several of us (including me) were asked to leave the school, grow up, and return when we were ready to apply ourselves in the classroom.

Coach Braun, unsurprisingly, was exasperated. "I'm extremely disappointed in you, boys. You've let your parents down. You've let your team down. And, most importantly, you've let yourselves down. You need to wake up, and you need to wake up *now*. You will learn that potential means absolutely nothing in this world. It's only what you do with that potential that counts."

I knew Coach Braun was right, and I knew I had no excuses. I was disciplined on the field, but had failed to use that same discipline in the classroom. I was determined to play football somewhere. Where that would be, I wasn't sure, but I knew I couldn't stop quite yet.

# THE HYDE PARK COWBOYS AND THE ARRIVAL OF DEMPSEY

*"As I watched the mayhem grow, I couldn't help but laugh. Only my coach could have been responsible for something like this."*
—Kevin Kelly

After flunking out of Bridgewater State—there's no other way to put it—I still had hopes of returning to college and playing football. I was attending Quincy Junior College and earning high enough grades to transfer, but I also needed to be playing football at the intercollegiate level.

It just so happened that my hometown team—the Hyde Park Cowboys—was joining the Eastern Football League, a New England semi-pro league.

These semi-pro Cowboys had the exact same uniforms as the NFL's Dallas Cowboys, and were the best-looking team in the league. Billy Mouradian, beloved in the neighborhood, sponsored the team. He owned a bar in Hyde Park called Billy's Saloon. He was a soft-spoken, quiet guy, and he loved his team and its players.

During the Cowboys' first year of play (1975), they marched into the championship game totally undefeated, only to lose it in triple overtime (that's seven quarters of football). I have never before or since heard of a game lasting that long. The final score was 10-7, with Charlestown pulling out a victory over Hyde Park in the final seconds.

During this time, I also spoke with Coach Currier about returning to a four-year college that played intercollegiate football. He informed me that the defensive coordinator at the University of Hawaii, Rich Blangardi, was a former player of his and that he was visiting New England, looking for players who might be interested in attending school out west. So I made contact with Coach Blangardi, and he told me that I'd have to improve my grades before he could help me out.

Despite this meager encouragement, I was out of my mind excited about the opportunity to play ball for the Rainbow Warriors. Suddenly, I had a renewed purpose and a clear goal. I knew I had to stay in shape while I hit the books, so playing for the Hyde Park Cowboys proved to be the perfect challenge.

The word was out that the Hyde Park Cowboys was the team to play for, so a lot of college graduates and former Park League players joined up fast. There were even a few players who had achieved All-American status, and a few more who had actually tried out for the pros. There was so much depth on the team that the third-string was easily as talented as the first. Players came from all over eastern Massachusetts. I was struck by their size, ability, and skill. I found myself hoping once again to just make the kick-off team.

I would be proud to play for my hometown, to play alongside some of the toughest and most talented players to ever come out of Hyde Park. Many of the Hyde Park players weren't just older than me—they were men I'd looked up to and even feared while growing up: Ricky McComick, Richie Flippen, Hunky Fisher, Frankie

Fanning, Bobby and Joey St. Peter, Bubba Lynch, and Larry Devoe. I was, to say the least, intimidated.

There were a handful of Hyde Park players my age as well: John "Oakie" O'Connor, Ronny Walsh, Dennis Hicky, and Jay Crowley. None of us had ever played together before, but we all knew each other from the neighborhood. I wasn't sure where I'd fit on the team or if I'd even get to play, but I knew I had to try. If I could compete in this league, it meant I had a chance to play ball in college in Hawaii.

The first few days of tryouts consisted of lots of no-pad conditioning drills and wind sprints. The head coach (also from Hyde Park) was Jimmy MacIntire, a solid coach and a good guy. He knew me as one of the little kids from the neighborhood, but always treated me with kindness and respect.

The first day of pads was a disaster for me. I had to buy my own helmet and find some pads quickly. My helmet was the first generation of AIR helmets, which require the player to put it on and then have someone pump air into it. The air enabled it to conform to your head size and create a snug cushion, displacing the impact of a hit more evenly. Unfortunately, someone had pumped my helmet full of air without the helmet first on my head, so when I tried to pull my helmet down to the appropriate position, which would have been even with my eyebrows, all it did was slide and puff back up to my hairline. I could snap on my chin-strap, but only barely.

Not only did I look like a goof, but the helmet actually made hitting *more* unsafe and the impact uneven. It was extremely frustrating, but there was nothing I could do about it at that point. To make matters worse, the only football pants I'd been able to find were an old pair from Pop Warner that had the thigh-pad pockets torn out. My only option was to take white athletic tape and wrap five complete revolutions around my thighs to hold my makeshift pads in place. On top of all that, I wore an old, heavy-knit, *bright* red football shirt decorated with dull gold satin numbers.

I looked like a total misfit and no one—and I mean *no one*—would talk to me.

All of the other players looked sharp, clean, confident, and experienced. They must have been laughing their asses off at me, wondering who the hell that clown was running around on the field.

After a few basic drills, we started into double-teaming, where a defensive lineman has to take on two offensive linemen at the same time. There are a few specific techniques that defensive linemen learn that are very effective against a double team, so that when this happens during a game, the defensive linemen don't get blown back five yards off the line of scrimmage or, worse, get knocked on their behinds.

At the end of the line, waiting my turn, I was really excited, eager to see how these well-established athletes would play. I knew I was going to get to watch some of the very best players in the region go up against each other—a rare and valuable opportunity.

The first guy up was the largest lineman on the team. Well before practice had started, I'd noticed him walk onto the field. He was six-foot-five and two hundred and seventy-five pounds, cut like a bodybuilder and wearing an Oakland Raiders jersey. He looked like a man who knew how to handle himself but, then again, so did the offensive linemen. At the snap of the ball, there was a massive collision, with the offense getting the upper hand. I was surprised to see this hulk of a man not using any particular technique against the oncoming players; brute strength alone can't win when it's two-on-one. Dempsey's never-ending preaching that technique always trumps size rang true yet again. The next few players came up and tried their hand, but still no one penetrated the line of scrimmage.

When it was my turn, I knew I wasn't going to out-muscle or out-tough any of these guys, so I instinctively did what I'd been taught. On the snap of the ball, I crabbed between the two linemen, basically getting on all fours while exploding between the two. The two offensive linemen didn't even touch me, and instead were left searching for me while I was already on the other side of the scrimmage line in a hitting position, looking to my inside.

When I returned to the back of the line, I got stares from a few of the other linemen. No one said a thing, but I could tell by their faces that they were impressed. I knew some of them thought it was just a fluke, so I decided to try another technique my next time up.

On my next turn, I lined up straight across from the lineman to my right. Both of the offensive linemen knew that I would have physical contact with that player first. This gave them a tremendous advantage because of the angle it would create. Instead of having two options for where I could go when the ball was snapped, I would have put myself in a position that left me with only one option, and that was to come straight across and into the lineman opposite me. As I stood ready, I imagined how both the offensive linemen and the players in line behind me were likely wondering what my reason for this could be. Why had I chosen to make things seemingly easier for my opponent?

But on the snap of the ball, instead of hitting the lineman directly in front of me, I exploded left and forward. The lineman to my left wasn't anticipating this, and so his body wasn't ready for the early contact I created. In an attempt to adjust, he rocked backwards. I slipped between the two linemen, again ending up on the other side unscathed. After three to four rounds of double-teaming drills, the other players finally started to talk to me.

A few wanted to know where I'd played ball in high school, but I didn't get the chance to answer before Coach Mac came over and said, "I heard you played for Clyde! I expect you to run through walls for me!"

After tryouts were all said and done, I made starting defensive tackle, despite weighing a mere two hundred and five pounds. But even then I couldn't take all the credit. I was part of the starting defense for one reason and one reason only: Dempsey, a master teacher, had taught me how to own the position.

There was one player on the team that could bench-press four hundred and fifty pounds. He could lift your car and throw you through a wall, and yet he hadn't mastered the techniques necessary to play the game at an expert level, so he sat on the bench.

The Cowboys were a racially diverse team, with both black and white players. Boston was still in the middle of its racial meltdown, and so many of the players had professional lives directly related to forced busing. But on the field, we never discussed our city's turbulent climate or let what happened off the field interfere with our team chemistry. When people work together, sharing sacrifice and experience, victory and defeat, they develop a bond, almost like soldiers in battle. Playing football, although not at all the same as dedicating oneself to a life-risking career, still creates an atmosphere that puts the mission ahead of any individual player. So when you're part of a team and you put your heart and soul into the attempt to win, that effort generates a tremendous level of respect between players. It's an unspoken connection that creates a special bond between athletes.

In 1976, the Hyde Park Cowboys became the perfect example of why and how race didn't have to be a source of conflict between us as neighbors, friends, or teammates. Firemen running into a burning building don't stop in mid-stride to wonder, "Wait a minute. Who's running in with me to save that child—a black guy or a white guy?" Football is all about the mission. When everyone sacrifices and works hard together, a bond is formed that's entirely beyond race.

Earl Garrett, an African American All-American defensive back from Boston State College, was a talented player, respected and well-liked by everyone on the team. He was probably about six or seven years older than me, but we still got along great and I often looked to him for guidance. Then, during one particular practice, we heard that Earl's mother had passed away and that the wake was being held that night.

There wasn't enough time for all of us to go home, shower, dress, and get to the wake in time, so six carloads of players, dirty, sweaty, and still in uniform, drove down to Morton Street in the middle of Roxbury, an all-black neighborhood, to pay our respects.

Standing outside the funeral home, we asked a relative if he could ask Earl to join us outside so we could offer our condolences. We weren't about to enter the wake in our sweat- and filth-stained uniforms. But when Earl's father appeared at the threshold, he must've seen our sincerity and the love in our eyes, because he said, "All you boys are welcome. Please come in."

We were greeted with endless smiles and appreciation by all. Earl hugged every one of us. Here we were, in the midst of one of the hottest racial periods in Boston's history, and yet we were sharing a beautiful moment of unity—racial differences be damned.

I now regret that, at the time, I never tried to make a connection with the *Boston Globe* so they could have written a story on the Hyde Park Cowboys. Our team unity and athletic success could've served as a model of peaceful action for our city. What Dempsey had told us back at Bosco rang true for the Cowboys: We didn't have black football players or white football players; we simply had *football* players.

With one victory under our belt, the next week of practice shouldn't have held too many surprises. But then, suddenly, there was a commotion on the field. Players were gathering around someone. Wandering over, I couldn't believe my eyes.

*What's Dempsey doing here?*

A swarm of guys had gone over to greet him, and a giant swell of pride swept over me as I watched the sincere respect everyone showed him.

He'd been slotted to play defensive nose-guard for the Cowboys, which meant we would play next to each other on the defensive line.

I had died and gone to heaven!

All through practice, I watched Dempsey like a hawk. During hitting drills, he was everything I'd thought and hoped he'd be: quick off the ball, flawless in his technique, and always displaying a kind of tenacity that can't be taught. It was rewarding to see my mentor execute all the techniques that he himself had coached.

One evening during practice, we set up for a pit-drill session, and Dempsey and I were lined up against each other. Feeling cocky, I went out on a limb and joked, "I've been waiting years for this moment."

Dempsey laughed, and we both came off the ball half speed.

Dempsey patted me on the helmet and winked at me. "You lucky bastard!"

But truly, I had no desire to go live against my coach. I had too much respect for him, and I knew he didn't want to embarrass his old pupil in front of the other players. Besides, it just didn't feel right to become violent with him.

By 1976, I had already heard plenty of stories about Dempsey's legendary fights and his connection to the mob as a collector. At Bosco, most of the Dempsey stories came from the Brighton kids. Some of the players seemed to know plenty of stories about Dempsey's street reputation, most of them about Dempsey as a collector for bookies in the area. Even my father was beginning to warn me to keep my distance from Dempsey. "I know you idolize your coach, and I know you're excited about playing ball with him, but you need to be careful." But I barely heard the warnings, so engrossed was I by Dempsey and the legend he'd become.

We had a player on the Cowboys (I'll call him John T.), who was one of the biggest and scariest-looking individuals I'd ever met. I heard through the grapevine that he and Dempsey often teamed up together when collecting money from people who were late, or who'd refused to make payments after borrowing from the bookies or the mob.

Personally, I think I would've sold my mother into slavery for petty cash if these two guys had ever come to my door looking for money—they were that terrifying. John was a white guy with an impressive Afro; wild, beady eyes; and a goatee topped with a thin mustache. He was a hunk of walking muscle just waiting to smash into someone.

One day during practice, John came up to me, put his arm around me, and said, "I understand you played for Clyde at Bosco. You know what that means, Kelly?" But before I could answer, he went on, "That means we're brothers. I love that guy," he said, sticking his thumb out toward Dempsey. "He taught me everything I know."

I smiled politely, thinking, *Thank God I know Dempsey,* for I couldn't imagine running into John in a dark alley. But, thanks to this connection, we ended up getting along just fine.

The first game Dempsey and I played together was truly memorable. He and I were on the kick-off return team. And as we peeled back to form our wall for the return man, Dempsey noticed that his player to block was running with his head down. Dempsey put on the brakes, then sprinted straight through him. *SMACK!*

The hit could be heard throughout the entire stadium. As the player lay unconscious, I looked over to our sidelines and saw the entire team hunched over, laughing and giving each other high fives. Dempsey's first hit in the new league signaled exactly what type of player he was: a man among boys.

As the two teams waited for an ambulance to take this poor guy to the hospital, some fans started a riotous bottle fight. It was a night game, so as the bottles crisscrossed from one side of the field to the other. With beer streaming out against the stadium lights, it looked like fireworks on the Fourth of July.

Watching the mayhem grow, I couldn't help but laugh. Only my old coach could be responsible for something like this.

The players eventually ran out to help break up the fight, but a few fans paid a heavy price. Some lay unconscious, and plenty had serious injuries.

During practice and in games, Dempsey was impressively quiet. I never saw him lose control on the field. He was like the lion surveying his kingdom from the top of the knoll, his game face saying it all. And during games, of course, he was a killer. He walked onto the field with the confidence of a heavyweight champion. His goal was simple: give one hundred percent for four quarters. *If you're not willing to hit me for four quarters, I'm going to be your worst nightmare!*

Once Dempsey knew a player was ducking him, he became like the shark that smells blood. He physically dominated that player, ready to punish him for giving up. Dempsey had zero respect for any player who quit on the field.

For me, it was pure joy to play alongside my old coach, having found a place where I was no longer the student to my mentor, but a teammate. Often after practice, he would stay behind to work on his own techniques or to teach other players new skills. He was truly a special guy. Even on my best day, I could never hold a match to Dempsey's quickness, toughness, and commitment.

Before the first play at many of our games, trash talking often took place on the line of scrimmage between opposing teams, but I never participated for two reasons: A) I'd been coached not to, and B) I really was too small to be taken seriously. Dempsey had taught us that, if you're going to talk trash, you better be able to back it up, because if you don't, the other guy will own you all day.

I may not have felt I could live up to the hype, but others sure did. During the championship game, there was plenty of it coming from both sides. I heard one player from the other team call out, "I'm going to tear your fucking head off!" to which one of my teammates jeered back about how good the sex was with the other guy's girlfriend.

What came next was a Dempsey classic.

He was playing against a center who weighed about two hundred and sixty pounds. The guy could barely fit into his helmet, his head was so big. Yet Dempsey, through all of the chatter around him, looked up to the guy and said, "Hi. How you doin' today?"

The center ignored him.

But Dempsey kept on, "You know, my mother's in the stands

and she would love to see me play a whale of a game today. I was wondering if you could take it easy on me so she can enjoy herself."

I couldn't restrain my laughter, and two fellow linebackers joined in.

The center looked up, confused and, with a high, squeaky voice said, "*What?*"

The ball was snapped and Dempsey ripped into the poor guy, hitting him so hard he actually unsnapped the guy's chinstrap and buckled his helmet halfway up his forehead. And, just like that, Dempsey owned him.

While in the huddle during a third quarter timeout, Dempsey turned, clearly frustrated with me, and said, "Kevin, tell me about the guy you're playing against."

"He plays flatfooted," I said. "He points his feet outwards. He gives plays away by shifting his weight. I can read him pretty easily."

"What's the down and distance?" said Dempsey.

"Third and eight."

"Then what the fuck are you doing messing with this guy? Blow through the guard-tackle gap and I'll meet you at the quarterback."

It was like something out of a movie. Just as he'd said, I blew the gap and we both hit the quarterback at the same time. While I was still on the ground, Dempsey turned and grinned, "Do I know what the fuck I'm talking about or what?"

We all laughed, even the quarterback.

I couldn't get over the fact that my old coach was actually keeping an eye on me during the game, while still playing well himself and even taking the time to *coach* me too. It was perfect!

I really pictured us playing together for years to come. But then, during the last few minutes of the game after we'd all but sealed a victory, players on both sides started to dial back their intensity a little. The Shamrocks ran a sweep left. Dempsey and I pursued the ball carrier. I was running behind Dempsey when suddenly, for no reason at all, this weasel lineman, this lowlife of a player, clipped Dempsey from behind, driving his helmet into the back of Dempsey's right knee.

Dempsey collapsed to the ground, reaching for his knee while grinding his teeth in pain. A clip that takes out a player's knee is one of the most cowardly acts in all of football. The lineman had done it purely out of frustration and his inability to accept a loss. Sure, it hurts to lose, but you don't *end someone's career* because the scoreboard isn't in your favor.

Dempsey ended up needing surgery to repair a knee that had already been injured once before.

The '76 championship game with the Cowboys became the last game he ever played.

The Cowboys won the championship 53-6. After the game, I refused to take off my sweaty, grimy uniform, instead walking around the locker room, showers, and coaches' offices to make sure I shook every hand on the team. I thanked every single player and all the coaches. I knew that championships were hard to come by and that what we had accomplished was special. I was one of the youngest players on the team and it was such an honor to be able to play with these great men who'd accepted me and treated me with respect. These were men who walked the walk. They were solid family and community men who played with an unselfish zeal.

Looking back over that season and the opportunity to play alongside Dempsey, I realize now just how rare an experience our season together truly was. Not too many players, at any level, get to share championships with a man as their coach one year and then as a teammate in another. As a person, he was the perfect teammate, always supportive and encouraging. As a player, Dempsey was calm and quiet, possessed of an unmatched discipline and focus. His air of confidence resembled what I'd always imagined General Eisenhower must've been like during wartime. Dempsey never worried about the score or how he was going to perform. The joy of playing was out-thinking the enemy and waiting for him to submit.

Another gift from that season was simply getting to watch Dempsey apply everything that he'd taught me, and everything that he'd preached to me, in his own game. It was truly something to see—Dempsey pursuing a running back and making a tackle twelve to fifteen yards down-field.

I've often wondered how I would've played against Dempsey if I'd had no idea who he was. I probably would've sized him up as many others had: a short, pudgy guy who looked odd in a football uniform. I'm not too sure how I would've reacted, however, when, after the first dozen plays, I realized he was quicker than I, employed flawless technique, and was plain beating the hell out of me.

After each Cowboys game, we'd head back to Billy's Saloon, all the players, fans, and Hyde Park locals together, to eat, drink, and share in the celebration.

Of course, it wasn't always that on the level.

There was always plenty of cocaine available in the back room for those needing a boost for the evening.

I was a straight kid and I never touched a drug, but both patrons and players coked up pretty frequently, claiming they could handle the "on-off" switch to cocaine.

In front of me, Dempsey always drank lightly and never took any drugs. He had preached to us in high school a never-ending sermon about staying off drugs. But, at that point in our relationship, he knew he could be himself around me, and so often unwound in front of me as he never would've back in our Bosco days. Even so, he was careful never to show his other side when I was present. Maybe it was important to him to keep up an image for me; I'm not sure. He knew I idolized him. And it's true; I would've been disappointed if I'd ever actually seen him snort coke. But it also never would've crossed my mind to confront him about it.

But for Dempsey, cocaine would eventually become his undoing. Some of the stories that began filtering through our circle of friends were *hilarious*, but unsettling. One story placed Dempsey in New York's Chinatown. Out of control in a Chinese restaurant, he suddenly stripped down and jumped into an ice fountain, completely naked. A call was made and a group from the Chinese mob showed up. It looked like things were going to get ugly until one of Dempsey's friends dropped a name from the Boston underworld. After a confirmatory call north, they got Dempsey into a private room and let him dress, drink, and eat with no further problems.

Another rumor had Coach and a friend stealing an eighteen-wheeler from New York and driving it up to Boston via Interstate 95. When they got the truck someplace safe, Dempsey, eager to see what they'd scored, went immediately to find out what the cargo was—perhaps a load of TVs, stereos, or appliances.

"What the fuck?"

"Jack," his buddy said, coming around back to see what they'd purloined. "What's the problem?"

Dempsey spat out another curse, adding, "It's nothing but women's dress shoes."

In the days before the booze and cocaine use got out of control, both with him and our society, it really was just part of our overall fabric. At most every bar, night club, or after-hours party I attended, cocaine was available. As players, most of us drank, and many snorted coke, but there was a natural flow to it, with no one judging another for what he did or did not do. We were teammates first, and deeply bonded by winning the league championship.

At the end of the night, players either went home to sleep it off or out to try to find a girl to spend the night with. Worst case scenario: An occasional fight might break out. But no one was going to end up in the hospital or go home missing an ear. At Billy's Saloon, fights were rare and no Cowboys ever misbehaved—they had too much respect for bar owner/team sponsor Billy Mouradian.

It was when Dempsey left the bar and headed, coked-out, into Boston that bad things sometimes happened. According to people close to him, he would become dangerously unpredictable, and people were advised to keep a safe distance from him.

Another alleged story about Dempsey's dramatic and violent behavior was told to me by a teammate who played with him in Boston's Park League. I won't name him here because he requested anonymity.

"Dempsey," he said, "was, hands down, one of the most talented and toughest football players I ever played with, and I retired at the age of 40, which allowed me to see and play with some exceptional athletes. But I say this as a good friend: When his switch was lit, there was no turning him off.

"At around 2:00 in the morning, I was driving home a carload of loaded guys, and Jack was sitting in the front seat. We were heading towards Kenmore Square when a guy in an Eldorado accidentally, or on purpose, cut us off. So for the next three miles, we took turns cutting each other off, and the guys in the car started to get really juiced up. Jack just sat there, staring at the guy in total silence. Finally, he said in a calm voice, 'Box this [profanity deleted] guy in at the next set of lights.'

"'Come on, Jack,' I said, 'It's late and I don't want any trouble. We're playing Southie in two days.'

"'No, no.' he said, 'It's all right. This will only take a few seconds.' He was waving his hand at me while looking over at the driver.

"So, what the hell? I boxed the guy in, just as Jack had asked, and suddenly Jack jumped out of the car. The guy rolled down his window, yelling at Jack. Jack pulled out a knife and stabbed the guy six times in the neck. Miraculously, the guy survived. Unfortunately for me, someone wrote down my license plate number and called the cops. Because Jack and I were built the same, I was ID'd as the attacker and was charged with attempted murder. I was panic-stricken when my lawyer informed me I was looking at fifteen years minimum. Thank God we had connections in town. It cost me $15,000 to buy the judge off and to get the charges dropped. All I can tell you is this: When Dempsey got that certain look in his eye, he was unstoppable."

As a kid, and as a player who loved the man, it was hard for me to separate rumor from fact. I never saw Dempsey act remotely like the guy in all the stories I'd heard, but I doubtless saw his *potential* to lose it. When he was my coach, I saw his anger. When he was my teammate, I saw his ruthlessness. But I never saw him attack someone on the street or spiral out of control due to alcohol or drug use.

But drugs and alcohol were indeed rampant throughout our society. A few weeks after the championship game, a group of players from the Cowboys and the Quincy Bulldogs went down to Baltimore to watch the Patriots play the Colts (back when the Colts were still in Baltimore). We left for Baltimore around midnight with all the food we could eat, all the booze we could drink, and all the cocaine we could snort. By four in the morning, many of the players were drunk out of their minds and exhausted. And by the time we pulled into Baltimore, many more were total wrecks. Three had passed out and never even left the bus—an eighteen-hour round-trip wasted. One of my teammates got arrested for running onto the field and hugging Horace Ivory, a Patriot player, after he scored a touchdown. During the game, we almost got into a fight with three rows of Colt fans.

As we drove back home through Connecticut, team members caught their second wind. Our captain, Larry D., who was the life of the party *all the time*, discovered that three of the players had never in their lives snorted cocaine. Larry searched out each player while the entire bus chanted the player's name and prepared them a line of coke. It was a brotherhood, and when the player gave in, the whole brotherhood cheered.

Out of respect for my father, the influence of my coach, and my own fundamental beliefs, I'd never taken drugs before, so when Larry finally got to me—the last player on his list—I knew what to do.

Grinding the coke as he looked at me and smiling craftily, he said, "Kel, I love you like a brother. Just a little pinch between your cheek and gum, and you're home free."

The entire bus was chanting my name:

*Kel, Kel, Kel, Kel—*

Peer pressure isn't when a social group dares you to do something you don't want to do. That situation is easy to say "no" to. True peer pressure is when your peer group *loves* you, you love them back, and you don't want to disappoint them, make them feel judged, or ostracize yourself from their trust. And I confess that I came close—very close—to taking a hit of cocaine myself. *What's the big deal? Just one time won't hurt me.* But then I suddenly thought that someday my own kids would look to me the same way I'd always looked to my father and to Dempsey, and they'd ask me: "Dad, did you ever take drugs?"

I smiled back at Larry. "Hey, Larry, do me a favor. Pass me a tuna sandwich, will ya? I'll get high on that."

A few guys laughed and, after a brief stand-off, everyone was back in their seats. I didn't feel in any way superior to these men, but I was proud that I hadn't caved in. Dempsey was not on that bus trip, but I've often wondered what would've happened if he had been.

I'm just glad I never had to find out.

# MY FINAL GOODBYE

*"I was the fat kid with glasses, walking home from school carrying my violin case. I got made fun of a lot, and that's when I learned to put down the violin and fight."*
—Coach Dempsey

After the '76 season ended, I refocused on returning to a four-year college. Aside from attending Quincy Jr. College to help boost my pathetic GPA, I'd also landed two great jobs: working as a bouncer at the Mad Hatter, the largest disco in New England, and working crowd control at Fenway Park, home of the Red Sox (a dream job for any Boston kid).

For a twenty-year-old, I felt I was at the top of the food chain. At Fenway, Crowd Control handled security inside the park. We wore beautiful, dark blue blazers highlighted by the Red Sox logo on the left breast pocket. Weekend night games were when we earned the real money. Fans, especially in the bleacher sections, would start drinking before they entered the ballpark and then try, with impressive creativity, to sneak in yet more alcohol.

Our job was to frisk every person entering the bleachers and grandstand sections. We found booze behind calves and triceps, in hooded sweatshirts, bras, pocketbooks, men's crotches, coolers, paper bags, and much more. We filled, on average, thirty different fifty-five gallon barrels of alcoholic beverages each night game, and *still* booze got through.

The Boston Police Department would send twenty cops to work every home game, and once in a while I'd even get the chance to work alongside my dad. But only once did we join together in breaking up a fight. He sat back and let the young guys handle the physical aspects, then took over after everything was back under control.

"Geez, what took you guys so long?" Dad said, pushing into the bunch as they cuffed the troublemaker. "Get out of my way. Let a professional show you how it's done."

Most of the guys didn't know it was a father ragging on his kid, so they just stood there, amazed, as I teased him back, "Yeah, old man, why don't you sit down and adjust that pacemaker, and maybe get involved earlier next time?"

My coworkers came away elbowing me, astonished and impressed, "Hey, why you talkin' to a cop like that for? Are you crazy?"

But before I could answer, Dad beat me to the punch as he cuffed the guy in tow. "Yeah, smart-ass, see if you get the family car next Saturday night!"

Working at the Hatter was also a high status job; the women were *beautiful* and more than available. Bouncers at the Hatter wore red and black rugby shirts, which opened doors to connect with women who otherwise wouldn't have given us the time of day. I actually used to have fun comparing how women would react to me when I was a customer versus nights when I was on duty. Sometimes the same girl who wouldn't dance or even talk with me on my day off would be flirting with me a few nights later when I was working the door—having no idea that she'd ever snubbed me. But we didn't care. It was just a big game, and we were trying to get as many dates as possible.

The club was so popular that there were actually bouncer groupies. A Wednesday group of girls, and a weekend group of girls, would regularly hang out with us. Twenty-six bouncers would be on duty at any given time to control a crowd of eighteen hundred. Of course, I was one of the smallest bouncers there, but many of the other bouncers were fellow Cowboys, so I never got much lip about it. The fights at the club were legendary; someone would bump into someone else, or two guys would go after the same girl and, after a few hours of drinking, it wouldn't take much to ignite the fuse. The fights inside the club always broke up quickly enough—there were quite a few of us working the floor.

But the club parking lot was a different story. After six months of fights and wild injuries, the police started to worry about the large number of people getting hurt at the Hatter. The clientele started to change; the crowd became younger, and more groups with larger numbers started to come in, which increased the number of fights.

One memorable night, the violence and forced busing dovetailed.

Many blacks and whites in the city at this point didn't trust each other. On both sides of the racial coin, many sought revenge whenever a relative or friend got mugged or jumped by someone of another race. A seemingly unending cycle of vengeance plagued Boston.

The Hatter was the first generation of multi-room night clubs. There was a game room, a projector room that streamed movies (a first of its kind), and a large lounge area for taking breaks from dancing and the loud music. The disco room, with a dance floor seventy-five feet long, had a "Saturday Night Fever" feel. The floor panels lit up with all the colors of the rainbow in sync with the music, and all of it was, of course, topped off with a giant strobe light beating overhead. Four speakers the size of refrigerators hung from the ceiling, overlooking hundreds of white kids from all over the city: It was disco heaven.

Occasionally, blacks visiting Boston and looking for a place to enjoy themselves would end up by chance at the Hatter. Other times, it occurred because some white jackass cabbie was intent on setting up an unknowing black kid to get the shit kicked out of him for walking into a white Southie disco.

"Your cabbie wasn't white and wearing a Shamrock clipped to his Scully Cap, was he?" I found myself asking that question all too often to any black guys brave enough to step up to the door. "Have you ever heard of South Boston?"

"Shit, man! Am I in Southie? I heard about all you crazy white folks beatin' up on blacks because of a school busin' thing, right?"

"Look, you're welcome to come in, but I gotta let you know that there's not one single black customer in this club. And these folks may not give you the warmest welcome you've ever felt."

All the bouncers at the Hatter, regardless of their own prejudices, knew that sending a black customer into the club unwarned was plain wrong. The Hatter bouncers were big and tough, but they were also great guys who acted with a sense of fairness. We didn't mislead anyone, and we were always careful to warn people whenever we thought it was warranted. We even went so far as to provide taxis and suggest somewhere safer for them to go clubbing. In return, we always got a sincere thanks for the heads up, and every black patron took our advice and went on their way—all except one.

One night, a group of four white college girls came in with a black male classmate from South Carolina. We went through our canned speech with the kid, but one of the girls said, "Nobody will touch him. We're from Quincy," and insisted he enter the club. I gave this chick a look like she'd lost her mind, but they went in anyway. We sent in six of our biggest bouncers to keep an eye out for them and to stay close.

As I was sitting by the center double doors, three Southie regulars approached me and asked if I would open the middle doors. I thought they were nuts. It was winter and freezing out. When I asked why they wanted them open, one guy said with a smirk, "We just wanna take the nigger out in the back alley and kill 'im."

"He's not even from around here—he's from South Carolina, for Christ's sake! What could you possibly have against him?" I asked, though I already knew the answer.

"I don't give a fuck where he's from. My younger brother got jumped by three niggers on the Orange line and needed nine stitches to close the gash above his eye. He's only twelve and they beat the shit out of him!"

"Listen, I understand why you're angry. I would be too. But this kid had nothing to do with your brother getting hurt."

"I don't care—I hate all niggers!" he said furiously.

"Let me ask you this: If a group of white kids beat up your brother, would you want to kill every white kid you saw?"

A few awkward seconds went by without anyone speaking until, finally, one of his buddies piped up, "C'mon, let's just try another door."

The Hatter dance floor could easily hold three hundred people, but when one of the white girls from Quincy and the black student got up to dance, every single person walked off the dance floor and encircled it, staring them down. This guy hadn't spoken to anyone or caused the slightest bit of trouble that evening, but the color of his skin changed the entire climate inside the club. It was really something to witness—something deeply disturbing. Maybe some of the people in the club felt as I did, but if so, no one dared speak up.

The dancing couple felt the intense hatred coming their way and quickly sat down.

"You satisfied?" I asked her, pissed that the girl hadn't listened to me in the first place. I told her about the kids who'd come around looking to kill her friend—I'm sure some of the Southie girls would've loved to have gotten their hands on *her* too. I've watched plenty of Southie, Charlestown, and Dorchester girls fight. Many of them could throw a punch just as straight and hard as any guy. Hell, even I would've thought twice before messing with some of those girls.

But this young woman would have lasted about three seconds before she lost some teeth, along with half her hair. We escorted her and her group to their car by sneaking them out the back door. Luckily, they were able to leave safely.

Although I was enjoying myself at both the Hatter and Fenway, both jobs meant working with obnoxious drunks day and night, and I quickly began to lose my patience with people. I started to lose my ability to empathize.

The bigger problem, however, was that I was simply unaware of this fact and of what it was turning me into.

But then, tired of my bravado, frustration, and trouble-making, my father finally stepped in and announced that my tough-guy days were over.

"Listen, it's only a matter of time before you cross the wrong guys. You smack one and then you have no idea that they're waiting for you after work. Three weeks later, we'll find you in a dumpster. Trust me, Kevin, you're not that tough. Keep your eye on the prize and go back to school."

My father gave all his kids plenty of room to grow, but when he stepped in to discipline or guide us, we listened.

And I knew deep down that my father was right. I had fully committed to moving to Hawaii, and I needed to be true to that. So, during the summer of 1977, I reached out to Dempsey for help.

"How was the T ride over from Hyde Park?" he asked, picking me up in his old Impala.

"Crowded and hot, but what else should I expect? Hey, Coach, this is the first time I've seen Boston College's football stadium. Christ! What a difference from Bridgewater State. Look at the size of this place! Outside of Foxboro, it has to be the largest stadium in New England. Look how far back the rows go—and four press boxes! *Shit!* Imagine playing here when the place is sold out. I've never played on AstroTurf, but I bet it feels like playing on a putting green. Players tell me you're faster on AstroTurf, and I can see why. The turf is so tight you can turn on a dime. Coach, how much do you think something like this costs?"

Dempsey stared straight into my eyes with that *let's get down to business* look of his, before flashing a small smile that softened his face. "Well, since BC played Notre Dame on national television in '75, BC's football program has exploded, both financially and talent-wise. I heard the price tag was about four-point-five million." Dempsey shook his head at the number, seeming as amazed as I was. "When you heading out to Hawaii?"

"I'll be leaving the first week in August."

"Great," he said, pulling into a parking space, "that'll give us eight weeks to get you ready for outside linebacker."

"Outside linebacker?" I said, baffled. "What're you talking about? I've been playing defensive tackle my entire career."

"Kevin, Hawaii is Division I, and regardless of what you or I might think, they will *never* consider playing a two hundred and ten pound kid at tackle. Don't worry, I'll have you ready. Let's stop shooting the shit. Go run a mile to warm up. We'll do our agility drills, then we'll review the basics to outside linebacker and end with conditioning. So, you're impressed with the size of the stadium, are you?"

"God, yeah! Just look at it!"

"Good, because over the next eight weeks, you'll run every single stadium step in here. Now get going!"

I'm sure the look on my face was hilarious. Eventually, though, I let out a long sigh and said, "Well, one thing is for certain."

"And what's that?"

"You're still the same ball-busting coach I had in high school."

"Ha! Were you expecting anything less?"

Every Friday for the next eight weeks, I met with my former coach and teammate to learn the ins and outs of being an outside linebacker. This was not going to be an easy adjustment. Defensive tackles have a three-point stance, whereas outside linebackers have a two-point stance, meaning they stand. A defensive tackle must focus on the opposing lineman's stance to pick up clues that might give him an edge. Outside linebackers, on the other hand, are looking for schemes in the backfield; the position demands a calmer, more strategic approach to the game. Defensive tackles must play an intelligent game as well, but at the snap of the ball, they have to be able to explode into the opponent's face or chest, before they can then *play* the position. Linebackers are responsible for both the run and the pass, so an overly aggressive linebacker won't last long.

Deep down, I was frustrated. I felt I had truly become confident playing the defensive tackle position, having played it the past three years. I had proven that size didn't have to mean everything. I'd proven it in high school during my senior year, in college during my freshman year, and at the semi-pro level as well. I kept wondering: If I'd been successful playing defensive tackle at the semi-pro level, then why can't I play tackle at the University of Hawaii?

"Yes, I preached and fully believe that size means nothing in the game of football," Dempsey sighed, rolling his eyes at my consistent complaints. "But I also made it clear that a good, big man will *always* beat a good, little man. This is most evident at the pro level. The pros bring to the game the entire package: speed, size, quickness, technique, intelligence, and lethal toughness. You have to be ready for that and you have to be able to adapt."

My last night with Dempsey was one I'll never forget. It was a perfect summer evening—warm with a slight breeze—and the type of weather that makes you wish you could sleep under the stars. The stadium was empty and quiet, with the perimeter's street lamps providing just enough light for us to see each other and do all the drills and coaching that we'd planned for the evening. It didn't matter that it was our last night together. Dempsey was his usual self: consistent, thorough, and unwavering.

"Come on! Quicker! You'll sit on the bench next year if you don't react quicker. Stop thinking—react!"

He put me through hell: agility drills, sprints, and running the endless stadium stairs. Then came the cerebral part of the game.

"Outside linebackers have to read their cues quickly. The tight end's head will tell you where the ball is going."

Dempsey was all business. I had matured as a football player and knew how everything we did here would affect any success I was to experience down the road. What was extra special for me was that I was fully aware of the unbroken bond that existed between Coach and me. I was also aware that what Dempsey was giving me at Boston College was rare. Not only was it the off-season, but I was also two years out of high school. These were his Friday nights, but he was giving them to me to help me get back to college and continue to play ball.

Deep down, I knew I'd blown my academic opportunity at Bridgewater—it had been entirely my fault. I'd lacked academic goals, lacked *life* goals. I wasn't sure exactly what I was trying to prove or what I really wanted out of life. Most of my friends were buckling down, finishing up college. They seemed to have a focus and direction to their lives while I was still just treading water, with nothing to show for my efforts but football.

But I always had this sense that everything was going to work out whenever I was around Dempsey. He had a way of communicating, without speaking, that what we were doing was what was most important. With Dempsey, you lived in the now. I knew that he believed every word he spoke. He was so detailed in his teaching that, for a little while, the outside world didn't enter my mind. Nothing was more important than what we were doing in that moment.

Dempsey radiated enthusiasm and intensity. Attentive to detail, he was, as always, the master teacher who demanded commitment, hard work, and focus from his pupils. I can only relate this intense connection to a father/son relationship. When I was a boy, I always felt safe when I was with my father. I always felt that no one could harm me. I believed all would be right with the world when Dad was home. Dempsey had this same effect on me.

In many ways, Dempsey anchored me.

I have no memory of Dempsey ever going through the motions. It was as if he was waiting the entire day for this time to coach. At the end of each workout, we would sit on the AstroTurf, stretch, and discuss life. We'd talk about how forced busing was tearing apart the fabric of our historic and beautiful city. We'd talk about football techniques and old games. Or sometimes I'd just sit and listen to him recount his own athletic past.

But during our last session, I was determined to confront him about the stories and rumors that had long been sullying his name. Though I knew I'd be crossing a delicate line, I had to know. I'm not sure where it came from, but somehow I mustered up my courage.

"Coach, you preached God, family, and country back when I was at Bosco, and I took the bait. I'm drug-free and I drink very little. Your influence and your mentoring have had a direct impact on how I choose to live my life every day."

"Well, that's great to hear, Kevin," he said.

"I do need to ask you something, though. There's a rumor about you that's been floating around the last few years."

"Yeah, what's that?"

"Do you work for the mob?"

Dempsey was taken aback, and I could tell I'd caught him off guard. Then he pinned me with his signature street-look, that *don't fuck with me* look. Still, somehow, I kept my gaze steady.

After an awkward pause, a long exhale, and a dropping of his massive shoulders, he spoke, "Yes, I do." I listened in stunned silence. "Look, these people I meet—they borrowed money to do something illegal, usually to sell drugs or to get involved with gambling. They knew exactly what they were getting themselves into. The first few times I visit someone, it's a business meeting. It's not like in the movies. If I hurt someone right away, then we'll never get our money. I sit down, pull out a briefcase, and set up installment payments. But if I'm coming to visit someone three, four times, and they haven't made a payment, well . . . things might get a little rough."

Dempsey explained his world in a flat, straightforward, no-apologies manner, as if everyone who gets involved in this business knows the rules and had better be willing to play by them.

"Makes sense to me, Coach," I said, my response surprising

even myself.

And that was that.

I had needed an answer, and he'd given me one that allowed me to keep him at least near the top of the pedestal I'd built for him and put him on.

Dempsey made the client out to be the bad guy, and justified his position in a neat and tidy way. He believed the service he provided was necessary. Dempsey had charisma and conviction in his voice and, as a kid still at the start of my twenties, I believed him—I believed him and let the matter drop because I wanted him to stay my coach, my mentor, and my role model. But, honestly, there was always a part of me that was drawn to his street side as well, that was drawn to the wildness and illegality of it all.

If he had said, *I'm going to collect some money tonight. Why don't you join me?* I could see a part of me wanting to go along. It would've been exciting to see Coach in action, strong-arming and scaring the shit out of some street punk. But I knew that in the long run, it would've been dangerous—not only because of the inherent legal and physical dangers of such a job, but also because of how it might've enticed me even deeper into that world. I'd had a taste of the street-life at the Hatter and, though it'd been exciting, it'd also changed me for the worse. Power, whether for good or evil, can become intoxicating and then addictive. I knew tagging along with Dempsey involved too many dead ends for me. That could never be my lifestyle.

What I didn't see coming, however, was what my confrontation with Dempsey would inspire: During the next few hours, Dempsey told me his life story. How much he embellished in order to impress me, I don't know. But I can replay to the word what was shared that evening—it's never left me.

"I was the fat kid with glasses, walking home from school carrying my violin case," Dempsey began, a story I quickly recognized as the one he'd also given to Abe Benitez a few years earlier. "I got made fun of a lot, and that's when I learned to put down the violin and fight. When I was nine or ten, I came home one day crying after getting picked on. I headed straight for my room and closed the door to be alone. After a few minutes, my father walked into the room. 'Clyde, stop crying,' he said.

"I lifted my head off the bed, and my father was holding the violin in one hand and a pair of boxing gloves in the other.

"We're not going to let this violin be the reason why you get beat up every day after school.

"I remember my mother standing on the stairs and listening to my father, then quickly heading for her room and closing her door. I was half afraid and half relieved to have my father teach and inspire me to stand up for myself. I had tremendous respect for him. Street fighting helped me develop a resilient attitude. If you beat me up one day, the next day I'd be at your door saying, 'Let's try that again!' Eventually, kids in the neighborhood figured I wasn't someone to fuck with."

Dempsey found his success and respect on the football field. In 1964, Boston English High School was so loaded with talent that it was ranked seventh overall in the entire nation. He developed into a two-time, high school All-American lineman. He didn't care too much for school, though, and hated time wasted on the smelly T train.

"I would rather steal a car than take the subway," said Dempsey. "I stopped counting the number of cars I stole at a hundred and seven. Of course, when my coach got wind of me skipping class and stealing cars, he benched me, and I went out of my mind. I thought he'd done it because I wasn't playing well enough. So I made sure I lined up against the kid that replaced me, and I punished that poor son-of-a-bitch *bad*. I loved football so much that if my coach had just sat me down and said, 'Dempsey, you miss one more class or steal another car, you'll never see the football field again!' then I would have gotten straight A's and never stolen another car in my life. But it never happened. We never talked. After two games, I was back in the starting lineup, and the most relieved player on the field was the kid who replaced me; I'd been tearing him up pretty good during practice.

"After high school, I attended Bridgton Academy in Maine for a postgraduate year, and later was lucky enough to attend Xavier College in Ohio. Unfortunately, things didn't turn out like I planned. When the coaches saw how small I was, they gave me the run-around. They sent me to the equipment manager, who sent me back to the coaches. Finally, I'd had enough. The equipment manager, tried to tell me that he didn't have any equipment for me when I was looking at a wall full of equipment behind him! 'I don't mean to be disrespectful,' I said to him, 'but what the fuck is all that equipment behind you?' I got so frustrated that I called my father and asked him to mail down my own shit.

"I finally got the chance to prove myself on the football field, though. Two seniors were fighting for the starting center position and I got the opportunity to meet each one by way of the pit-drill. I was so fired up, I could've taken on King Kong and killed the son-of-a-bitch! I exploded out of my stance, drilled the first senior, and nailed the running back! I was so revved. I turned to the coaches and said, 'Let's do that again!' So the next senior jumped in, and it looked like an instant replay. I drilled the second senior and nailed the back again. My adrenaline was running so high that I actually turned to the coaches and said, 'Gentlemen, I have arrived.'

"One of the coaches came over and said, 'That was impressive, Dempsey, but these guys aren't going to go up against anyone your size.' Soon, the team started scrimmaging and the coaches just ignored me. After that, it was all downhill. I couldn't get on track academically and, after a few months, I wanted to call it quits and go home. My father wanted me to stay, and things got heated on the phone. I ended the conversation by saying, 'Fuck you,' and I hung up on him. Later that day, while changing a flat tire, he dropped dead from a heart attack. After my father's death, I made a commitment to take care of my mother. Years later, I bought her a house and I promised never to leave her."

We sat in silence for a moment. I had always looked at Dempsey as solid, both physically and emotionally, but here he was, letting me view a part of his life that few people—and none of his players—had ever had access to. I was discovering that he had scars from old wounds that had never fully healed. We were both from similar backgrounds. I could tell that the finality of his father's death had badly affected him. When you realize that you can never speak to your parent again, it's gut-wrenching. I understood, but still I didn't tell him, and never did tell him, of my mother's death—this was Dempsey's time. He was opening his inner world to me, and I didn't want to redirect the flow of the conversation. But he was quick enough to do that for me, changing the subject on a dime:

"So, Kevin, you ready for Hawaii?"

Looking back, I now understand that, at that moment, Dempsey had shared enough of his past with me. He didn't have it in him to give me any more than that.

"I'm not sure if I'm ready, to tell you the truth, Coach," I said. "But if I was ever gonna be ready, it's because of you. Seriously, thank you again for everything you've done for me."

With both hands, Dempsey grabbed me by my shirt, shook me, and barked, "I didn't spend my Friday evenings all summer long getting you ready if I didn't think you could play! Remember what I've always told you: They put their pants on one leg at a time, just like you, Kel."

Then the shaking stopped and he wrapped me up in a hug. I knew I would really miss him, but I had no idea it would be the last time I'd ever talk with him.

On August 19, I boarded a United Airlines 747 feeling excited and ready. This was my first time flying, and I was headed to beautiful, exotic Hawaii.

As the plane pulled away from the gate, I saw my entire family, a few friends, and my high school girlfriend all waving goodbye. I saw Anne, my sister—still only six years old—pressing her hands and face against the window, seemingly wondering, *Why would he choose to leave us?*

I'd been so self-absorbed that I hadn't thought much about this moment until I was already knee-deep in it, and suddenly I felt a lump in my throat.

Some of my friends and neighbors were very confused about my decision to move to Hawaii.

"Why would you want to live there, for Christ's sake? Apply for a Civil Service job, get married, raise a family here in Hyde Park where you belong, put in your years, retire, and collect a pension."

"What're you going to do if things don't work out?"

"Stay with your own kind, Kev."

"What're you running away from?"

But still I struggled to see what was so complicated. Who in their right mind would give up an opportunity to live in Hawaii? I never wanted to look back on my life with regrets, and so for me the decision was easy.

Now there was no turning back—I was headed for a new life on the other side of the world.

# DOWNFALL

*"Are you Clyde Dempsey?"*
*"No, I'm Ronald Mior. I'm Canadian. I've never been to America."*
　　　— Detective Sid Millin, Ontario, Canada


From 1977 through 1980, Dempsey's use of cocaine only intensified. He took to carrying his gun more often when he was out at night. People close to Dempsey were starting to see him more frequently out of control and even completely unglued.

He began to struggle with his role as mentor and coach at Don Bosco.

"There were times when he didn't show up for practice," Sylva later told me. "It was so unlike Dempsey, and no one knew exactly what was going on, but it hurt us as a team."

Dempsey had always had the utmost respect for Coach Currier, and though Currier knew this, there was no way Dempsey could continue on at the school as unhinged as he'd become. In 2001, Currier and I met in Brighton for lunch and he told me, "I think Jack knew he was heading down a different path. There were areas in his life that I stayed away from. And if we ever did talk about his darker side, then the conversations were always initiated by him. Then one night, near the end of the season, we were sitting at a bar in Quincy Market and he promised me he'd never do anything to hurt me, the team, or the school. So our last year coaching together at Don Bosco was 1979."

In 2012, Skip and I met at a local pub in Waltham, Massachusetts. He reflected on bumping into Dempsey again in 1980.

"I don't think there was any player closer to Dempsey than me," Skip said. "He took me under his wing and shaped me from being a boy to becoming a young man. My ability to attend college and play ball was all due to him. But then in 1980, I was back home in Brighton visiting my mother. One night, while I was at Sammy White's bar with a group of friends, I saw Dempsey off in the distance. I stood up, waving, 'Hey, Coach, how you doing?' Dempsey quickly turned and looked at me as if he'd never known me. The look on his face was like 'Don't fuck with me.' He never said a word. He just turned and walked away, and I've never forgotten the look on his face. I sat back down, bewildered, wondering, *What the hell just happened?*"

Coach Currier explained what it was like to watch Dempsey zero in on someone. "Many times, I'd seen Dempsey enter a bar, pick out the biggest guy, and wait for the right moment. Dempsey would sit up at the bar and eye the guy throughout the evening while having a few drinks. Dempsey loathed muscle-heads who purposely wore overly tight shirts to try to impress the girls. Late into the evening, Dempsey would saunter up to the unexpected target, slap him on the back, and offer to buy the guy a drink. When the muscle-head scoffed at Dempsey and said, no thanks with a dismissive tone, Dempsey would turn it up a notch.

"What's the matter? Too good to have a drink with me? Come on: I said I want to buy you a drink.

"After a second refusal, Dempsey would unleash on the poor

son-of-a bitch. At times, Dempsey would simply punish people. It was truly something to watch," Currier said, as I shuddered at the thought of seeing Dempsey beat someone to such an extent that they ended up needing an ambulance.

During Dempsey's lifetime, he would find himself in front of a judge fourteen times. From 1963 to 1973, he was arrested nine times. Most were DUIs, one was for operating to endanger, and one was for assault and battery. But in 1978, his rap sheet would start to look different. That year, Dempsey was arrested for discharging a firearm and an assault with a dangerous weapon. Though the charges would eventually be dismissed, it was barely a year before Dempsey was arrested again for assault and battery with a dangerous weapon. Somehow, though, these charges were also dismissed.

On July 1, 1981, however, Dempsey made a decision that would change his life forever.

Edward White (not his real name) was big for twenty-four. A resident of Dedham, Massachusetts, he stood 6'3" and weighed close to two hundred and thirty pounds. White had been a regular at a bar called Mr. McNasty's in downtown Boston. According to management, White was a good kid. He had never caused a problem at the bar and was viewed as quiet and friendly. Dempsey had just begun hanging out at McNasty's after being introduced to the place by a new acquaintance, a taxi driver and part-time bouncer named Sawyer.

Life can involve a series of complicated intersections and, for White and Dempsey, theirs would end up being catastrophic. To this day, no one can say for sure whether or not Dempsey and White had ever met prior to July 1st of that year. But that evening, Dempsey was with a small group of friends, drinking White Russians and working the room, socializing with his friends and with Meany, McNasty's 6'6" bartender.

When interviewed by police, Meany reported that, "Dempsey came up and introduced himself to me and, throughout the night, bought me a few beers. I couldn't drink on the job, though, so I put the beers on ice to take home for later. Dempsey appeared clear-headed and calm throughout the night. I didn't sense any hostility at all from him. If he was agitated, in a bad mood, or looking for trouble, it didn't come across to me."

But waitress Allison Towne picked up a different vibe from Dempsey. "He called me a bitch for not smiling at him after he made a comment to me," she said. "He wasn't the typical Mr. McNasty's customer. He made me feel uneasy."

What first lit the fuse between Dempsey and White, no one knows for sure, but a few words were tossed back and forth before someone eventually approached Sawyer to intervene.

"Mr. Sawyer, please tell us exactly what happened when you first approached Mr. Dempsey," Detective O'Halloran said, waving the cigarette smoke from his face while sitting at a private table in the back corner of McNasty's.

"I walked over to Dempsey," Sawyer said, "placed my hand on his shoulder, and asked if everything was okay. Dempsey shrugged and said he was fine and that it was White who was having the problem. So I approached White and told him that Dempsey didn't want any trouble and everything would be okay."

Having been a bouncer at the Hatter, and having worked crowd control at Fenway Park, I had broken up plenty of fights. On a scale of 1-10 (10 being the worst), White and Dempsey's interaction to that point seemed like it should've been somewhere around a 2. But I had seen plenty of disputes escalate with devastating results, where people got knocked out, lost teeth, had their noses broken, were hit with pipes, bats, tire irons, and so forth, but those fights were usually triggered by an emotional outburst that turned red-hot real fast, much more intense than what was initially going on between Dempsey and White (at least according to witness accounts).

Case in point: One Friday night when the Hatter was packed, four Boston College football players arrived. One of the players was Fred Smerles. Smerles stood 6'4" and was two hundred and eighty-five pounds of solid muscle. He was enormous! He was also an All-American defensive tackle who'd go on to have an NFL career with the Buffalo Bills at nose guard.

Fights inside the Hatter didn't last long, what with twenty-eight bouncers on duty, but on this particular night, Smerles and his teammates had a problem with a group of kids from Southie. After the first punch was thrown, the club exploded and, for the first time in my career there, we couldn't shut the fight down. Over forty Southie kids swarmed over the BC players. After ten minutes, each of which felt like an eternity, we managed to regain control of the club. But five bouncers still had Smerles up against a wall.

"Freddie," pleaded Billy Bragger, one of our biggest bouncers, "just stay right here, *please*. Someone's gonna get really hurt if you don't stop."

"Okay, okay, we'll leave," Smerles said, relaxing and putting his hands down by his sides.

Suddenly, though, a Southie kid ran up behind Bragger, jumped up, and threw a punch straight at Smerles' face. Without looking or skipping a beat, the kid flew out the front door into the parking lot. Smerles snapped. He was so enraged that, as he chased the kid into the lot, I thought to myself, *If he ever gets his hands on this kid, he'll kill him.* That level of anger made sense to an outside observer given the brawl's build-up.

But to the witnesses at McNasty's, the interactions between

Dempsey and White hadn't come anywhere close to the Smerles incident. Dempsey and White's comments were short and comparatively light. And, what's more, a bouncer was there to intervene. So the million dollar question is: What made Dempsey, a man who could easily take care of himself in a fistfight, a man who was legendary for it, pull out a *handgun* so soon?

It's a mystery we may never find the answer to.

But, no matter the reasons, around eleven-thirty that evening, someone heard Dempsey say to White: "You fucking asshole, you want to fuck with me now?"

Witnesses then saw Dempsey holding a snub-nosed .38 caliber pistol just three feet away from White, who replied, "Put that puny thing away."

"I'm going to kill you, motherfucker."

Then Dempsey aimed the gun at the floor and pulled the trigger. The bullet hit the ground between White's feet, causing him to jump back, but then, to everyone's surprise, White turned around, bent over, and jeered, "Why don't you stick it in my ass and pull the trigger?"

For someone who'd just had a gun fired at them, this was a more than bizarre response, and one that only heightens suspicions that perhaps there *was* some prior connection between White and Dempsey.

I'd once had a gun pulled on me back in 1987. I was line-striping a parking lot for a bank on Route 9 in Framingham. We could work only when the parking lots were empty, so we arrived no later than five in the morning to get started. The bank guard working inside the bank had no idea who we were, though, that first morning, and so he called the local police.

It was obvious the cop who arrived had been sleeping while on his shift—his hair was a mess and his eyes were still adjusting to the lights in the parking lot as he squinted blearily at us. In fact, it was easy to tell he'd been in a lousy mood even *before* he climbed out of his cruiser, given how he came tearing into the lot. Screeching to a halt, he jumped out of his cruiser with his gun already drawn.

"Hit the ground *now,* motherfuckers! *Now!*"

Having a gun pointed at you, realizing your life could end in an instant, made the size of the gun increase tenfold. To me, that barrel looked to be the size of a howitzer. Scared shitless, I hit the ground just to get out of the line of fire.

What enabled White to remain so relaxed after the gun was fired at him is mind-boggling.

When White then turned around and laughed in Dempsey's face, Dempsey fired one shot directly into White's chest.

White stepped back and looked at the bartender, and then at the bouncer. His expression was one of disbelief, as if he was thinking, *Can you believe he just shot me?*

White took one step forward toward Dempsey. Dempsey fired a second shot into White. The kid spun quickly to his left, and that's when Dempsey fired his third and final shot into White's body. White stumbled backwards and collapsed near the front door.

Dempsey stepped over White and, in a fit of rage, took two swipes at him with his gun, missed, and then pushed White back into the floor. Someone moved quickly toward Dempsey's right side, perhaps in an effort to wrestle the gun from him, but then Dempsey raised his weapon again and the man immediately stopped and threw up his hands.

"Hey, no problem here!" the man said.

Dempsey finished his drink, placed the empty glass on the counter, shook hands with the doorman, and told him he'd see him later.

Patrons were stunned. As Sawyer later testified, "At first, I thought it was a joke." Some people thought someone had lit firecrackers inside the club, which is actually fairly reasonable since it was so close to the Fourth of July. One witness thought White was dead before he hit the ground, but then two patrons (both with medical backgrounds) opened up his shirt, saw three holes in his chest, and said he was having trouble breathing. They yelled out for someone to call 911.

White never said another word. He died on the way to the hospital.

Dempsey, in the meantime, worked his way to another bar and had a few more drinks to calm himself down and try to make sense of what had just happened. He eventually made his way to a friend's home in Stoughton, a small town outside of Boston, and stayed for a day or two. The shooting made the papers and the local television news. Dempsey then headed for Maine and stayed with his lifelong friend, Mike Kelly, who was there on vacation with his family.

Dempsey told Mike Kelly that he'd had a bad beef in Boston and needed to stay out of the city for a while. Kelly testified that he never asked for any specifics, and that Dempsey never gave them. After a few days, Kelly told Dempsey that he might want to leave the states entirely if he was really in that much trouble. So Dempsey called a friend for some money and jumped on a bus to Canada with twenty-eight hundred dollars, a stolen Vermont driver's license, and a loaded gun. Dempsey eventually made his way to Toronto and stayed in a few halfway houses, quickly realizing that he needed to establish a new identity.

But he couldn't live that way for long.

Desperate, Dempsey visited a Canadian cemetery and found the grave of a baby who'd died in 1953 at the age of eleven months. He then visited a local library, looked up the baby's obituary, and discovered which parish had performed the child's baptism: Saint Mary of the Angels. He then filed for a new birth certificate, which allowed him to apply for a driver's license, which in turn made him eligible for legitimate employment in Canada.

In this way, Dempsey began creating a new life for himself and, for the next nine years, he worked as a successful real estate agent. He even fell in love with a woman named Sylvia Vaughan and, after seven years, became engaged to her—all under the name of Ronald Mior. Dempsey knew he had only one chance to start a new life, and that required him leaving Boston and the murder behind him.

Turning on the "good" Dempsey was easy for him. He could be kind, funny, and very generous with both his time and money. It was easy to like Dempsey—this guy with the thick, square glasses and his seemingly non-threatening personality.

But that didn't mean Dempsey's murder case was filed away and vanished in some back room filing cabinet at Police headquarters. After the Boston Police Department's thorough investigation and tireless search for Dempsey in the Boston area, the consensus among the investigative team was that Dempsey had skipped town and was on the run. After three years and no leads, Dempsey's case was transferred to the "cold case" files.

State trooper Frank Matthews got a lucky break when he was invited to work on the Massachusetts State Police's Violent Fugitive Arrest Squad (VFAS). The VFAS worked closely with the Boston PD on its cold cases.

It would be by chance that Frank and I would meet. It was the result of the typical "what a small world it is" situation. My former boss's son purchased a home next to a good friend of Frank and, because a friend of the friend had obtained a preliminary copy of this book, they found themselves discussing Dempsey. Two weeks later, Frank and I were talking on the phone, and instantly I was excited to meet the guy. To "talk Dempsey," Frank and I met in September of 2015 on the Mass Pike at a pull-over service station in Westborough.

Over the next four hours, we looked at each other in disbelief as one connection after another was established.

"Frank, where did your dad grow up?"

"He moved to the Old Colony projects in Southie in 1960, and I was born there."

"You're kidding. That's where my dad grew up as well."

"I have little memory of Southie. We moved to Hyde Park when I was a kid."

"Hyde Park? Where in Hyde Park?"

"Off River Street. Why?"

"I grew up next to Moynihan Field, off of Truman Highway.

"You're kidding me!"

"What did your dad do for a living?"

"He was a State Police captain."

"My dad was a Boston cop—43 years of service."

"Frank," I said, "my father thought he'd died and gone to heaven when he moved out of the Southie projects and purchased his home in Hyde Park in 1953. He couldn't get over the fact that he had a front lawn and a back yard, though both were tiny."

"Kev, when we were kids and in the family car getting ready to head home after a night out, my father loved our home in Hyde Park so much he would turn to my mother and say: "Mary, time to head back to the castle.""

"I have a feeling my dad and your dad would have been great friends! Where did you attend high school?"

"I went to CM and played football for the legendary Coach O'Connor."

"Stop it! No way!"

"What? Why? What school did you go to?"

"Bosco."

"Don't tell me you were on that '74 team?"

"I was. The '74 game against CM, to this day, is the number one athletic highlight of my high school career and the greatest football game in Bosco's history. I will say, however, that Coach O'Connor was one of the most respected coaches in the Boston area. Nothing but class. Great coach!"

"Kev, he was all that and more."

"Frank, tell me how special was it to work at the same place as your dad?

"You don't know the half of it. My older brother Stevie was on the force as well. I got on the force right after high school at the young age of 19. Stevie and I are only two years apart. Not only are we close, but I have a tremendous amount of respect and admiration for him, personally and professionally. He was an exceptional investigator. We both recently retired from the State Police as lieutenant colonels. For my dad, it was a dream come true. He loved being a 'Statee.' It was his whole life, but having his two boys on the force was an indescribable joy for him. I learned more from my dad and brother about the force, investigation work, life, being a husband, being a parent, and how to treat others than from anyone else."

"So tell me, how did you get involved with the Dempsey case?"

"I picked up the file in 1984. By that time, there were all types of rumors going around about Dempsey's whereabouts. We were hearing that he was hiding in Ireland. We also heard he'd often been in and out of Boston. Another rumor had Dempsey sneaking in and out of Boston dressed as a woman, which would have been something to see—he was 5'-7", weighed over two hundred pounds, and was built like a fire hydrant."

"I'm curious: Where do you even begin to investigate after a case has gone cold for so many years?"

"Actually, there's quite a bit we can do. First, we do good ole, tried and true, police work. My job is not to see if Boston PD missed something. We have a great relationship with the Boston PD, and we're not going to rock the boat. My job is to simply grab the file and start from scratch. We start with Dempsey's inner circle and interview everyone. I met with friends and relatives, fellow coaches, childhood friends, peers from work. I also met with Dempsey's mother, but I walked gently with her. She'd already been through enough and my few conversations with her were always short and respectful. I eventually stopped visiting her.

"Today, technology is frequently a blessing to criminal investigators. You can't believe how many criminals use social media. They use an alias or delete what they write or post, but the truth is, there's no such thing as a fully deleted message or posting. But back in the mid-80s, we were all using landline phones and postal mail to connect with one another.

"We asked the Post Office's Mail Cover unit to monitor mail with the people Dempsey was most close to. Mail coming in from overseas, out of state, or from over the border would be pulled. Once a week, we would collect any pulled mail to see if it was coming from Dempsey.

"Court orders to allow phone taps are extremely difficult to obtain. It's not like in the movies where tapping someone's phone is approved in hours. In real life, your liberty rights are fully protected under the law, and unless we have evidence that a phone is being used in a criminal enterprise, a wiretap is impossible to obtain. However, it doesn't mean we couldn't pull phone records. We had legal access to all phone records, and if Dempsey made a call from out of state or outside the country, we would have tracked him down. We were convinced that Dempsey would slip up. Truth be told, most criminals eventually do.

"But year after year went by and we had nothing. I even started to believe that perhaps he was indeed hiding out in Ireland. Dempsey became an obsession to me. As I continued with my career and worked on some high profile cases, Dempsey never left me. My mother, who had a tremendous sense of humor, would send me a Christmas card each year, and each one would read something like:

*Dear Frank,*
 *Merry Christmas! Enjoying my time in Paris!*
*Hope to see you soon!*
 *—Jack Dempsey*

"Your mother sounds like a gem! Frank, let me ask you this: What drove you not to give up on the case?"

"Kev, in the fugitive unit, there's a sign for everyone to see, It says: 'We work for God.'"

"I don't get it. What does that mean?"

"It means we work for those who no longer can work for themselves. It's our commitment to the victim and to the victim's family never to quit on a case. In the Dempsey case, our last best hope arrived when we were approached by 'America's Most Wanted.' We knew they had a strong track record identifying criminals, what with millions of viewers exposed to the original show and then a re-run of the show. For them, we rented a bar in Boston to reenact the crime. There, and on the televised episode, they did a terrific job portraying the crime accurately. We waited, and fourteen months later, all our (and their) hard work paid off!"

One fateful evening in December of 1990, while relaxing with a group of friends, an episode of *America's Most Wanted* came on. To the surprise of the group and to the shock of Dempsey, he was one of the evening's featured fugitives.

But even this wasn't enough to overturn Dempsey's new life, for he'd inspired the same type of loyalty in his new friends and family as he'd always managed to inspire in his friends and students back in Boston. However, a few weeks after the show aired, the police conducted a large drug bust that involved a member of Dempsey's social group—a member who'd seen the broadcast, who knew Dempsey's secret, and whose girlfriend ultimately turned in Dempsey in exchange for a lesser charge for her boyfriend.

| D-4 | 11457959 | BOSTON POLICE DEPARTMENT CONTINUATION SHEET | | 2 | 4 |
| --- | --- | --- | --- | --- | --- |
| 7/2/81 | HOMICIDE | assailant produced a firearm, discharged one | | | |

assailant produced a firearm, discharged one round into the floor of the premises and then fired at point blank range, 3 additional rounds into the body of the victim, causing the victim to stagger backward and fall to the floor of the premises in the vicinity of the main entrance. The assailant then fled on foot out the main entrance on to Queensbury Street and into an alley behind the premises. A thorough search of the area was made for the assailant by units of Area D to no avail. The victim was transported to the Brigham & Womens' Hospital by the Health & Hospital units for treatment of gunshot wounds of the chest one of which pierced the victims heart. The victim was pronounced dead at 12:50 a.m., 7/2/81 by Dr. Walker of the Brigham & Womens' Hospital. Positive identification of the victim was made by the deceaseds' brother, one Roger Widden, of 3 Briar Road, Canton, Ma.

DET. SGT. JAMES CHAISSON, HOMICIDE, V-951 responded and conducted his investigation. Det. Sgt. P. Maloney, V-981 responded to the scene and assisted in the investigation. The D801f (SHEEHAN & CONNELLY) responded to the scene and as a result of investigation by them it was determined that the assailant later identified as one John Dempsey, of 49 Willow St., W. Roxbury, had been using a 1972 Plymouth, M.R. 301 EMJ, which was found at the scene and to ed to Area D-4 for fingerprints in the A.M. of 7/2/81.

The SD-61 (Flanagan & Drown) responded to the scene and conducted their investigations. Det. Sgt. Chaisson, will seek a warrant for Homicide against #25 later this A.M.

#22. Concinued: Mary Gorman, 16 Queensbury St., Boston tel;267-8034

Scott Eckhoff, 41 Palmer St., Medford, Ma.     391-4272

Ron Cheney, 41 Park Drive, Boston, MA     536-3454

Henry Iadonisi, 59 Vincent Rd., Dedham, MA.     326-9259

John L. Meany, 49 Ward St., Lexington Ma     362-3936

Robert O'Dwyer, 64 Hemenway St., Bos.,     266-7035

Allen Davidson, 1. Evans Rd., Brookline, MA     734-8315

Philip Monica, 15 Anderson St., Boston, Ma     367-3576

11457959

HOMICIDE    0711    7/1/81

88 QUEENSBURY STREET    na    11:20    11:20

NA    X    W

3 BRIAR ROAD, CANTON MA    NA    MECHANIC    24    6/11/57

YES

| | | | | | |
|---|---|---|---|---|---|
| LLIAM DONNELLY | NA | #08 | 225 Nichols St Raynham | 823-8447 | XX YES NO |
| LLISON TOWNE | NA | #08 | 457 PARK DR. CIT. 2 | 267-2759 | |
| AURIE MARGOLIN | NA | #08 | 1661B Comm.AV. CIT. | 7874614 | XX YES NO |

DEMPSEY JOHN    CLYDE

49 WILLOW ST. W. ROX.    X    W    35-40    5'7 unk

IRE RIM GLASSES/DK CURLY HAIR WHITE SHT    230    stky    curly    unk

NA    YES NO

X    NA    301EMJ    PASS    DUSTER

PLYMOUTH 72    2 dr.    BLACK

NA    NA    NA

JOHN PITMAN    28 TAPPIN ST. ROSLINDALE    X
NA    YES NO

X
YES NO

FIREARM    RES-COMM    BAR    NA

CLOUDY    ARTIFIC.    FOOT    DRINKING

UNK    YES NO

X
YES NO

About 11:20p.m.,7/1/81, the D-911 (Sgt.T.Maloney) along with the
D201f (Conlin & Furlong) and the D-304f (Sergei & Adduci) responded
to Mr. McNasty's at 88 Queensbury St. relative to a man having been
shot. Upon arrival the officers observed the victim lying on the floor
inside the premises with apparent gunshot wounds in the chest area.
DEPT. of HEALTH & HOSPITALS UNITS 20-A-4 (DiMAURO & KLEAMINAKIS),
20-P-3 ( HOLLAND, ZARRILLO & AHERN), 25MD5 (Dr. SINCLAIR), responded
and attended the victim. William Donnelly, the manager of Mr. McNasty's
reported to the officers that about 11:20p.m, the victim was drinking
in the bar with his assailant, when without apparent provocation, the

D-911f    3    6660

7/2/81    HOMICIDE/IDENTIFICATION/ AREA D DEP. SUP. FLAHERTY/ N.E.'s

4:00    Sgt John E. Sudatone    6257

HEADQUARTERS RECORD

# MASSACHUSETTS STATE POLICE
# WANTED FOR MURDER

## CLYDE JOHN F. DEMPSEY

AKA:    JACK DEMPSEY

DOB:    3/29/45    WM    200 LBS.

BROWN HAIR, BROWN EYES,  5'8"

LKA:    49 WILLOW STREET, WEST ROXBURY, MA

WARRANT IN EFFECT AT BOSTON, PD #5379 of 1981.

ISSUED OUT OF BOSTON MUNICIPAL COURT.

SUBJECT WANTED FOR MURDER IN BOSTON, MASS. ON JULY 2, 1981.

ANYONE HAVING INFORMATION CONTACT THE FOLLOWING:

John R. O'Donovan
Lt. Colonel
Mass. State Police
Invest. & Intell. Oper.

617-566-4500

Cpl. Kevin Horton
Mass. State Police
Violent Fugitive Arrest Squad
508-820-2370    or    1-800-KAPTUR

M S P  2/26/90

# CLYDE JOHN F. DEMPSEY
## Murder
### (Dec. 7, 1990)
Data from the Mass. State Police

e: 45  DOB:3/29/45

8"

0

own eyes
own hair

joys sports, especially football
y be coaching football
kes to gamble
inks, especially Scotch
es drugs
y be working in ski resort
y be working as a ski lift
  operator
kes to work out with weights
y be dealing drugs
y be working as an enforcer
y be working with kids in
  an inner-city program
y be working in a school
y be working as a bartender

Tatoos: none
Scars:  none

CIC: 14 TT TT 06 11 10 55 04 04 15
A: Boston, Mass.
: Colorado

Clyde John F. Dempsey is wanted by the Massachusetts State
lice for the murder of ███████████.

On July 1, 1981, Dempsey walked into Mr. McNasty's Cafe for
few drinks. When he spotted an unidentified man who owed him
ney -- reportedly $150 -- he walked over to him and demanded the
ney.

Several minutes later, ████████████, a tall young lad who
rked as an automobile mechanic in the neighborhood, stepped
tween the two men in an effort to persuade Dempsey to leave
████ alone.

Furious, Dempsey pulled out a handgun from his waistband and
red a warning shot into the floor at ████████ feet, according
polce. Dempsey them slowly lifted his arm and fired three
dditional shots into ████████ chest, killing him.

Reporter: Cabell Bruce
Trooper Frank Mathews (508) 820-2370
Massachusetts State Police

On February 28, 1992, Sid Millin was in his eighth year as a detective for the Hamilton-Wentworth police department in Ontario, Canada. That day, Millin drove up to South Hamilton and knocked on an apartment door.

"Excuse me, I'm Detective Millin from the Hamilton-Wentworth Police. I'd like to ask you for your I.D. please."

Wordlessly, Dempsey produced his driver's license.

"Any additional I.D.? How about a birth certificate?"

Without the slightest hesitation, Dempsey opened his briefcase and, from its upper left-hand pocket, pulled out "his" birth certificate.

"I was shocked," said Millin. "I have never in my life seen anyone who could put their finger on their birth certificate so quickly. It was my first inkling that maybe Dempsey was not who he said he was."

"Mr. Mior, have you ever been to America?"

"No, I'm a Canadian."

"Where were you born?"

Dempsey wasn't giving up. "Toronto," he said calmly.

Millin must've sensed Dempsey's toughness, so he cut to the chase: "Are you Clyde Dempsey?"

"No, I'm Ronald Mior. I'm Canadian. I've never been to America."

"We think you're Clyde Dempsey. We'd like to take your fingerprints."

Maintaining his claim of innocence as well as his identity as Mior, Dempsey willingly complied with the fingerprint request. After a few hours, the police came back into Dempsey's room and informed him that the prints were a match. The jig was up. Dempsey had gone to the police station willingly. He knew that the game was over and signed voluntary deportation papers. On March 30, 1992, Dempsey found himself en route back to Boston.

Before Dempsey's trial, Dempsey's lawyer informed the judge that Edward White's father had verbally threatened to shoot Dempsey in the courtroom. The lawyer was not only concerned for Dempsey's safety, but for his own as well. He didn't want to be sitting too close to Dempsey if White's father was going to be seeking revenge.

Acknowledging the severity of the threat, the judge agreed that, even though people would already be passing through a metal detector on the first floor, everyone entering the courtroom would have to submit to a second search. They also agreed to meet with White's father to make him aware that the court knew of his threat.

After all of the prosecution witnesses completed their testimonies, Dempsey took the stand in his own defense—a rarity in murder cases.

Dempsey was first asked questions aimed at establishing all of his most basic information: when he was born, where he was raised, the level of education he'd achieved, and what he did for work, including his time at Don Bosco.

The state's prosecutor was Phyllis Broker. And she was *tough*.

"Mr. Dempsey, you told the Canadian officials your name was Ronald Angelo Mior. Is that right?"

"Yes, I did."

"That was a lie, right?"

"At the time it was, yes."

"It is not true today, is it?"

"No, it's not."

"You took the identity of an eleven-month-old child who had

died," Broker continued, unrelenting. "Is that correct?"

"Yes."

"And that, too, was a lie. Is that correct?"

"That's correct."

"Now, in July of '81, did you carry a gun?"

"I carried it from time to time," Dempsey conceded. "For my bar-tending duties."

"And you carried it loaded?" she said.

"Yes, I did."

"Fully loaded?"

"Yes, I did."

"Did you have a license to carry a gun in 1981?"

"No, I didn't," Dempsey admitted.

"And you know it is illegal to carry a gun without a license?"

"Yes."

"How many drinks did you have that evening?"

"Several."

"What were you drinking?"

"White Russians."

"Top shelf?"

"Yeah."

"You weren't drunk?"

"Well," Dempsey said, "let's say I had a glow on."

Dempsey had gambled by putting himself on the stand, but he'd had to. There was no one to testify in his defense. However, Dempsey still had his personality and charisma on his side, a powerful and potentially persuasive combination. People took to Dempsey quickly; he could be charming, funny, likable, and very caring.

But Broker wouldn't bite.

"You had no difficulty leaving the bar, did you?"

"No, I did not."

"And you had no difficulty shooting Mr. White?"

"I was saving my life, Ms. Broker," he said, agitated, sitting up straighter and crossing his arms defensively.

"You had no trouble shooting him, did you?"

"I tried to stop, but…"

"Did you have trouble shooting him, sir?"

"I was in fear of my life, Ms. Broker," he said, leaning forward, refusing to back down.

"Did you have any trouble shooting him?"

"I fired the gun, and I saved my life," he said, looking Broker straight in the eye.

"In fact, when you shot and killed Edward White, you had to take the gun from your right hip where you carried it. Is that correct?"

"That's correct."

"Fully loaded, right?"

"Correct."

"You first aimed the gun between his feet. Is that correct?"

"I fired a warning shot between his feet."

"You aimed between his feet?"

"To tell him to get away from me."

"Did you aim at him?"

"After he threatened to cut my throat, I put one [bullet] between his legs and told him to get away from me. Yes," Dempsey said, raising up both of his hands as if to say, *I had no other option.*

The dialogue between Dempsey and Broker demonstrated a clear game of intellectual chess, with Dempsey fully aware of the road Broker was trying to take him down. She wanted to convince the jury that Dempsey was deliberate in his thinking and decision-making, while Dempsey wanted them to believe that his response had been instinctive, driven by fear and a need to survive.

But despite Dempsey's testimony, each prosecution witness had painted a picture of White as non-aggressive the night of the killing.

Bartenders, bouncers, and waitresses alike testified that White had been a customer there for six months and that he'd never created a problem at McNasty's.

Broker broke down the case frame by frame, recreating every second of Dempsey's exchange with White. She brought Dempsey back to each shot he fired; what was he thinking, what was his intent, why didn't he seek help, why wasn't there an alternative way to deal with White? Most importantly, however, she exposed Dempsey as a liar, as a man who cared for no one but himself.

"After July of '81, did you ever go home again?"

"No."

"Never?"

"I never went back," Dempsey said, growing irritated again.

"Have you ever had any contact with your mother since July 1st of 1981?"

"I didn't want her to be harassed by the police any more than she has been. No, I did not."

"Is your answer no?"

"No."

"You never called her?"

"No," Dempsey said, crossing his arms as he sat back in his seat, looking intently at Broker. Dempsey could handle any question pertaining to him, but when Broker brought up his mother, she was coming close to a line that no one would've ever crossed with Dempsey on the street. I thought back to our last evening together, when he'd at last opened up to me about his past and about the promise he'd made to his mother.

*After my father's death, I made a commitment to take care of my mother . . . I promised never to leave her.*

Broker paused briefly, then went on to expose Dempsey's life on the run, his stealing the identity of a dead child to become a successful businessman, a man who'd lived safely and comfortably in Canada.

"You knew there was a warrant out for you, did you not?"

"Yes, I did."

"And that is why you fled to Canada, is it not?"

"Absolutely."

"Where did you get the gun?"

"From my friend, Mr. Sampson."

"Who paid your half of the mortgage [on your Boston home] while you were up in Canada?"

"My mother."

"She went into a nursing home, did she not?"

"Correct."

"Can you tell this jury what you went through to get a certificate of baptism in the name of Ronald Mior?"

"Well, when I was moving around, living from one boarding room to the next, I did a lot of reading. I read mystery books. I took a name off a gravestone, went into the obituary columns, and filled out an application. I found out when he died, when he had church services, the church he was baptized in, and went and got the certificate."

"You had done it several times?"

"No, but I intended to do it again after seeing the TV show. I was never coming back."

"You had begun to create yet another identity for yourself, is that correct?"

"That's true."

"What name were you going to use?"

"Gary Adeem."

"Did Ms. Vaughan know you were planning a new identity?"

"She did not," Dempsey said, suddenly sheepish.

"Were you planning on taking her with you?"

"No."

A particularly damaging part of Dempsey's murder trial was the non-appearance of Sylvia Vaughn, his fiancée of seven years. The only witness who could have testified on Dempsey's behalf, who could've testified to the positives in his character, had decided to not even attend the trial.

Dempsey's demeanor started to show a slight annoyance at being rifled with what seemed to him to be meaningless questions, especially when posed by a woman. But the questions were unrelenting—it was as if Broker embodied justice's gavel itself, hammering away at Dempsey until each tiny detail suddenly took on new and damning weight.

"You created a life of lies in Canada because it was in your best interest, isn't that correct?" Broker insisted.

"It was."

"And you created a web of lies in front of this jury again because it's in your best interest. Isn't that correct?"

"That is not correct!" Dempsey protested, raising his voice defensively.

"You heard the medical examiner testify that Mr. White was shot under the right armpit and that the bullet exited above his right breast?"

"I heard."

"He was shot in the back, sir."

"No, he wasn't. He was facing me. I'm not an expert in medical testimony."

"But you're an expert with guns, are you not?"

"No," Dempsey said, growing edgy. "I'm not an expert with guns. I've fired guns, but I'm not expert. If I didn't have it on me that night, I wouldn't be here answering your questions."

"That's probably true, Mr. Dempsey. But, in point of fact, you did have it on you."

"If I didn't, I'd be dead," Dempsey said, looking with confidence at the jury.

"After you shot into the floor, you raised the gun and shot him in the chest."

"So I wouldn't get my throat cut, Ms. Broker," Dempsey said, leaning in, his massive shoulders tilting forward and inward.

"You shot him in the chest. You shot him in the stomach. And, as he bent forward and spun around, you shot him in the back."

Dempsey sat up straight, his eyebrows pushing down and coming together as he pointed a finger directly at Broker. "It did not happen that way. He came at me. I don't know what happened. I pulled the trigger. I was backed up against the bar, and that's the only thing I remember. That man threatened to cut my throat."

Crossing her arms, Broker approached Dempsey. "When this was happening, did you go over to John Meany and say, 'John, you're the bouncer here. Help me out. Get this guy away from me.' Did you do that?"

"Mike Kelly went over to get Sawyers."

"And?"

"Mr. Sawyers asked if there was a problem. I said no, but you better check with him. As soon as I pointed at him, he got angry. He got crazy."

"And Mr. Sawyers was standing right there when Mr. White got angry and crazy. Is that correct?"

"Mr. Sawyers walked away. When he walked away, [White] came towards me."

"And, before that, you had no trouble with Mr. White?"

"None whatsoever."

"And, all of a sudden, he snaps the top off of a brandy snifter and comes at you with a stem? Is that what you are telling this jury?"

Dempsey paused as he adjusted his position on the stand. He looked down at the floor with a quick glance and, for the first time, there was a noticeable moment of reflection. Dempsey's breath quickened and his words came out in a race, "He came at me with a glass."

"For no reason whatsoever?"

Looking at no one in particular, Dempsey said, "The guy pointed at me and said, 'Does he want a piece of my ass?' That's what he said."

It was clear by then that, of the two lawyers involved in the case, Broker was the more aggressive, more outspoken, and more driven to win. On the opposite end of the spectrum, Mr. Jubinville, Dempsey's attorney, didn't pose a single objection during Broker's entire line of questioning. Broker's commitment to putting Dempsey away matched (and perhaps even surpassed) the same drive, aggressiveness, and intensity that Dempsey had always preached to his players as he readied us for an upcoming opponent. She was *prepared.*

"Did you know the name Edward White from previous occasions?"

"I never knew Edward White before in my life," Dempsey said, though he looked away, his arms folding tighter across his chest.

"You never met Edward White before?"

"I never saw him before."

"And your testimony is you never had any difficulty with him that evening?"

"I had no difficulty until he came at me."

"And, out of the blue, you're telling the jury he wanted to cut your throat?"

"That's exactly what he said to me."

"And the only other person alive that you told this story to is your fiancée?"

"I told her I killed in self-defense, yes."

"And you and she are still on good terms. Is that correct?"

"Correct."

"But she's not here today, is she?"

"No, she's not."

"While in Canada, did you ever anonymously try to call the police and say 'This is my version of the story'? Did you ever do that?"

"No, I did not."

"Did you ever ask someone to look into the circumstances of Mr. White's death?"

"No, I didn't."

"When you walked out of that barroom and onto the street, were you in fear for your life?"

"I shot Edward White in self-defense. I was in shock after it happened. I can't recall every detail. I walked out the door and I've been walking ever since."

"So you don't want the jury to believe that you voluntarily came down here to straighten out the record? That's not what you want this jury to believe?"

"I want the jury to believe the truth."

"You want the jury to give you a break. Isn't that right?"

"I shot that man in self-defense, Ms. Broker. I wouldn't be alive today to testify if I didn't."

"Mr. Dempsey, is there anyone in that bar that you're aware of, that you *know*, that saw any brandy glass in Mr. White's hand?"

"Mr. Kelly saw it."

"He's the only one?"

"He threatened to cut his throat as well."

"There were a lot of people in that bar, correct?"

"Yes."

"And you're telling this jury the only person in the whole wide world that saw this brandy snifter was Mr. Kelly? Is that your testimony?"

"Yes."

"But Mr. Kelly testified he left the bar early and was not present at the time of the shooting. Is Mr. Kelly lying?"

"I know what I saw," Dempsey said, averting his gaze and studying his hands.

On cross examination, Jubinville, Dempsey's attorney, basically replayed Dempsey's side of the story: that he shot White in self-defense, that he'd had no other choice, that his escape to Canada was driven by a fear of not receiving a fair trial in Boston, that after *eleven years* of running, of hiding and lying, he *now* wanted to do the right thing. It didn't sound plausible. There was no punchline, no reflective consideration of the facts, no reason for sympathy that could have swayed the jury.

Our judicial system is far from perfect. Juries are made up of people driven by emotion. Regardless of the evidence, a strong closing argument can potentially sway a jury's determination. A good lawyer can make a jury pause, become emotionally charged, and even create doubt. It's the ultimate sales pitch.

"The only thing you were thinking about was protecting yourself. Isn't that fair to say?" Broker demanded, nearing the end of what had been a truly merciless interrogation.

"At that time, I wasn't thinking," Dempsey said.

"And isn't that what you're doing today, sir? Looking out for yourself?"

"I'm testifying to the truth, Ms. Broker."

"The truth. You're here to save your neck, aren't you?"

Broker continued to question Dempsey relentlessly, demanding to know how he'd gotten up to Maine and Canada in the first place, where he'd gotten his phony driver's license, and where he'd procured all his cash.

"I have nothing further, Your Honor," Ms. Broker announced.

The judge leaned forward, "Mr. Jubinville?"

"Nothing further," Mr. Jubinville grunted in reply.

"You may step down, Mr. Dempsey," the judge said. "Any further witnesses, Mr. Jubinville?"

"No. The defense rests."

The judge looked back at Broker. "Anything further from the Commonwealth?"

"No, Your Honor. The Commonwealth rests."

For her closing statement, Broker took her time with the jury. She asked its members to go back and replay each witness' statement in their minds, to look for inconsistencies in their testimony, and then decide.

"Is that witness telling the truth? Most importantly, you're going to ask yourself: Does the witness have a reason to make it up or lie? Because that's what you are best at—your collective common sense is most useful for finding the truth, dismissing the lies. Because Ronald Mior was a lie, and I suggest to you that Jack Dempsey is a *liar*. Ronald Mior lied. He lived a lie because it was to his benefit to do so. Only when he is backed into a corner does he tell the truth. I suggest that he realizes now that he is in yet another corner here, and so he creates another lie, a lie of self-defense.

"You heard Mr. Jubinville say he lied, and saw him shrug his shoulders, as if to say, *No big deal*. He became Mr. Mior simply because he lied. His whole life for the last *eleven years* has been a lie, and he continues that strategy here in this court. One of the things you can't do is to make your verdict based on any sympathy, bias, prejudice, or speculation. Base your verdict simply on what you've heard in the courtroom. I suppose it would be nice to think, *Well, this was eleven years ago. That's a long time ago. A lot has gone on since. And we could just shrug our shoulders.*

"But you can't do that because Edward White is *dead*. We can't simply shrug our shoulders and forget. If you believe Mr. Dempsey's testimony, that he acted in excessive self-defense, then your verdict needs to be manslaughter. But I'll also say to you, if you find this man a liar and that he lied to you, then you *must* dismiss his testimony. And, based on the evidence you have heard, your verdict *must* be guilty of murder."

On April 6, 1992, by a jury of his peers, Clyde "Jack" Dempsey was found guilty of carrying an illegal firearm, and guilty of committing murder in the second degree. Before Dempsey left the courtroom, he was made to listen to a handwritten, heart-breaking statement from the White family, read by Broker:

> *No parent wants to outlive one of their children. Only a mother or father who has lost a child, no matter what age, knows how devastating this loss truly is. It's a part of you that is gone and can never be replaced. To know he is healthy and strong when he leaves for work in the morning, and then to get that nightmarish phone call that he's gone—and all in a senseless shooting . . . It's a feeling that's indescribable.*
>
> *It's not something that goes away in a few months or a year. It takes forever. Only some of the pain goes away—and only very, very gradually.*
>
> *It also takes a toll on the rest of the family. Edward's three brothers and sisters have felt a terrible loss. They were all close growing up, playing sports together, working and enjoying life. And then, all of a sudden, it's all over. A large part of them is now lost.*
>
> *Thank you for permitting us the opportunity to*

*make a statement to this honorable court. The jury has spoken, and now you must impose a sentence. Edward White's family stands before you today and prays that you impose the maximum sentence possible under our laws.*

*On July 1, 1981, our son and brother, then only 24 years old, was brutally murdered in cold blood by the defendant, Clyde Dempsey. The defendant fled to Canada to evade the United States' judicial system. While in Canada, he illegally established himself as a Canadian citizen and became an entrepreneur in real estate. Newspaper accounts of activities in Canada indicate that he amassed and then lost a sizable fortune.*

*During the past eleven years, the defendant has enjoyed his freedom. Edward was not permitted this luxury of life, of living. Tens of thousands of man-hours and an abundance of thousands of dollars have been expended in the investigation, search, apprehension, and trial of Clyde Dempsey.*

*The action you take today, after eleven years of pain and anguish, may finally put this issue to rest for the White family, but we can never forget that July day when our Edward was brutally murdered by Clyde Dempsey. No more life—no, never, over, done, the end. No more laughing, crying, working, playing, dancing, loving. No more. Never a parent, never get to grow old, grow wise, never to know his full blooming, never. Over are the joys, difficulties, pains, gains, wonders. Over are the benevolent hard works, the forever friendships, the brotherly loves, a son's grin. None. The end.*

*Still so much pain for the living, forever empty, forever lost, forever sorrow, forever anguish for those who knew him. Friends go without. Siblings still sob. Nieces and nephews never knew him. Parents can only endure. And, from his life, we live on with his memories as a guide. Family and friends are much better for having known him. We are here in the service of spirit and the service of others who need to be protected from the man who took his life.*

*As much as we have learned and as much as we have life and love, there is still so much to do. One final step is to remove Clyde Dempsey from society for the maximum term allowable without parole. Even with maximum sentencing, the scales of justice cannot possibly come into balance, for there is still so much for the living and there is no more living for Edward White, our murdered son. No more life. No, never, over, done. The end.*

*Your Honor, we are a law-abiding family with due respect for you, this court, this process. Our family asks, insists, respectfully, that justice be served for our son Edward.*

*Thank you.*

If only the hands of time could be wound back to that terrible night. Imagine either Dempsey or White leaving the club early or becoming lost in deep conversation with a girl, or Dempsey staying longer, sitting at the bar and shooting the breeze with Meany—a thousand different scenarios are possible such that Dempsey and White's violent altercation never took place.

Where and what would they be doing today? As of this writing, White would be fifty-seven years old. Would he be a father? A grandfather? What direction would his life be heading in? Dempsey would be sixty-eight years old. How many young boys would he have been able to help shape into young men? How many kids would have benefited from his coaching and mentoring? How many kids would have gone to college because of Dempsey's commitment to his players? What legacy would he have left for Boston's inner city kids?

For Dempsey and White, sadly, we'll never know.

On April 21, 1992, Dempsey was given a life sentence to be served at Cedar Junction (Walpole) for second degree murder. But before Dempsey was sent to Walpole, he was held at the Nashua Street Jail located in Boston's North End.

On November 6, 1992, at seven-thirty in the morning, Dempsey instigated a jail house riot. Of course, according to Dempsey's statement, that's not what happened. As Dempsey told it, a prisoner got out of his seat to have a cup of coffee, when a guard took the coffee away. So the prisoner reached over and tried to get it back. Suddenly, the guard grabbed the prisoner by the arm. The prisoner winced in pain and told the guard that his arm had just come out of a cast, but the guard continued to put him in "a hold," twisting the man's still-tender arm.

"You're breaking my fucking arm!" the prisoner cried. The prisoner was forced up the stairs, screaming, "You're breaking my arm!"

Dempsey recalled hearing the guard say, "Shut the fuck up—you're going to your cell!"

A number of prisoners stood up and began yelling at the guard to leave the guy alone.

In the dining room, it was a major violation of the rules to stand up at your table. All prisoners needed to be seated at all times. When someone stood up, six to seven guards came running into the dining hall to restore order. After Dempsey stood up, he claimed that he was overrun and knocked to the floor.

"I was put in a headlock, someone had their fingers in my eyes, my arm was twisted behind my back, and a third guard had my legs. I was struck in the face and kicked in the ribs. Someone was straddling me and hitting me in my face."

Dempsey was shackled by the waist and sent to cell thirty-eight, the same cell where Dempsey later claimed he'd been kept shackled and naked for five days.

"I was kept in solitary confinement, cold and without a blanket. I wasn't given any medical attention and, for a week, they only fed me sandwiches and juice."

But according to Rob MacIntosh, a guard working the night shift at the Nashua Jail, there were a few facts missing from Dempsey's account of the story.

"Guards never put their hands on a prisoner. It's against protocol as well as straight-out dangerous to a guard's health. We're simply outnumbered. Guards are trained to communicate with prisoners under the following criteria: Ask, Advise, Order. When an emergency occurs, the SERT"—Severe Emergency Response Team—"is called in to restore order but, in this case, the prisoners held the unit captive and an 'All Call' went out. Approximately forty guards stormed the unit. Dempsey was out of control. He took one of the guards, Chuck Wheeler, knocked him to the ground and bit the upper third of his right ear off. Dempsey knocked another guard unconscious, which sent him to Mass General Hospital. Dempsey was so strong and his bone structure so thick, they couldn't fit the handcuffs around his wrists.

"When I came onto my shift, I could feel something was up," MacIntosh explained. "Everyone seemed to be on edge, even the prisoners." To find out what had happened, MacIntosh naturally turned to his sergeant.

"How you doing, Sarge?"

"Better now that Dempsey's locked up."

"Dempsey? What are you talking about?"

"You haven't heard, Rob?"

"Sarge, I've been working the night shift for four years. I just came on duty fifteen minutes ago. What the hell is going on here?"

"Okay, okay, relax. Everyone is on pins and needles and a little edgy right now. Dempsey incited a riot this morning, and he sent a few guys to the hospital. Jesus, he's a God damn animal. Are you ready for this: He bit Chuck Wheeler's ear off and sent Johnny O'Driscoll unconscious to Mass General. We lost the unit for ten minutes and had to put out an All Call."

"An All Call? Shit, when was the last time Nashua had to do that? It hasn't happened during my time."

"It's been eleven years. The veteran guards were just trying to remember during dinner."

And to add an extra twist to the story, it just so happened that Rob MacIntosh was also the head line coach at Bosco, and that he'd had a strong desire to connect with Dempsey prior to the inmate's arrival at the facility. Rob had played for and later coached with Bob Currier at Bosco. Additionally, Rob's mother had grown up in Brighton and had gone to school with Currier at St Columbkille's.

"My father was built strong," MacIntosh said, "but it was my mother who was the tough one in the family. She was a Marine during the Korean War. She was so tough that years later, after we moved to Charlestown, she had a heart attack and *walked* to Mass General Hospital.

"But what really made me want to connect with Dempsey was a desire to pick his brain on coaching, on teaching the offensive and defensive linemen. I had heard of Dempsey for years while at Bosco. In 1992, Skip would take over as head coach at Bosco and all I heard was 'Dempsey would do it this way.' 'Dempsey would do it that way.' 'We'll do it the way Dempsey did.'"

"Where's Dempsey held up, Sarge?" Rob asked.

"Cell number thirty-eight. Why?"

"How long has he been locked up?"

"Since eight-thirty this morning."

"Sarge, give me the keys, will ya?"

"Give you the keys for what?"

"I think I can reach Dempsey."

"Reach Dempsey! Are you out of your mind? The guy will kill you."

But MacIntosh was adamant. Grabbing the keys and donning a Bosco football jacket, MacIntosh made his way to cell number thirty-eight.

"Are you Jack Dempsey?"

"Why?"

"We have a mutual friend."

"Yeah? Who's that?"

"Bob Currier."

Dempsey, looking out his window at the pedestrians on the street, responded, "How do you know, Bob?"

"I played for Bob at Don Bosco and later coached with him."

But when Dempsey finally turned to him, it wasn't as an old high school football coach, recalls MacIntosh. "When our eyes first met, I felt like I was looking into the eyes of Satan. But then

Dempsey saw my football jacket and, instantly, he transformed into Dempsey the coach."

"What do you want?" Dempsey asked.

"I wanted to know if I could pick your brain about coaching both sides of the line."

"Well, nice to meet you," Dempsey said, extending a hand. "Pull up a chair."

"And although I was nervous," MacIntosh said, "realizing this guy could kill me at any moment, I spent the next five-and-a-half hours in his cell. During that time, I learned more about coaching football than I have in thirty years. I stood up to leave, ready to lock Dempsey in. His closing statement will stay with me as long as I live: 'Remember, the secret to great coaching is loving your kids.'"

# Reconnecting

*"We did it all together—teacher, teammate, brother.*
*Love, Coach Dempsey"*

While Dempsey was on the run in Canada, I and my teammates were still on the treadmill of life attempting to make something of ourselves. We had gone our separate ways and, for the most part, lost contact with one another.

A year after Dempsey killed White, I was back at Bosco coaching with Currier. I knew very few of the specifics of Dempsey's fatal encounter at Mr. McNasty's. All I knew was that Dempsey was in Canada and that he occasionally had contact with Currier. There were even rumors that he drifted back into Boston from time to time. We all acknowledged that the death of White was a game changer for Dempsey. All of the legendary street fights and romantic tales about Dempsey collecting for the mob were now put aside, tainted and darker. And we all knew, no matter how it pained us, that Dempsey now would never be able to coach, mentor, or inspire kids again.

I had ended my football career in 1980 when the Hyde Park

Cowboys won their third championship in five years in the Eastern League of New England. In 1981, I went into business for myself, applying all the skills and determination I'd learned from football to become a parking lot maintenance contractor. I'd made plenty of mistakes, but I'd gained two core gifts given me by football: perseverance and commitment. I wouldn't accept being defeated, although I didn't spend too much time looking back.

It's hard to recall exactly what I thought of Dempsey during this period in my life. I'm sure I put his act of murder into a place and framework that worked best for me. Dempsey's actions went too far, of course, but perhaps he'd been justified somehow. Maybe the guy he shot had been a bad guy—just like all those borrowers he'd once told me about. Maybe the guy he'd shot had known the rules of the game but simply refused to play by them. Maybe Dempsey had just been performing some kind of street or mob justice I couldn't understand.

I had no knowledge of White, so it was easy to create a character or personality that justified Dempsey's deciding to kill him. It wasn't difficult for me to root for "Street Dempsey" and somehow glorify his being on the run.

Regardless of how I portrayed Dempsey, he was still rooted deep within me. I coached football for a number of years at different schools and, when I did, I was Dempsey. The same speeches, the same connecting of lessons learned on the field to lessons learned in life, and, of course, the same endless mantra: *Size means nothing in football. It's all about quickness, technique, and desire.*

The more I coached, the more I felt drawn to make a change in my life. I decided to work with kids full-time. So, in 1990, I sold my business and returned to school at the University of Maine to pursue a degree in teaching. While working out in the gym, I shared some Dempsey stories with a few fellow students with whom I'd become friendly. I was in my thirties, and they were much younger—

somewhere in their early twenties. When I told them about Dempsey, they had looks on their faces I knew all too well: shock, surprise, and awe. It made for great theater, and I loved playing my part.

Before the Christmas break, one of my lifting buddies, Kapoula Thompson, found me leaving the library.

"Hey, Kev, did you catch *America's Most Wanted* this evening?"

"No, why?"

"Your coach—that Dempsey guy you told us about—he was the featured fugitive! They talked about him coaching at Don Bosco and how all the players loved him. They think he's on the run in Canada."

It was only after Dempsey had been caught, tried, and sentenced to Walpole that I suddenly felt the gravity of White's murder. Even so, a life sentence for Dempsey was impossible for me to comprehend.

"I just can't believe that he'll spend the rest of his life in prison!" I said, shaking my head incredulously as my parents listened to the entire, wild tale.

"Dempsey will handle Walpole with no problem," my father said, laughing as he glanced through the *Boston Globe*. "Give him some time and he'll be running the place."

The funny thing was, I didn't laugh back. Instead, I could only turn and walk away, conflicted.

What did Dempsey really mean to me after all these years?

In April of 1996, the 1974 Bosco champions finally got some well-deserved recognition. We were inducted into the Bosco Hall of Fame. For me, it was a highlight month: I married my wife, Xiaofeng, on April 7; ran the Boston Marathon on April 15; and capped it all off on April 29 by gathering with old teammates I'd not seen in twenty-one years. But while our head coach stood with us for many of the photos, we all felt the discomfort and strangeness of knowing that our beloved line coach was locked up behind bars.

Unfortunately for me, I was unable to spend much time reconnecting with my teammates. My wife and I had to work the next morning and had a two-hour drive back to Deerfield. So, after some quick handshakes and photos, I was out the door.

My wife and I settled in beautiful western Massachusetts. We started a family, and both began to work in education. Xioafeng taught Chinese at Deerfield Academy (a world-famous private school) and I became the Assistant Principal of Deerfield Elementary School, a public school. Life was good for the Kellys.

But then another rock dropped into the Bosco pond: in 1998, after forty-three years of educating and shaping the lives of thousands of inner city kids, Bosco closed its doors.

Immediately, I was back in 1974. My teachers, teammates, coaches, the championship year—all of it wiped out and gone forever in one quick swipe.

I realized then that we—*my* team—would forever own the distinction as the only Bosco team to ever win the Catholic Conference. I also realized that we were going to evaporate into obscurity if we didn't do something soon to preserve this legacy. I decided then and there that I wasn't going to allow our memory and achievements to slip away, and the first person I knew I needed to contact was Coach Dempsey.

Sitting in my office, I wrote Dempsey a letter. It was a perfect, cloudless spring morning, the air was crisp, and the sun shone brightly through my office windows. Tulips—red, yellow and purple—were pushing up through the ground. A dogwood tree was budding dark red, and the birds sounded like a symphony warming up before a concert. Reclining amid all this idyllic scenery and beauty, I wondered what Dempsey was doing, seeing, and hearing at that same moment in his prison cell. What was he thinking about? What beauty was in his life? Would he remember who I was or even care?

*Dear Coach Dempsey,*

*I hope this letter finds you well.*

*You may not remember me, but my name is Kevin Kelly and I played for you at Don Bosco and was part of the '74 championship team. We also won a championship together as teammates in '76 with the Hyde Park Cowboys.*

*I have coached high school football off and on over the last twelve years, and have had the opportunity to work alongside many accomplished coaches. However, I have never before met anyone who coached line technique with your level of knowledge. You were an outstanding motivator and teacher to me. The smallest details were always addressed: stance work, reading the opponent's body, watching for shifts in a lineman's stance, focusing on the lineman's hand for quickness off the line. You punched into us that the average play lasts only three and a half seconds, and that if you can't give a hundred percent for three and half seconds, go play tennis! And, most importantly, you drilled into us that size means nothing in the game of football. It's all about quickness, technique, and desire.*

*I teach all of these strategies and principles as a coach today.*

*I can't help but reflect on the number of high school players who've missed the opportunity to have you as their coach. I, along with many other Bosco players, feel that our championship never would have happened if we hadn't had you as part of the coaching staff. You and Coach Currier were the perfect balance.*

*I'm planning to write a book on the '74 Bosco team and feel that you and your life story are a critical part of that story. With your permission, I'd like to come and visit you for an interview.*

*Looking forward to hearing from you.*

*Respectfully,*

*Kevin Kelly*

A few weeks later, I received the following letter from Coach Dempsey:

*Dear Kevin,*

*Great to hear from you and of course I remember you. The '74 season was one of the most enjoyable and satisfying years of my coaching career. The memories of the players and coaches coming together for a common goal will stay with me for the rest of my life.*

*I'm also glad to hear that you are coaching. The "ME" athlete is so difficult to watch on TV. The pros are hurting the purity of the game. Playing with an unselfish attitude, sacrificing for the good of the team, and connecting the lessons learned on the field to the real world, all seem to be fading.*

*Keep the game pure!*

*You are the only player that I ever celebrated championships with as both coach and teammate!*

*Write the book!*
*We did it all together,*
*Teacher,*
*Teammate,*
*Brother,*
*Love,*
*Coach Dempsey*

Later, as I sat in my comfortable office looking out my window, taking in all the beautiful sights and sounds, I thought of my coach sitting in his dirty, tiny cell in Walpole. I was stunned and emotionally moved by what I'd just read. The letter brought tears to my eyes. *What a tremendous waste!* I thought, suddenly overwhelmed. *A waste of talent, a waste of potential and, mostly, a waste of a life! How could he have thrown it all away?*

Dempsey had self-destructed—taking drugs, committing murder, breaking every rule in the book while evading arrest in Canada, and all to end up with a life sentence in prison.

Yet here he was, writing me as if from the back porch of his childhood home; reflective, insightful, and caring. He worried about the future of his sport and about those who played it. Where had *this* Dempsey been during those critical moments back at McNasty's?

A few months went by before I wrote Dempsey again to set a date for our interview. In the meantime, I decided to meet with Currier. Currier was a man who, if nothing else, could always be depended upon for the truth—and the truth was just what I needed. After all, though I was by then a mature, mid-forties adult, there was still that part of me that wanted to see Dempsey through the eyes of my eighteen-year-old self. And Currier knew it.

"Kevin, I know you're excited to see Dempsey, and I know you're going to look at him only as your coach," Currier said, reading me with stunning ease. "But be careful. Coach Dempsey is only part of who he truly is. There's a dangerous and unpredictable Dempsey as well. You have a family. If Dempsey gets out of prison, he'll gravitate to those he can reach out to. Ask yourself: If Dempsey were at your door and told you he needed a place to stay, would you invite him to live with you and your family? How would you get him to leave if he overstayed his welcome or became unstable?"

Coach Currier sobered me up. He was absolutely right. I needed to keep my emotional distance from Dempsey.

Dempsey had recently appealed his case. There'd been some sticky, legal loophole for him—the judge may not have correctly explained to the jury the differences between murder one, murder two, and manslaughter. Dempsey and his lawyers were convinced that his verdict would be overturned. If so, he could be free within four years.

No matter how I felt about Dempsey, I had to admit that he was a master manipulator. And, for my family's sake, I couldn't afford to get sucked into his world.

So I let more time pass and didn't worry much about why Dempsey hadn't yet responded to my last letter. My life as a school administrator was busy enough as it was, and, besides, being a dad and husband were my first priorities.

It wasn't until the fall of 2001 that I prepared to mail out my next letter to Dempsey. First, however, I called Walpole to make sure that Dempsey was still there—I was told it was not unusual for prisoners to be rotated periodically from prison to prison across the state of Massachusetts.

"Hi, I'm just calling to see if Jack Dempsey is still being held at Walpole."

"Do you mean Clyde Dempsey from Allston Brighton?" asked the operator.

"That's the one," I said, laughing to myself. Why had I assumed that the operator would automatically know who Dempsey was? His legend didn't stretch *that* far!

"Clyde Dempsey died last month. Are you a relative?"

My heart fell. How was this possible? Coach Dempsey dead?

I felt a sudden, tremendous guilt settle upon me. I felt selfish. I wondered who'd been with Dempsey when he took his last breath. How had he died? Why hadn't I tried to visit him sooner? During his many years locked up in Walpole, some of my teammates had. If I hadn't thought of writing the book, and if Bosco hadn't closed its doors, would I even have thought to visit Dempsey at all?

The answer was painful: probably not.

As a player and teammate, I'd idolized *Coach* Dempsey. But, like my beloved mother before her death, I'd pushed aside *Street* Dempsey, *Dark* Dempsey, *Depressed and Angry* Dempsey, into whatever compartment had worked best for me. I'd felt comfortable remembering the man who'd coached me and whom I adored in high school and after. I'd relished the memories of playing a glorious year with him as a teammate. And I honestly hadn't wanted to see Dempsey behind bars.

Would he have felt humiliated by such a visit, or had I just been too afraid of recognizing my coach for the murderer he was?

Either way, I'd made it work in my mind. It was the easy way out.

As I struggled with the news, I found that I also felt robbed—I hadn't gotten the chance to speak with him one last time. I hadn't gotten the chance to give him a voice through this book, or to thank him again for all he'd done for me.

I had wanted to discuss his childhood at length, to know more about his relationship with his father, his mother, and his friends. I had wanted to dig into his past so I could better understand the devastating decisions he'd made after I graduated from Bosco. What had driven Dempsey to be so disciplined in one area of his life (football and coaching) but be so dramatically chaotic and destructive in others?

I had wanted to ask the tough questions about what really happened between him and White. Had they really known each other prior to that July night? Had Dempsey been on cocaine that evening? What ultimately made him pull out his gun, and why the hell had he pulled the trigger three times? I wanted to know if he regretted that evening. I wanted to know if the statement made by White's family, read in court prior to sentencing, had troubled him. I wanted to know if the reflective and mentoring Dempsey could speak to the Dempsey who had so completely failed to live as he'd always instructed us to.

Could Dempsey look into the mirror and be honest with me? Could he look in the mirror then, in his prison cell, and even be honest with himself? Coach, Collector, Friend, Teammate, Dempsey, Mior, Murderer, Prisoner—who *was* he exactly?

Finally, I had to accept the reality that I'd missed the chance to see my coach one last time. I had to accept the reality that one of the most influential men in my life was now dead.

Later that year, I called the legendary Will McDonough, sports columnist for the *Boston Globe* and color analyst for ESPN. I was looking to speak to Steve DeOssie. Steve had played for Bosco and was the only player from our school to ever make it to the pro level. Recently retired, DeOssie was just beginning his career as a local sports announcer for the Patriots. I was hoping to get a statement from Steve about his relationship with and views on Dempsey. So when McDonough asked why I was looking for DeOssie's number, I dove right into the meat of the story and how I was writing a book about Don Bosco's '74 team and our legendary coach.

"Who was your coach?" McDonough asked.

"Jack Dempsey from Brighton."

"You mean Jack Dempsey from Boston English? Kevin, I attended Boston English and was a three-star athlete there. I later coached Dempsey when he played football for English!"

I laughed directly into the phone. I couldn't help myself. "Is there anyone in Boston who *doesn't* know this guy?"

"Jack Dempsey was, pound for pound, one of the toughest and most talented football players ever to come out of Massachusetts," McDonough said. "Boy, was he one hell of a tough kid!"

"Coming from you, Will, someone who's seen decades of top-flight athletes in Massachusetts, that's one hell of a compliment!"

After a few months passed, I sat down, pulled out my yearbook, and opened it up to the football section. As I looked over the photo of my old teammates, I realized that over thirty-eight years had passed us by. Don Bosco had held no reunions and, with many of my old teammates, I'd lost total contact. *Where are these guys now?* I wondered. *What have they done with their lives? What went through their minds if and when they heard about Dempsey's death?*

I was determined to find out.

# CLOSURE

*"If our Bosco experience gave us anything, it allowed us to believe that if we could survive playing football at Bosco, we could survive anything in life."*
—Al Libardoni

Googling old teammates and catching up with people-who-knew-people, I set to work tracking down the '74 team. From 2001 to 2003, I touched base with Al Libardoni, Coach Currier, and Peter Masciola, and though time and life dimmed my commitment to write the story, Max Williams wouldn't let me quit or let the book die. Throughout the first decade of the new millennium, Max would call often from his home in Los Angeles.

"Kev, how's the Dempsey story coming?"

"Max, I haven't written much, but every time I tell the story about Dempsey, Bosco, his *America's Most Wanted* appearance, and the '74 team, people always have the same response: 'Boy, you should write a book!' It doesn't matter if they're young or old, male or female—everyone's response is always the same."

"I'm telling you, Kev, *stay with it*."

The problem was, I wasn't a writer. As a matter of fact, writing was (and is to this day) my biggest weakness. I was intimidated by the very notion of trying to write it all down and couldn't see the forest through the trees. It seemed a herculean task.

Then finally, in 2010, Max had had enough.

"Kev, I'm coming out there. Either you write the story now or you never will. Try to find as many players as you can."

A few weeks later, Max came to Boston just as he'd promised, and a handful of us met near the Charles River. It would be the first of four meetings, with each meeting successfully growing in number of players found. Over the next three years (and with the help of a fairly large number of people), I slowly began locating all of my teammates from the '74 team.

In 2010, through Richie Moran, I found Skip Bandini.

"Kev, Skip is head coach at Curry College, my alma mater. I've even attended a few coaching clinics with Skip."

Skip had likewise stayed in touch with Frank Marchione.

Then a lifelong friend of mine from Hyde Park, Jack Shea, came forward, saying, "Hey, Kev, I met this guy who's playing in a band with my brother, Rick. He said he played ball with you at Bosco."

"No kidding! What's his name?"

"Vinny O'Brien."

And, just like that, I had Vinny on the phone.

"Hey, Vinny! Geez, how the hell are you?"

"Great, Kev! I'm married with three boys, all grown up and doing well. I hear through Jack that you're writing a book on the '74 team."

"I'm really trying to track down as many of the guys as possible. We haven't seen each other in so many years, though, so it's difficult to know where to begin. I assume we're located all over the country. One guy no one seems to have heard from is Abe Benitez. I wonder whatever happened to him."

"Ha! You wanna talk to Abe? I have his number. We've often played music together over the last ten years."

I would later discover that Vinny lived down the street from Ski. Ski had access to Chester Rodriguez, our wide receiver and defensive back, who was living in North Carolina. Chester and I spoke over the phone, but he was the one player who showed no interest in reconnecting with us. It was a shame, I thought. He'd always been talented, well-liked, and highly respected by his teammates.

As for Chris Staub, I simply Googled him and got lucky.

"Hi, I'm sorry to bother you, but does a Chris Staub live here?"

"Who's calling, please?"

"This could be an old friend, Mrs. Staub. Did your husband attend Don Bosco?"

"Why, yes he did."

I also had an old number for Paul Carouso and hoped he still lived in Somerville (he did!).

I had contact information for Tommy "Yogi" McGregor from my hometown of Hyde Park, as well as for Eddie Dominguez. Eddie was now working as a Boston cop and had kept in touch with John Sylva, now a Massachusetts State Trooper.

Eddie also knew how to get in touch with Colie McGillivary, who lived in Dorchester. Colie, adding his own link to the chain, had contact information for Shawn Murphy. While having lunch with Colie and Shawn at the Holiday Inn in Dedham, I wondered aloud, "Whatever happened to Billy Elwell?"

"Billy Elwell?" Shawn said, grinning. "He lives in Tewksbury."

"Jesus," I said. "No kidding! I can't believe we're finding so many of us so quickly."

"I think Stevie Riley still lives in Dedham, Kev," Colie chimed in. "He used to live off Route 1. His house should only be about three miles from here."

"Have you heard from Cemate?"

"Last I heard, Cemate was in Atlanta. I wonder if Sylva can track Craig down."

It wasn't long after that before I was yet again on the phone and on the hunt.

"Hello, is this Craig Cemate?"

"Who's calling, please?"

"I'm an old teammate of Craig's. May I ask who I'm speaking with?"

"Yes, I'm his son."

"Well, is your dad home?"

"Yes, but who should I say is calling?"

I couldn't help myself: "Tell your dad the MVP lineman from the '74 Bosco team is on the phone looking for the MVP running back!"

"Last I heard of Gary Green, he was living in Reading," Craig said, the both of us still high from all our reminiscing and joshing around. "He works for the Post Office."

"Reading?" I said. "Jack Shea lives in Reading!"

"Hey, Jack, do you know a Gary Green?'

"You mean the mailman?"

Gary and I connected via email, and he forwarded me an old phone number belonging to Richie Abner, one of our linemen (and a lineman whom Dempsey had particularly loved. His physical size and build resembled Dempsey's from his high school days).

Sadly, I also discovered that one of the brotherhood, Derrick Martini, had died in 2007. Derrick had been short and powerful. He was part Samoan and part Italian, with jet black hair, a million dollar smile, and a thick, muscular body. He'd made one hell of a nose guard. Over the years, however, he'd put on a large amount of weight and died of a heart attack at the still youthful age of forty-eight.

That left only our lineman, Jerome Frazier, and our inside linebacker, Eddie Trask, to locate. I had one phone number for a Jerome Frazier living in Dorchester. I called that number many times over a six-month period, only to hear the phone ring and ring, and never even reaching an answering machine.

Eddie Trask, on the other hand, simply hadn't been heard from in years.

Eddie wasn't always the easiest guy to warm up to. He had a surly disposition, but he had been one great linebacker. Eddie was plagued with injuries throughout his playing career, but he never missed a game. He'd come lumbering up to the field looking like a mummy, with yards of white athletic tape wrapped around his body. It must've taken about forty-five minutes just to tape him up for a game.

"Eddie and I were good friends," Chris reflected, "and hung out with each other after high school. At one point, we were even going to join the Marines together. But then we slowly lost contact with each other. Last I heard, he was living in Plymouth."

It was rumored that Eddie had been in a bad fight that had left the other guy dead and Eddie in prison. In January of 2013, I found three Eddie Trasks living in Massachusetts, but none from Plymouth. I wasn't very optimistic, but I had nothing to lose, so I hand wrote a letter to all three. I let them know that if they'd attended Don Bosco and been a member of the '74 team, then we were holding a reunion and would love for him to join us. I left my contact information and crossed my fingers.

I quickly heard back from two Eddie Trasks, both informing me they had never attended Don Bosco but wishing me luck in my search. There was never a response from the third letter, so Eddie was out. I was disappointed. I knew the guys would love to see him. Everyone I interviewed remembered Eddie warmly. His commitment to the team (and the way he'd made two crushing tackles on the one-yard line against CM) kept him rich and fresh in everyone's memories.

As I sat in my office and checked over the team photo, I was shocked to discover that we had found almost every starter from the '74 Bosco Bears. It was a remarkable feat that, perhaps not so ironically, had taken a team effort to accomplish.

I realized then how much I'd loved searching, finding, connecting with, and interviewing the players from the '74 team. I had always held the deepest admiration and respect for them.

In February of 2013, the reunion for the '74 Championship team was set. Thirty-nine years had passed and yet there we were—twenty-three players, along with Coach Currier and Al Libardoni's brother, Billy (an assistant coach during the '74 season)—all finally in the same room again.

Skip had offered to hold the reunion at Curry College. "If we're going to do this," he'd said, "then let's do it right. I don't want this to be some drunk-fest with no meaning. I want each guy to get up, talk about what Bosco meant to them, how Dempsey impacted their lives, and what the championship means to them today."

Skip ordered new game jerseys for all of us, so everyone got to wear their old high school team number at the reunion.

Then, three days before the reunion, we got the news I'd feared most: A major snowstorm was predicted to hit New England the day of our planned gathering. Three players were flying in, their tickets already purchased. Some of the guys would have to drive hours to get to Curry College. Bruce Bortz, my publisher, who had stuck by my side for years believing in the Dempsey story, also had reservations to fly in with his wife from Baltimore to meet the team members.

It had taken *months* to coordinate this day, and for many, this was a one-shot deal. Fortunately, we were, by this time, all connected by group email. So, the night before the reunion, Abe, who would have to drive a particularly long distance, sent the group an email I dreaded to read: "Kev, if it snows too hard, are we canceling the reunion or do we have a back-up date?"

My thinking was not to have anyone drive in potentially dangerous conditions, no matter how badly I wanted us to reconnect. But then Frankie Marchione stepped in and, in true Marchione style, sent everyone the following reply: "What the fuck is wrong with us? When did a little snow ever stop us from practicing down at Science Park? We're from *New England* for Christ's sake! Everyone BE THERE!"

I was up by five-thirty the next morning. After a stop for breakfast, I was heading toward my car and going over my mental "To Do" list, when suddenly my phone rang. "Hi, is this Kevin Kelly?"

"Yes, it is. Who's calling please?"

"Kev, this is Eddie Trask. I received your letter. Not sure how you found me, but it was nice to hear from you!"

I almost fainted.

"Eddie?" I said, floored. "Jesus, I can't believe we found you! How the hell are you?"

"Everything's going well. I'm married, and we have a terrific daughter. Unfortunately, I have a family obligation and can't make the reunion today, but please tell everyone I said hello and wish them the best."

What a feeling! *Three years!* We had done our best to search out and find the entire '74 team and, by February 16, 2013, we had done it!

I stopped by Dedham to pick up Stevie Riley, and we both headed over to Curry College together. As I pulled into the lot, I was both excited and nervous. Slowly, players started to show up. We gathered first in Skip's smallish office, exchanging hugs and slaps on the back. And, finally, by three o'clock, we were all together again. Every player wore their new Bosco football jersey, and everyone looked terrific.

Eddie Dominguez couldn't make the reunion, but he had shocked all of us by handing over the '74 Championship banner to Peter Masciola. That banner hadn't been seen by many of us for close to forty years. We laid it out on the floor and stared at it in total silence.

Settling back into our memories and old friendships, I made a simple request: "Fellas, I purchased twenty-three footballs. You'll notice that each ball has '1974 Catholic Conference Champions' written on its side. If you could take a minute and sign each ball, then each of us will have a team ball with every player's signature."

After the ball signing, we all took a seat in Curry's football film room. It was a small auditorium, but perfect for our occasion. Then, one at a time, each player got up and shared how he'd picked Bosco as a school. He described his football experience and his memories of and relationship with Dempsey, and, of course, his recollections of our championship season. Something special started to emerge that was totally unplanned; players started to share not only where they'd come from, but their families and how they'd lived as kids, how they'd scraped by and fought their way through one mess after another. Players reflected on their adult journeys to success and how all of it was directly tied to the lessons we'd learned on the football field.

All of us sat transfixed as each player got up and spoke.

It started to become obvious that the seniors and juniors had had two significantly different experiences playing football at Bosco.

The seniors had two miserable seasons with no team unity. Playing football at Bosco had been a challenge, and the negativity that'd hung over us going into our senior year had been palpable. We'd had few indications that we were special in any way or that we'd even be competitive. The juniors, though, were *champions!* They'd confidently walked into their senior year on fire. They'd known who they were from the start, and then gone out and proved it.

First to speak up was Paul Carouso.

"My older brother, Richie, played with Kevin's older brother on the '69 team. So attending Bosco was an easy choice for me. I remember going to camp as a freshman weighing about a hundred and twenty pounds, and getting pancaked by Bruce McDonald.

"By the end of my sophomore year, however, I never doubted that we could be something special. I simply loved playing."

But what kept our undivided attention wasn't the power of Paul's honesty, but the knowledge of Paul's personal history. Paul had always been a gifted running back and an intelligent, hard-hitting defensive back. He'd served as captain his senior year and had had dreams of playing in college. But then the summer of his senior year, he was struck by a hit-and-run driver and left for dead. Both legs were amputated and, as if that wasn't enough, his younger brother had died only a year prior, a young life taken by an arsonist's fire. When asked if he held any bitterness to the hand he was dealt, he replied simply, "Are you kidding? Every day is a gift to me! I'm lucky to have lived, and I've never forgotten that. Never will."

"I was also driven by the worry I felt for my father," Paul continued, captivating us all. "We had eight kids in my family. We lost our mother early, and my dad struggled to keep everything together. Then suddenly, within one year, we lost our brother and I lost both my legs. The look of worry and hurt on my father's face was a constant, and it bothered me terribly. I was determined not to become a burden to my father. I was desperate to prove to him that I was alright. I biked, swam, skied, mountain climbed—I was driving my doctors crazy—but it gave me purpose and took some of the burden off my father."

Following Carouso at the rostrum was Abe Benitez. Abe's father had been a factory worker in Boston for thirty-five years and, although there was freedom for him and his family in America that they hadn't known in Cuba, it was still an economic struggle for his family of six. Being a non-white with a Spanish accent didn't open many doors for the senior Mr. Benitez, either. For Abe, watching his father struggle in America was difficult, but sports, and especially football, gave him the opportunity to escape and vent his aggression.

"It was therapy. It was stability. I mean, growing up at home was unnerving. My father, who has always been a good man, was a different person when he drank. His drinking brought fear to all of us at home, like being at the edge of a cliff on a windy day. I will always love my papa for all the good and realism that he taught me—I would not change my past for anything. I am who I am, in large part because of him. But those times—they were hard, and Bosco gave me what I needed. Bosco gave me a taste of how greatness is born from within and of how to keep that fire burning."

Abe always carried himself with class. After Bosco, he received his CPA from Bentley and now manages six billion dollars for an investment firm. What's more, Abe's married, and is the father of two daughters.

Ski, our team's quarterback, was next to speak. Ski entered Bosco during his junior year and, though he'd never played quarterback before in his life, he led us to our greatest football run in the school's history, an 18-2 record, during the first two seasons of his career. Ski was also a standout baseball player, but it was hockey that landed him a four-year scholarship to Boston College. During his freshman year there, Ski was drafted by the NHL's Philadelphia Flyers, but upon his mother's request, he stayed at BC and finished his college education.

"Of all my accomplishments at the college level and of all the teams I played for, nothing has meant more to me than the '74 season and winning the Catholic Conference Championship."

It was a statement that surprised many of us but, deep down, we got it. The championship had unlocked a well of confidence in each of us.

Ski now works for an investment firm, is married, and has three children, all of whom are outstanding athletes.

Next was Frank Marchione. By the time Frank arrived at Bosco, he had established himself as a clean-cut kid and a hard-hitting football player. Even so, he got himself into some trouble during his senior year and, not long before graduation, was expelled. Lost and confused, and with parents devastated by the expulsion, Frankie wasn't sure where to turn. Once again, it was Dempsey who jumped in, feet first, to rescue one of his boys.

Dempsey immediately took it upon himself to haul Frankie up to East Boston High and demand a diploma.

"Hi, how can I help you?" asked the school secretary.

"We're here to see the assistant principal, Johnny Bartiloni," Dempsey said.

"Is he expecting you?"

"No ma'am, but you can tell him that Jack Dempsey needs to see him."

Just like that, Dempsey was meeting with the assistant principal.

"Jack, how the hell are you? It's been what? Ten years? What in God's name are you doing here?"

"Listen, I have a good kid here who got into a little trouble. He just got kicked out of Bosco. You need to take him in for the last few weeks of the semester so he can graduate from East Boston."

What else is there to say to such a demand but: "Are you nuts? There's no way he can receive a diploma with just three weeks of school left—you know that. He needs to be enrolled for over thirty days or he has to repeat next year."

"Johnny, listen, that's not an option," Dempsey said flatly. "You need to work with me on this. I'm not taking no for an answer. This boy is bright and has a future, and I don't want to lose him to the street."

Frankie, meanwhile, sat uncomfortably, alone, outside the assistant principal's office, listening to the slow escalation of voices out through the door.

"All I heard was a lot of yelling," Frankie later told me, "and most of it was coming from Dempsey. Three weeks later, I graduated from East Boston High School. I didn't take a single exam, and most of my teachers were just getting to learn my name."

Frank subsequently embarked upon a colorful and fantastic journey, working as a bar owner in Arizona, a mud engineer in Wyoming, and then as a successful entrepreneur in the restaurant business.

Peter Marciola, our tailback, went on to play hockey at Stonehill College. After Stonehill, he went to law school and became a military lawyer with the Air Force, achieving the rank of General. At the age of fifty-four, he became the oldest ranking officer serving in Afghanistan.

"Football gave me my foundation," Peter told us. "Football is very much like the military in some ways, except that, in the military, the consequences are real. But the togetherness—everyone with the same common goal and working together as a team—that leadership came to me from football. The synergy that makes a group successful is a powerful connection. The discipline I learned at Bosco, I took with me into the courtroom and into Afghanistan."

John Sylva stepped forward after Marciola.

"I wasn't sure how a freshman was going to be received by varsity players," he recalled. "But I've never forgotten the support

BOTH SIDES OF THE LINE

and endless encouragement you all gave me."

Chris Staub, along with teammate Eddie Trask, was thinking of joining the Marines. But when Dempsey found out, he demanded that Chris meet him at Bosco the following Monday. Dempsey, from the passenger seat of his old Chevy Impala, told Chris, "Get in," and Chris hopped in without a word of protest. Chris had never met the guy in the driver's seat. Dempsey and the driver were laughing while sharing war stories about a bar fight in Brighton from the night before. Chris just sat there and listened, clueless as to why and where they were going. Then, after a ninety-minute ride, they pulled into the University of Rhode Island and walked into the football coaches' office. Together, Dempsey and the driver introduced Chris to the head coach.

Dempsey and the URI head coach moved to the far corner of the office and spoke as Chris waited. They looked over at him periodically but never acknowledged him. After several minutes, the coach finally came back, sat behind his desk, folded his arms, and studied Chris carefully. Then, after what seemed like an eternity, the coach spoke, "Alright, I'm going to give you a scholarship from September to January. If you can prove yourself on the field and in the classroom, I'll extend the scholarship for your full freshman year."

Chris was dumbfounded.

When he got home, his parents wanted to know where he'd been all day.

"I was offered a football scholarship to URI!"

Chris' parents were floored. They had ten children and knew there was no way they could ever afford to pay all that college tuition. Chris made it through the entire four-year program and became a football standout, graduating with a business degree. Chris is now an international businessman, traveling and connecting with people from all over the world.

"I can't imagine how my life would have turned out if I had instead entered the military," Chris told me. "What I do know is, if it hadn't been for Coach Dempsey, I never would have had the life I have today."

Vinny O'Brien, who played line at one hundred and fifty pounds and later captained his college team as a running back, graduated from law school and opened his own firm. Vinny is highly successful, but has never forgotten where he came from. Generous, funny, and a talented musician, he's simply a great guy.

By the time he stepped behind the reunion microphone, Skip Bandini had coached football at both the high school and college level, and was then the head football coach of Curry College. An endless giver to his players, to his community, and to the sport he loves, he exemplifies the very best of what *real* coaches stand for.

"One day after my senior year, Dempsey told me out of the clear blue that we were going to go for a ride," Skip told me. "We drove three and half hours to Bridgeton Academy in Maine. Dempsey told me he'd played a postgraduate year at Bridgeton and knew the coach. I had no idea where or what Bridgeton Academy was, but Dempsey showed me around and, after meeting with the coaches, I decided I liked the place and was accepted. I was stunned and wasn't sure exactly what to say. Dempsey told me they were going to give me fifteen hundred dollars towards the school's $3,000 tuition. He asked me if my family could pay the rest, and I told him my mom made three thousand *a year* while trying to bring up two kids alone.

"So I knew, and told him, that paying any amount towards tuition was simply impossible. Dempsey just said, 'Okay, no worries. They're going to have another meeting about your financial aid situation later this week, and I'll be back in touch with you after I hear from them.'

"That following Thursday, Coach Dempsey called me, 'You're all set! You don't have to pay anything. You just have to work in the kitchen—you know, a work study grant.' So, I headed off to Bridgeton thinking everything was hunky-dory. Later that year, Dean Whitney called me into the financial aid office.

"'Hey, Skip, great season this year. Glad to have you on board at Bridgeton.'

"'Thank you, Dean Whitney. I'm thankful for the opportunity.'

"'Skip, it appears we have a problem, however. You continue to have an outstanding tuition balance of fifteen hundred dollars.'

"'I'm sorry, Mr. Whitney. I know nothing about this.'

"'Skip,' he said, 'I don't mean *you* in particular, but Coach Dempsey: He told me back in the fall that he would be paying the remainder of your tuition.'

"'Coach Dempsey? Really? I'm not sure what to say, Dean Whitney. I was told everything was all set and I just needed to work in the kitchen to pay off my tuition.' So, after an awkward silence, Dean Whitney excused me.

"Later that summer, walking into Sammy Whites' bowling alley in Brighton, I bumped into Dempsey.

"'Hey, Coach, what happened at Bridgeton? They said you owe the school fifteen hundred dollars for my tuition.'

"He just laughed and said, 'I knew they would never kick you out. You were too good a football player. Congratulations! I hear you're going to be playing ball at Mass. Maritime Academy!'

"Dempsey never had any intention of paying that balance! He was banking on Bridgeton stepping up and taking care of me."

Skip would become an All-American football star at the Massachusetts Maritime Academy and graduate with an engineering degree.

"I owe everything to Dempsey," he said. "I started out as a young boy and ended up a man."

I was next, though I knew I wasn't (and couldn't) compete with Skip's words and message.

But, of all the things I could have said, what I felt most was the astonishment that we were all actually together again. So I started off with an observation I'd had while listening to the players talk—so many of us were happily married, with kids. Considering where many of us had come from, we should've had a high divorce rate and been lousy parents. Yet player after player spoke highly of the joys of being a parent and of the love and pride they felt for their children.

Due to the snow, we'd all just assumed that Al, our captain, hadn't been able to make it. But as I was finishing up, Al entered the room wearing his Don Bosco Championship jacket.

"When I think of Science Park," he said, "no athletic facilities, and the fact that we still won every game in one of the toughest conferences in the state—it allowed me to come to this conclusion: *If we could survive playing football at Bosco, we could survive anything in life.*"

It was the perfect closing statement.

Everyone stood and cheered.

To cap off the night, we all sat back and watched film footage of our big win over CM and of our championship game victory against Archies. There were occasional comments, compliments, and even some applause for particularly great plays. But mostly the room was silent, transfixed by the power of the moment. We were being transported back in time, four long decades ago. It was magic.

When the lights came back on, there was another round of applause followed by a deep, natural silence. Any additional words would have been inappropriate or inadequate.

As we sat in silence, the light of the screen illuminated our faces, and the DVD player stopped with a click. None of us said a word. I examined the weathered faces of the men sitting around me, the faces of my teammates, the faces of old friends. We hadn't seen each other for decades and yet, in this moment, time wasn't a barrier any more. A common experience had bonded us together—an experience that had transformed us from young boys to young men.

After a few moments more, we all knew it was time to go our separate ways. We had spent seven hours together and the time to leave had come. Each player made sure to say his goodbyes with promises of staying in touch and of seeing each other again soon. When the room was nearly empty, I walked over to Skip and said, "We couldn't have done this without you. No one could have united us together like you did tonight."

When I stepped outside into the dark February night, the cold wind blasting against my face and my adrenaline still flowing, I realized that it was the same sensation I'd once felt after a hard-fought football game. I smiled. It had stopped snowing. In the end, our "big storm" had produced only three inches of snow.

I laughed. Thank God for Frankie!

Warming up my car for the long drive home, I took a moment to reflect. The day had been perfect. Everyone had had their say, and we were all truly brothers again. And yet, in the back of my mind, I was still very much aware that a towering presence had been missing. Listening to my teammates that night, it became abundantly clear to me that while Dempsey's boys had been striving to do good with their lives, Dempsey had been self-destructing.

For years, I'd struggled to find an answer that would satisfy me, that would answer all my unanswered questions and erase all my doubts. After that night, it became clear to me that in some way we were truly Dempsey's boys, his sons. He had no family, no wife, no kids—everything outside of football had been a struggle or a failure for him. But on the football field, he was at home, confident, complete, respected, and admired. He did more than coach his boys; he cared for and nurtured them, and gave them opportunities he'd never had. He wanted the best for us, just like any good father. Right or wrong, I once again made the explanation work for me.

After that night, I knew my search was over. No more wondering, no more speculation, no more pain.

For one glorious season, it was Dempsey who cast a wide net over a group of raw, undersized, inner city boys, who together accomplished the unthinkable. He gave us something that could never be taken away: The belief that hard work and togetherness could trump size, speed, and talent. The belief that we could accomplish and achieve anything in life if we had the drive and commitment to do so. The belief that even *we* could be champions.

Sitting in the car, running the heater, I pulled out our team photo. I no longer had to wonder about what had happened to my teammates, how they'd made out in life, or what the '74 season had meant to them. I no longer looked at the faces in the photo as young boys from long ago. I now saw men—men who had lived good lives, men who had never forgotten their roots, men who had never forgotten their school, men who had never forgotten their teammates, men who had never forgotten Michael Monahan, and men who had never forgotten a very special coach who'd lived on both sides of the line.

# EPILOGUE

In 2014, Max Williams returned to Boston. He wanted to walk our practice field and visit the public swimming pool at Science Park. The last time I'd walked the practice field myself had been back in 1982 when I'd spent a year coaching for Bosco. So I jumped at the opportunity to also pay the ol' stomping grounds a visit. It was July, so I had visions of hundreds of inner city kids swimming at the MDC pool. I knew we wouldn't be able to walk into the girls' locker room, but we could certainly still get a feeling of what it'd all been like back in 1974. I was excited to point out to Max the Lechmere clock that hung across the Charles River, to see the torn up grass, and to see everything that had changed. Little did I know just *how much* it had all changed.

Pulling into Science Park, we discovered that the pool had been closed for years. The doors and windows were all boarded up and the thick metal doors of the entryway were covered in rust. Untended weeds and vines had grown through the concrete sidewalks and woven themselves along the brick façade. Lechmere no longer occupied the building across the Charles, and even the clock had been removed. A Staples now was in its space. The trees, so small forty years ago, were now so thick and tall that they totally blocked our view of Cambridge. *And our practice field?* What had once been a wide expanse of grass was now a series of baseball and softball diamonds laid out in opposite corners.

But there was one saving grace: our oldest practice area, the area that had held no grass until my senior year, the area that was forty feet from Storrow Drive and speeding traffic, the area that was in plain sight of the Charles Street Jail, the area where I'd learned to play football—it was still intact, unchanged by time.

I walked the field with Max, pointing to specific areas that triggered memories and stories: getting kicked in the ass by Currier my sophomore year, remembering the dust in August, the mud in October, and the snow in November along with all that freezing wind coming off the Charles. I pointed out the tragic location of Michael's accident, and we both paused a moment in silence.

"And this is where Eddie Trask said, 'Fuck 'em! Let's start practice without them!' and set up a pit-drill after the Malden Catholic game."

I was flooded with memories and could have stayed for hours, laughing and tearing up at the sight, smell, and feel of it all.

"Kev," Max said, reading me and all the excitement and nostalgia pumping through me, "I know this sounds like bullshit, but I'm telling you—I can feel Dempsey on this field with us. I can truly feel his energy and his presence. And he's sending both of us the same message."

"Yeah, Max?" I smiled. "What message is that?"

"Tell the story!"

Tommy & Kev & Mom

Easter Sunday 1960. I am three years old and my brother Tom is seven. My beautiful [mot]her was then but thirty years old. Who could have ever predicted that, four short years [later], she would take her own life.

father holding me. My brother Tom looks on.

My mother and father (Tom and Christine Kelly) on a night out.

The Kellys on their honeymoon 1953.

The Kelly family home in Hyde Park.

My dad, in uniform, is holding me. My father would serve on the Boston Police force for forty-three years. He died on February 4, 2015, just as this book was being completed, at the age of 85.

JFK and TJK  Tom Kelly and John F. Kennedy

My grandmother worked at the Kennedy compound in Hyannis when she was a young woman. Years later, my dad met John F. Kennedy when he was a U.S. senator for Massachusetts and running for the presidency. This picture was taken in 1959.

At my wedding, my wife Xiaofeng and Dad

My girls: Michelle, Tianyao, an
Bailey the do

My family today

# Afterword

# Michael Monahan

In February 2014, Colie McGillivary notified several team members that Michael Monahan had just passed away. For ten years, we had tried to find Michael, only to discover that he lived outside of Boston, a two-hour drive from my home.

After work on a Tuesday afternoon, I packed a suit in the trunk of my car and started the drive to Norwell, Massachusetts, hoping to pay my respects. I drummed my fingers on the steering wheel, turning over in my mind if this was the right decision. Is this what the Monahan family would want? Was I overstepping boundaries? Was I reopening old wounds?

I had gotten in contact with Eddie Dominguez, our captain on the '74 team, and he informed me that he was also planning to attend the wake. Together, we would represent the Don Bosco team. This time we would not turn our backs on Michael.

We were apprehensive about how the family would view us, but they welcomed us with open arms and appreciated knowing, after forty years, that none of the players had ever forgotten Michael. The Monahans are a tremendously close family who cared for and loved Michael. They certainly had the right to feel anger and bitterness, and we the team players represented the anguish, sadness, and tragedy that had altered their lives. The actions of Don Bosco's coaches, and the neglect of our teammates, had changed the course of Michael's life, and left the Monahan family with a broken son. If anyone had a right to be angry at God, at the team, and at its coaches, it was the Monahans. But instead of carrying feelings of bitterness and anger, the family was at peace that day. They seemed the very embodiment of empathy and understanding.

Michael's sister looked me in the eye and said, "You have to learn to play the hand you're dealt."

A freshman when I was a senior, Michael's brother Brian felt no bitterness toward the school. "Bosco," he said, "wrapped their arms around our family. There was total support for us."

And Michael had apparently remained positive and upbeat throughout his life. When we entered the funeral home, we saw a series of pictures that spanned Michael's life. Every picture showed Michael with a smile. The strength of a family is truly tested during moments of adversity. When I looked into the eyes of the Monahan family, I saw a resounding strength, a directness, that was almost piercing.

Eddie and I put up a good front, but we were both deeply troubled. I had attempted to find Michael ever since beginning to write this book. In 2013, after three years of hunting players down from all over the country, we finally reunited as a team at Curry College. To discover Michael was just down the road, and then to discover he had died, bothered both of us terribly. I should have looked harder for Michael. We all wanted Michael to know how sorry we all felt for not only the incident, but for not reaching out to him over the years. It's a burden I will always carry, and perhaps it's justified.

It's the hand I've been dealt.

# MY MOTHER

In January 2014, I received shocking information surrounding my mother's death. For fifty years, I had lived with the belief that my mother's death was a personal decision. No one had given me any information to think otherwise. My dad, at the age of eighty-four, was of no help. He had full-blown dementia, though he still lived at home in Hyde Park. My sister Ann and her husband Derick had moved into the house five years earlier to take care of him full-time.

Dad was known for never throwing anything away. Having absorbed junk for more than sixty years, our basement had lost every square inch to boxes, tools, old newspapers, photographs, National Geographic magazines, broken furniture, and appliances that he never got around to fixing. You name it and we had it. Dad was the modern Sanford and Son. Now wheel-chair bound, Ann had the green light to begin the unimaginable task of slowly sifting through the basement and once again regaining some usable space.

During a Sunday afternoon visit to Dad's house, Ann nonchalantly handed me a thick envelope. "Kev, I found this in the basement. I haven't looked through any of it, but there are some old photos. Perhaps some of your mother." At the time, I had very few photos of my childhood and only two of my mother. Starting that day and over the next five years, my sister Ann would discover seventy-seven photos taken of her from 1950 to 1973.

I took the large envelope home and later that night, with a cup of coffee, slowly began to pull out the contents. My mother's nursing diploma, a title to our 1963 Chevy Impala, some old stock certificates, a photo of Frank Baker, our grandfather in 1905, bare-chested before a wrestling match. Suddenly, my heart skipped a beat. On a white, 4x5" inch piece of paper was my mother's suicide note to my father.

Darling,
Please forgive me. I've always loved you and the children. I have never harmed them intentionally. I could never prove I am innocent.
Love,
Chris

I was completely puzzled. What did this mean? I frantically emptied the remaining contents. I discovered an official note from the courthouse in Boston, dated June 5, 1964. My mother had been charged with an assault and battery! On June 12, she resigned from her job at Peter Bent Brigham Hospital. On June 29, she was dead.

This is what I was able to piece together: My parents had rented the second-floor of our home to a young couple. In the beginning, everything appeared to be fine. After a year, my parents raised the rent. Even though I was young, I remember one day running out of my bedroom, drawn to the yelling coming from the kitchen. As I peeked around the corner, my mother and father were trying to close the kitchen door while the upstairs neighbors were trying to push the door open. Suddenly, when they noticed I was standing there, everyone stood still. No one said a word to me. The neighbors turned and went upstairs. "Kevin, everything is okay. Go back to your room and play." I just looked at my mother, turned, and walked away.

Even if the matter went to court, nothing was going to happen to my mother. Hell, my dad was a cop; this would have been a minor issue in their lives. The case would have been dismissed, or a restraining order might have been issued. The worst case scenario would have been probation, and even that was highly unlikely. I sat in numbed silence. This was surreal. Fifty years of not knowing? Chemically jolted, I sat digesting a flood of flashbacks; year after year of asking if there had been any reason behind her decision. A surge of anger began to well up inside me. Why hadn't my father come clean with Tommy and me, especially when we grew older? I get that he wouldn't want to tell us when we were kids, but damn, I think we could have handled this information as adults!

The note and the suicide simply didn't make sense. Something wasn't adding up. What did my mother mean when she wrote: "I would never hurt the children intentionally. I could never prove

I'm innocent." Were they two separate statements, or was the loud, raucous, and possibly physical dispute with the tenants connected in some way? Our mother never hurt us. So it makes no sense that the charges were connected to us. If they were, the court's wording would have been abuse, neglect, and child endangerment, not assault and battery. Why would she take her life because of these charges? She was a very proud woman, and family image was very important to her, but suicide?

After all this time, I had put my mother's death neatly away in a small box in a far corner of my mind. I had moved on. My dad had started a new family. Tommy and I loved our new mother and were excited when Kathy, John, Tricia, and Ann came into our lives. We had lifelong friends, went to college, married, and raised our own kids. We had rewarding careers. Everything had turned out fine. My mother on occasion would pop in and out of mind but never in a troubling fashion. I had searched long enough for an answer, and had come to an acceptable conclusion about why she took her life at such a young age. I was at peace with all of it. Now at the age of fifty-seven, I had to try to digest this unsettling knowledge that there was an external trigger to her death.

My brother Tommy passed in 2008, and because of my dad's dementia, he doesn't even know my name as I write this. There is no one to seek out for an answer. I was disrupted and out of balance for a few days, walking around in and out of a fog. My own family could only hear a limited amount of this new discovery. If I felt helpless for an answer, they felt totally unhelpful. They couldn't and didn't want to jump into 1964, and were unable to care about a person they had never met and who had died fifty years ago. I could see it in their eyes.

# NOTICE TO DEFENDANT
## Commonwealth of Massachusetts

SUFFOLK, TO WIT:

The MUNICIPAL COURT OF THE WEST ROXBURY DISTRICT OF THE CITY OF BOSTON, holden in said district in the County of Suffolk for the transaction of criminal business.

To

Christine Kelly

You are hereby notified that an application for a criminal complaint to issue against you

for Assault and Battery

has been made in this Court and a hearing thereon will be had on Friday the 5th day of June in the year one thousand nine hundred and sixty-four at nine of the clock in the forenoon, at which time you may appear and present such evidence as you desire to have considered before said Court, or the Clerk thereof.

WITNESS, DANIEL W. CASEY, Esquire, at Boston aforesaid, this 1st day of June in the year one thousand nine hundred and sixty-four

*Vincent A. Mannering* CLERK.

Court House, Arborway and Morton Street, Forest Hills.

**Please bring this notice with you and present it at the Clerk's office.**

CP 9/62/2M

I am still close to many of my childhood friends from Hyde Park, but what could they possibly say or do? "Geez, Kev, pretty amazing to find that out after all these years. You okay? Hey, how 'bout those Patriots?"

My brothers and sisters would always laugh when talking about how our father would never throw anything away. That illness, or now, that gift, allowed me to learn something of the truth surrounding my mother's death and put some closure to a lifelong question.

Regardless of the reason or reasons why she took her life, the end result was the same. The best I could do was to look at my wife and two wonderful daughters, hold them tight, and move forward.

# LETTERS

Hi Bob,

Happy St. Pats day. How've you been? I guess good old John Maloney has pumped you full off the atrocities I'm accused with or of or whatever.

Well I've always felt that you and I transcend accusations. I can tell you one thing Bob Maloney is a fucking two faced conniving asshole! The face you see next to you on the bar stool is the face he displays outside of here. This is a punk jail and Maloney is just the fucking punk to run it!! He's a yes man and all the credit he's taken with you for the so-called favors was done thru a friend to a friend on Beacon Hill to Rufo directly. Maloney received the instruction but I'm sure told you I'm taking care of ~~Bob~~ Clyde Bob! He Blames it on Belly & me and Belly's friend they what happened but his fucking unsupervised staff who enforces whatever policy & procedure they feel like according to how they feel that day because of their hangover or lack of getting their. These guys don't do a fucking thing but read smut Books play cards bust inmates balls for entertainment. They like to ransack your room let you visit with your 81 year old mother

293

cuffed behind your back + shackled.
the same way I have to visit my
attorney. Send out addresses to the
D.A. who monitors your mail. None of
them would go ~~one~~ one on one + settle
it like a man they rather use kindergarten
psychology and group force to reenforce
their already infantile egos. But what
the fuck that's jail! These are Sub-
Fucking Human beings Maloney Included
and you can tell him for me Bob after
my case is over one way ~~&~~ or the
other, I'm going to stick it up Maloney's
ass and Brasil can fuck Reyo's
political plans. I want him to know
it and think about it Bob so do
me one last favor and deliver the message
Tell him Brassil and himself better
talk to their accountants. I know why
the authority is in such an autocratic
stupor. It's because keep the peons confused
with insignificant duties and petty disturbances
and administrative confusion while they rob
the place fucking blind. I'm
going to have some very very
good old friends up on Capitol Hill
crawl up the Suffolk County jail
System's _ass_ with a microscope.

3.

Tell him he forgets who he is fucking with I'm not some street punk wannabe niggeraround you know my influence straddles both sides of the "Coin". Why is this being said thru you! I'll tell you #1 To enlighten you as to his real character whether you care or not and to hope that you will drop me a line or visit when I head to my new home.

He's just done the biggest insult he ever could to me he's moved all the Stool Pigeons fags + Scumbags Cowards up on the same tier as me and my Co-defendant and when I see him Bob I'm going to break his Fuckin jaw Even if I'm 65 years old, He's a Piece of Shit! And if he comes between our friendship I'll be very disappointed in you. He's probably told you I can't have visits being the fucking liar he is but I've been able to have them since Dec. 23rd.

I pick a jury March 19th Monday My Trial Starts March 22 in Suffolk Superior 4-10 days max then which - ever way the scales of justice tip so well I, Bob you provided one of the key moments of satisfaction for me

4

my years of Coaching with you and I'll always Cherish the victories the foibles and the friendship. I'll understand if I don't hear from you anymore. We are in different worlds now and survival tactics and approaches to life differ greatly. I wish you the best and continued good health and peace of mind.

Your Friend
Jack

P.S
Deliver the MESSAGE
+ DESTROY The LETTER!!

Yours In Chains
"The Hydrant"

296

Sept 18 - Friday

Dear Bob

Just a note to say I still think
of you fondly and cherish the memories
of our coaching experience. We were certainly
a great Combination. I learned alot from
you, Organization, Poise legace Scouting
and enjoyed the leeway, respect and
confidence you displayed in me.

Bob, please forget that Nashua
Street stuff and Maloney. The case is
over and I got convicted on all four
counts. Hey That's life in prison!
I was angry then and spoke in
frustration. I don't want to lose
you as a friend ever! and I still
think of you often, especially when the
Fall rolls around. Two segments of
my life that meant the most to me
all my psyche. The Engbik - Later years

297

The Don Bosco and West Roxbury and St Colls, years! Alot of ffaall with alot of great Coaching experiences, alot of great friendships. I remain as always your Friend, first and your line Coach second!

Yours Forever
Jack

Dear Coach,

I hope this letter finds you well. I have been spending time interviewing many of the Bosco alumni pertaining to their memories of Bosco and their relationship with you. What is striking is how consistent everyone views you as a coach and as a person. You certainly impacted a tremendous amount of people. Stevie Deosie mentioned you as the most important coach in his carrier. Coach Currier was inducted into the Mass. Coaches Hall of Fame and in front of a thousand people from around the state he mentioned that "the best assistant coach I ever coached with over the years isn't here tonight and his name is Jack Dempsey."

I still would like to extend the invitation for you to be part of the book. Your feelings on football, coaching, your experiences, and your life are an important dynamic to this book. Every player that I have spoken with feels strongly that the championship would never have happened if it wasn't for you !!!! Besides being a coach that cared for his players you were an outstanding motivator and teacher!! The smallest details were worked on, stance work, reading the opponents body, watching for shifting in a lineman's stance, focusing on the lineman's hand for quickness off the line, punching into us that the average play lasts three and a half seconds and if you can't give a 100% for three and a half seconds .........don't play!!!! I use all of these strategies as a coach today.

Don Bosco closed its door for good in 1998. The 74 squad is the only team in the school's history to win the Catholic Conference. (out right) The 75 team, although a much better team, ended up co-champs. Not only do we go down in history but we also dive into obscurity and that is the driving purpose behind the book; to keep that from happening!!!!!

Hope all is well and I hope to hear from you!!!

Respectfully,

Kevin Kelly

# WHERE THEY ARE NOW

| PLAYER | COLLEGE | PROFESSION |
| --- | --- | --- |
| Mike Ewanoski | Boston College | Investment Manager |
| Al Libardoni | Springfield College | Retired Teacher/Coach |
| Stevie Riley | | Roofing Contractor |
| Colie MacGillivary | Mass. Bay C.C. | Boston Gas |
| Paul Carouso | | Deceased, 2015 |
| Peter Marciola | Stonehill College | Retired Air Force General/Lawyer |
| Craig Cemate | American International College | Security Specialist |
| Chester Rodriguez | Boston College | School Counselor |
| Shawn Murphy | Harvard University | President Mass. Retirement |
| Chris Staub | University of Rhode Island | Businessman/Entrepreneur |
| Skip Bandini | Mass. Maritime Academy | Engineer/Head Coach, Curry College |
| Tommy McGregor | | Manager |
| Derrik Martini | | Deceased, 2007 |
| Abe Benitez | Bentley College | CPA |
| Ed Dominguez | Boston Police Academy | Boston Police (Retired), MLB Investigator |
| Kevin Kelly | University of Maine | Educator/Coach |
| Billy Elwell | Northeastern University | Graphic Designer |
| Eddie Trask | | Contractor |
| John Sylva | UPENN | Mass. State Trooper |
| Vinny O'Brien | Fairfield College | Lawyer/Entrepreneur |
| Frankie Marchione | | Entrepreneur |
| Richie Abner | | IT Specialist |
| Gary Green | | U.S. Postal Supervisor (Retired) |

Legends live on:

*The Boston Globe Magazine*, August 16, 2015

Above: Keith Tillman, left, and teammates celebrate Billy's Cowboys winning the Boston Park League championship in 1976. Facing page: Jim McIntyre, the team's first head coach, in his furniture restoring studio.

black players signed on as the years passed, helping fuel the team's success.

Billy's Cowboys would exist for about 25 years, and then later for a few final seasons as a team that DeVoe coached in Braintree. Along the way, they would endure many highs and lows—a move from the Park League to the broader Eastern Football League, inductions in the Semi-Pro Hall of Fame, serious injuries, defections, divorces, a schism at Billy's Saloon, and bitter disagreements about the team's direction. (DeVoe fired his brother from the team on three separate occasions.) "It was like one big family," says Kevin McCarthy, who helped start and manage the Cowboys.

They would also write a Cowboys chant, to be performed in falsetto:

*Go back, go back, go back to the woods*
*Your team is too short, you ain't got the goods*
*You ain't got the rhythm, you ain't got the jazz*
*You ain't got the class that the Cowboys has*
*I like it, I like it, I like it like that*
(There's one final line, but it would never pass

my censors.)

After that stinging loss to Charlestown in 1975, revenge was the Cowboys' first order of business. They returned in 1976 more determined than ever to claim the Park League title. They had more talent now, not least Garrett, a kick returner and tight end who'd been drafted by the Minnesota Vikings in 1974. After a narrow win to start the season, the Cowboys began bowling over opponents, including the Townies, routing them 44-6. "We rolled," says Garrett, a longtime physical education teacher, coach, and referee in Boston.

When the Townies lost unexpectedly in the playoffs, the Cowboys faced the South Boston Chippewas in the championship game, which drew 8,000 people to Franklin Park's White Stadium in late November. It wasn't close. The Cowboys destroyed the Chips, 53-7.

It had taken them two years, but the title was finally theirs.

**BOTH GREW UP** in working-class Boston. Both were raised, in their teenage years, by single mothers. Both loved to hit people on the football field. Both wore No. 60 in their careers. Their stories are so intertwined, in fact, that when Rich Young has a health issue, he often calls Larry DeVoe first, because DeVoe's probably had it, too. "Sometimes I don't even have to go to the doc-

tor," Young says. "He's my Siri."

DeVoe, now 64, is stocky, has piercing blue eyes, and still wears the goatee of his younger years. He lives in Braintree with his wife, Deborah, and is largely retired. Young, 63 an[d] divorced, has a thin layer of dark curly hair, a[ ]warm smile, and a few more pounds than he [ ]in his playing days. He retired in 2010 after a[ ]long career as a Boston physical education tea[ch]er and coach.

In the 40 years since DeVoe brought Young onto the Cowboys, they've shared countless holidays, cookouts, football games, and escapades, including the time they filched a goril[la] suit for DeVoe to wear at his wedding rehears[al.] It was Young whom DeVoe's wife once called [to] hunt DeVoe down after a serious bender. DeV[oe] turned to Young when he wanted a godfather [for] his son. A few weeks ago, they traveled to Can[ ]ton, Ohio, together for a Hall of Fame ceremo[ny.]

Sometimes Young bristles at what comes o[ut] of DeVoe's mouth. (Politically correct Larry De[ ]Voe is not.) "He says things I wouldn't let no[ ]body else say to me," Young says. But he has n[o] doubts about DeVoe's heart. "There's nothing [ ]wouldn't do for me," Young says.

DeVoe, whose playing career spanned from the days of leather helmets through his 40th birthday in 1990, has the longer injury ledge[r,] which includes eight operations on his ankle[s,] five on his knees, a bicep reattachment, a sho[ul]der replacement, and a shoulder reconstructi[on.] Nerve damage from compressed vertebrae gi[ves] him pins and needles in his hands and make[s] walking difficult. "I didn't think it was going [to] be this [expletive] bad," he says. "But I would[n't] change it."

I'm not sure he could have anyway. DeVoe['s] passion for football, the pure joy he derived, [the] itch to play he felt every year—it's hard to ima[g]ine him resisting any of it. "Football is an anal[o]gy for life," he told me when we first met las[t] fall. You keep good people around you. You s[how] loyalty, respect, and caring. You work hard. De[ ]Voe will admit there were times he didn't live [ ]up to those ideals himself. But in one import[ant] way, he did. And at a time in Hyde Park when [it] wasn't necessarily easy to do.

In recent years, when DeVoe has seen Billy Mouradian around, the former saloon owner still embraces him like a proud papa. Mourad[ian] can't recall much anymore, DeVoe says, but t[he] team—that's burned into his memory.

"Hey, hey, how good were them Cowboys?" Mouradian asks him.

"We was real good," DeVoe answers. ∎

*Scott Helman is a Globe Magazine staff write[r.] E-mail him at scott.helman@globe.com and follow him on Twitter @swhelman.*

1976 Hyde Park Cowboys: Champions! I am at the far right, still in my uniform.

# Acknowledgements

No book can ever be written without a team of people pushing you and giving you a tremendous amount of support. The dream to write this story started seventeen years ago. Throughout that time, my team has been an important piece of this project. Without the team's support, this book would never have been written.

Thus, thanks to:

My wife Xiaofeng and my daughters, Yaoyao and Michelle, who weren't afraid to be honest or to criticize my writing when needed.

My brother John, and my sisters Kathy and Ann, for their unending support.

Bruce Bortz, my publisher, who stood by me for years when it would have been easier to walk away from this project.

Michele Capobianco and Katie Mead-Brewer, whose editing skills are unmatched, and who greatly helped me bring this story to life.

Michael Crocker, who nudged me to believe in and write this story.

John Palmer, who spent months helping me craft language for it.

Danny Sayer, who told me: "You have a story to tell, so tell it."

My teammates and Coach Currier, who spent time being interviewed, and who showed remarkable patience awaiting a final product.

But if any one person needs to be singled out, recognized, and thanked, it's Max Williams. Max spent an entire decade calling me and pushing me to write this book. While jumping on a 2010 flight from California, Max made me finally commit to this, in no uncertain terms. It truly wouldn't exist without him.

To Wayne Lynch and the 1965 Bridgeton football team: Thank you for providing such a vivid account of Coach Dempsey and the legacy he left at Bridgeton Academy.

To Frank Matthews, retired Massachusetts State Police lieutenant colonel who, just in the nick of time, came to me with a lot of valuable information, and who allowed me to understand the commitment and perseverance the force brings to cold cases like the one involving Dempsey.

Finally, thank you, everyone—family and dear friends.

Thank you!

# About the Author

Son of a Boston Irish cop, Kevin Kelly was born and raised in Hyde Park, Massachusetts. With the sudden tragic death of his young mother, he and his older brother Tom quickly learned how to adjust and navigate through their formative years. Fortunately, they had a rock-solid father, a tight neighborhood of lifelong friends, a beautiful and loving stepmother, and football.

Following in his brother Tom's footsteps, Kevin attended Saint Don Bosco Technical High School in downtown Boston from 1971-75. Approaching his senior year, he saw himself on the brink of quitting the football team, but was inspired to continue playing by his older brother's single comment: Quitting would be a decision he would regret for the rest of his life. Undersized and unappreciated, and with a coach named Jack Dempsey who inspired a group of nonbelievers, Don Bosco went on to win the Catholic Conference

Championship in 1974. On the strength of that, Kelly continued to play football at both the college and semi-pro levels.

A rare and cherished moment came in the summer of 1976, when, by chance, player and coach played side by side for the Hyde Park Cowboys, in New England's semi-pro league. Together, they shared a second championship and solidified a bond that lasted a lifetime. Today, Kelly continues to pass on the knowledge and inspiration of Dempsey, the coach, to *his* players.

When Don Bosco closed its doors in 1998, Kelly felt the strong need to write down the Bosco/Dempsey story, lest the'74 championship team fall into obscurity. There was also a desire to try to understand why Dempsey, the boys' mentor who did so much good for so many, could turn out to be so bad.

Kelly received his undergraduate degree in Special Education from the University of Maine.

Since 1980, Kelly has coached football at the elementary, middle school, and high school levels. His coaching resumé includes: Don Bosco, Madison Park, Catholic Memorial, Tyngsboro High School, Frontier Regional, Northfield Mt. Hermon, and Deerfield Academy.

After a life as owner of his own construction company, Kelly went back to school and earned his Master of Education degree from the University of Massachusetts.

From 1998 to 2010, he made a career switch, eventually becoming an Assistant Principal and Principal at Deerfield Elementary School. Leaving the public school system in 2012, he accepted the opportunity to return to the high school level as Assistant Dean of Students at the prestigious Deerfield Academy, a boarding school founded in 1797 and located in Deerfield, Massachusetts.

He is married to wife Xiaofeng. They have two daughters, Tianyao and Michelle. They live in Deerfield, Massachusetts.

8/2016